MOBILE TECHNOLOGY AND SOCIAL TRANSFORMATIONS

This book investigates the ways in which the mobile telephone has transformed societies around the world, bringing both opportunities and challenges. At a time when knowledge and truth are increasingly contested, the book asks how mobile technology has changed the ways in which people create, disseminate, and access knowledge.

Worldwide, mobile internet access has surpassed desktop access, and it is estimated that by 2022 there will be in excess of 6 billion mobile phone users in the world. This widespread proliferation raises all sorts of questions around who creates knowledge, how is that knowledge shared and proliferated, and what are the structural political, economic, and legal conditions in which knowledge is accessed. The practices and power dynamics around mobile technologies are location specific. They look different depending on whether one chooses to highlight the legal, social, political, or economic context. Bringing together scholars, journalists, activists and practitioners from around the world, this book embraces this complexity, providing a multifaceted picture that acknowledges the tensions and contradictions surrounding accessing knowledge through mobile technologies.

With case studies from Hong Kong, South Korea, India, Syria, Egypt, Botswana, Brazil, and the US, this book provides an important account of the changing nature of our access to knowledge, and is key reading for students, researchers, activists and policy makers with an interest in technology and access to knowledge, communication, social transformation, and global development.

Stefanie Felsberger is a Bartlett Fellow at the Access to Knowledge for Development Center, American University of Cairo, Egypt and PhD Researcher at the Centre for Gender Studies, Cambridge University.

Ramesh Subramanian is the Gabriel Ferrucci Professor of Information Systems at the School of Business, Quinnipiac University, Connecticut, and A2K Fellow at the Information Society Project, Yale Law School.

RETHINKING DEVELOPMENT

Rethinking Development offers accessible and thought-provoking overviews of contemporary topics in international development and aid. Providing original empirical and analytical insights, the books in this series push thinking in new directions by challenging current conceptualizations and developing new ones.

This is a dynamic and inspiring series for all those engaged with today's debates surrounding development issues, whether they be students, scholars, policy makers and practitioners internationally. These interdisciplinary books provide an invaluable resource for discussion in advanced undergraduate and postgraduate courses in development studies as well as in anthropology, economics, politics, geography, media studies and sociology.

Using Evidence in Policy and Practice
Lessons from Africa
Edited by Ian Goldman and Mine Pabari

Southern-Led Development Finance
Solutions from the Global South
Edited by Diana Barrowclough, Kevin P. Gallagher and Richard Kozul-Wright

Introducing Forced Migration
Patricia Hynes

Mobile Technology and Social Transformations
Access to Knowledge in Global Contexts
Edited by Stefanie Felsberger and Ramesh Subramanian

For more information about this series, please visit: www.routledge.com/Rethinking-Development/book-series/RDVPT

MOBILE TECHNOLOGY AND SOCIAL TRANSFORMATIONS

Access to Knowledge in Global Contexts

Edited by Stefanie Felsberger and Ramesh Subramanian

Routledge
Taylor & Francis Group
LONDON AND NEW YORK

First published 2021
by Routledge
2 Park Square, Milton Park, Abingdon, Oxon OX14 4RN

and by Routledge
52 Vanderbilt Avenue, New York, NY 10017

Routledge is an imprint of the Taylor & Francis Group, an informa business

British Library Cataloguing-in-Publication Data
A catalogue record for this book is available from the British Library

Library of Congress Cataloging-in-Publication Data
A catalog record has been requested for this book

ISBN: 978-0-367-54522-2 (hbk)
ISBN: 978-0-367-54524-6 (pbk)
ISBN: 978-1-003-08957-5 (ebk)

Typeset in Bembo
by Taylor & Francis Books

CONTENTS

ILLUSTRATIONS

Figures

Tables

CONTRIBUTORS

Colin Agur, Hubbard School of Journalism & Mass Communication at the University of Minnesota—Twin Cities, USA

Dennys Antonialli, Executive Director at Internet Lab, Law and Technology Research Center, São Paulo, Brazil

Enrique Armijo, Associate Professor of Law and Associate Dean of Academic Affairs, Elon University, USA

Celina M.A. Bottino, Project Director, Institute for Technology & Society of Rio de Janeiro (ITS Rio), Brazil

Rishika Czarzasta, Global Coordination & Reporting Specialist, Mercer, Warsaw, Poland and Indian Institute of Technology Madras, India

Stefanie Felsberger, PhD Student, Center for Gender Studies, Darwin College, University of Cambridge, UK

Shubhangi Gokhale, Research Assistant Professor in the Public Administration Department, Sejong University, South Korea

Harry Halpin, Visiting Researcher, Programming Securely with Cryptography, Inventeurs du Monde Numérique, Paris, France

Arun Kumar, Professor of Finance & Accounting, Department of Management Studies IIT Madras, India

William O. Lesitaokana, Senior Lecturer, Media Studies, University of Botswana, Gaborone, Botswana

John B. Lourdusamy, Department of Humanities and Social Sciences, Indian Institute of Technology Madras, Chennai, India

Saji Matthew, PhD, IIT Madras, India

Beatriz L.M. Nunes, Institute for Technology & Society of Rio de Janeiro (ITS Rio), Brazil

Nagla Rizk, Founding Director, Access to Knowledge for Development Center (A2K4D), American University in Cairo, Egypt

Jacqueline de Souza Abreu, Researcher, InternetLab

Carlos Affonso Souza, Director, Institute for Technology & Society of Rio de Janeiro (ITS Rio), Brazil

Ramesh Subramanian, Quinnipiac University, Hamden, CT, USA

ABBREVIATIONS

A2K	Access to Knowledge
A2K4D	Access to Knowledge for Development Center
AANES	Autonomous Administration of North-Eastern Syria
ACEL	National Association of Cellular Carriers / National Association of Cell Phone Operators
ADI	Ação Direta de Inconstitucionalidade
ADSL	Asymmetric digital subscriber line
Anatel	National Telecommunications Agency
AGPL	Affero General Public License
APK	Android Package Kit
b2b	Business to business
BBS	Botswana Building Society
BOCRA	Botswana Communications Regulatory Authority
BoP	Bottom of the pyramid
BTC	Botswana Telecommunications Cooperation
BTS	Base transceiver station
CAPMAS	Central Agency for Public Mobilization and Statistics
CCP	Code of Criminal Procedure
CIA	Central Intelligence Agency
CIT	Egyptian House Communication and Information Technology
CSA	Service Centre Agency
CSC	Common Service Centers
DDoS	Distributed denial-of-service
DECT	Digital enhanced cordless telecommunications
DRTS	Department of Road Transport and Safety
EGP	Egyptian Pound
FCC	Federal Communications Commission

FNBB	First National Bank Botswana
FSA	Free Syrian Army
GCMA	Greater Cairo Metropolitan Area
GDP	Gross domestic product
GPS	Global positioning system
GSM	Global system for mobile communications
H2MI	Human–human-machine interface
HDI	Human Development Index
HMI	Human-machine interface
IACHR	Inter-American Commission on Human Rights
IBGE	Brazil's Statistics and Census Institute
IBOPE	Brazilian Institute of Public Opinion and Statistics
ICT	Information and communications technology
ICT4D	Information and communications technology for development
IITM	Indian Institute of Technology Madras
IMEI	International mobile equipment identity
IMF	The International Monetary Fund
IoT	Internet of things
IP	Intellectual property
ISP	Internet Society Project
ISPs	Internet service providers
IT	Information technology
IT-BPM	Information technology–business process management
ITU	International Telecommunications Union
MCIT	Ministry of Communication and Information Technology
MCST	Minister of Communications, Science and Technology
MERS	Middle Eastern respiratory syndrome
MOESD	Ministry of Education and Skills Development
MSC	Mobile switching center
MTRST	Ministry of Tertiary Education, Research, Science, and Technology
NATO	North Atlantic Treaty Organization
NeGP	National eGovernment Plan
NGOs	Non-governmental organizations
OAS	Organization for American States
OCLP	Occupy Central with Love and Peace
OECD	Organisation for Economic Co-operation and Development
OONI	Open Observatory of Network Interference
PAN	Permanent account number
PBX	Private branch exchange
PKK	Kurdistan Workers' Party
PNAD	Household Analysis National Research / Pesquisa Nacional de Análise de Domicílio
PPP	Purchasing power parity

SDA	State designated agency
SIGA	Sistema Integrado de Gestão de Aparelhos / Handset Management Integrated System
SIM	Subscriber identity module or subscriber identification module
SMS	Short messaging services
SPREADD	Storage, processing, retrieval, exchange, access, display, and dissemination of information
STF	Federal Supreme Court / Supremo Tribunal Federal
STJ	Superior Court of Justice
UN	United Nations
UNDP	United Nations Development Program
VAT	Value Added Tax
VLE	Village level entrepreneur
VNI	Virtual network(ing) index
VPN	Virtual private network
WIPO	World Intellectual Property Organization
WWW	World Wide Web
YPG/YPG	People's Protection Units

ACKNOWLEDGEMENTS

The creation of knowledge is always a deeply collaborative and never a solitary process and our book is no exception. Many people have contributed to and shaped this book from the very start to its final output.

The idea for this book was born from a discussion between Jack Balkin, the founding director of Yale Law School's *Information Society Project* (ISP), and Nagla Rizk, founding director of the *Access to Knowledge for Development Center* (A2K4D) at the American University in Cairo. We as editors are deeply indebted to the support both the ISP and A2K4D have provided to make this book a possibility. Colin Agur, Pranesh Prakash, Nagla Rizk, and Lina Attalah all were central in shaping the call for chapters which was developed collaboratively between us. We then shared the call with the wider Access to Knowledge Global Academy, a global, collaborative network of academic and research centers focusing on research and policy promoting access to knowledge (A2K). Its members include centers in Brazil, China, Egypt, India, South Africa, and the United States who all helped to shape the call as well as the ensuing book. Valerie Belair-Gagnon and Rebecca Crootof have both supported this book and its progress as Executive Directors of the ISP, and we are both extremely grateful. We would also like to thank Rosie Anderson, Elizabeth Cox, and Helena Hurd at Routledge whose advocacy and support for this book help make it a reality. And a big thank you is owed to Mohammad M. Rabea for taking the amazing cover image for this book and to Ehab ElShazly for lending a hand.

Finally, we would also like to extend our sincere thanks to all the wonderful contributors, who patiently responded to our urgent requests, frequent comments and suggestions, and demands on their already busy schedules. Without their excellent contributions, there would be no book to speak of. And last, but most definitely not the least, we would like to express our sincere gratitude to Laura DeNardis, our long-time friend, enthusiastic supporter, for so graciously and generously offering to write the Foreword for our book, despite her incredibly busy schedule. The book is so much the better due to her contribution!

We also extend our deepest gratitude to Richard Bartlett without whose generous support this book would not have been possible.

Stefanie Felsberger and Ramesh Subramanian

In the Summer of 2016, my wonderful friends and colleagues Colin Agur and Valerie Belair-Gagnon, Executive-Director of the Yale Law School's Information Society Project (ISP), came to me with an interesting proposition. Colin had been slated to co-edit a volume under the ISP's auspices, but he could not work on it as he was about to join the University of Minnesota as a faculty member. Colin and Valerie decided to ask me if I would be willing to take Colin's place and co-edit a book titled "Mobile Technologies and Access to Knowledge." The book would curate interesting and exciting research works from around the world on various aspects connecting mobile technologies to A2K. Having been a member of Colin's doctoral committee, I was well-versed on mobile technologies in India, and was intrigued by the promise and potential of mobile technologies on access to knowledge around the world. I was also delighted at the opportunity to publish my third book under the ISP umbrella, and gladly accepted the gracious offer. Thus, began another exciting journey which has brought me new, life-long friends from all over the world. So I first thank Colin and Valerie for offering this project to me. Through this project I was introduced to my wonderful colleague and co-editor, Stefanie Felsberger, a researcher at the American University of Cairo and currently a doctoral scholar at Cambridge University, UK. She has been a wonderful colleague and friend who has been at the forefront of every step that we have taken these four years in getting this volume in shape. This book would simply not have happened without Stefanie's enthusiastic and skillful collaboration. I would also like to thank Rebecca Crootof, who took over as Executive-Director of the ISP after Valerie, for her unstinting support during the early stages of the project. The Yale Law School's Information Society Project would not exist but for the untiring and inspiring leadership of Prof. Jack Balkin. Over the years of its existence, Jack has guided and inspired hundreds, if not thousands of academics, researchers and activists around the world. My sincere thanks to him for providing me a second home at the ISP all these years.

Ramesh Subramanian

My first thank-you goes out to Dr. Nagla Risk, director of the Access to Knowledge for Development Center (A2K4D) who gave me the opportunity to work on this project when I was a researcher in Cairo. I will be forever grateful to her for placing this trust in me and the support she has given to me as an academic. Working alongside her and my colleagues in Cairo has deeply shaped my understandings of the world, power, and knowledge—both at the level of the personal and the political. I also want to express my gratitude to Joey Shea who helped with editing, formatting, and citations. A special thank-you is also owed to Fernando Revelo La Rotta whose help in editing and with citations was indispensable, but who was also there to discuss and debate many ideas related to this book. His insights were extremely helpful. I want to thank Lina Attalah whose ideas and writing have been a constant inspiration and motivation for me to grow and develop my own thinking and politics. Her contribution to shaping the focus of this book and reminders to pay attention to the details have been central. I want to thank Pranesh Prakash who also shaped the call for chapters of this book in its early stages. His insistence to interrogate things as they are and not to rest on well-trodden paths of explanations has been a guide for the analyses this book hopes to provide. Finally, I want to thank my friend and co-editor Ramesh Subramanian, professor at Quinnipiac University and A2K Fellow at Yale ISP. He has been an invaluable source of advice and support during the editing process. As this is my first time as editor of a book, I could always rely on his wonderful advice and experience to navigate the long path of getting from a book idea to publication.

Stefanie Felsberger

THE AMERICAN UNIVERSITY IN CAIRO
100 YEARS
School of Business
Access to Knowledge for Development Center

FOREWORD

Laura DeNardis

In the darkness of refugees' first steps onto new soil after an ocean journey, it is not uncommon to see mobile phones powering up along the shore. This is both a powerful and poignant 21st-century image. Those fleeing violence and political oppression in their home countries can carry very little with them. Those who are able, grab their mobile phones as their lifeline into a new world. The ability to access maps, connect with loved ones, search for information, and locate humanitarian assistance all hinge on this technology. Those reaching humanitarian aid camps immediately seek out electricity to power their phones.

The next billion Internet users will primarily come from developing countries accessing the Internet from smart phones via wireless access rather than home computers connected to a broadband cable. This wireless connectivity opens up access to educational resources, healthcare information, and entertainment. And it provides political and economic opportunities for many.

Yet the same mobile technologies that provide unprecedented access to knowledge are also being co-opted to restrict access and exert social control. Arrangements of mobile technologies are also arrangements of human rights. They are points of censorship in authoritarian countries. They are points of surveillance and authoritarian control. And they bring privacy considerations into an entirely new realm. In an Orwellian turn, a police search of a mobile phone raises vastly more privacy considerations than even searching someone's home. Phones contain medical records, financial data, locational data, personal pictures, schedules, and intimate communications.

Wherever one is in the world, and for good or bad, mobile phones are ubiquitous and entangled with every intimate aspect of human existence. Even Chief Justice John Roberts, writing in a United States Supreme Court ruling, observed, "Cell phones … are now such a pervasive and insistent part of daily life that the proverbial visitor from Mars might conclude they were an important feature of human anatomy."[1] Anyone who has temporarily misplaced their phone understands this dependency and the panic of losing access. Mobile telephony is now the gateway to sending email to a prospective employer, accessing social media and news, working remotely, listening to music, sending money to family through a cash app.

During the COVID-19 pandemic that kept so many across the globe from their schooling, work, and social life, mobile phone access became their window into the world and into vitally important news and health information. Without mobile technologies and the access to knowledge these technical architectures afford, the experience of the pandemic would have been much different, and people far more isolated and even more cut off from work, resources, health information, and education. Mobile phone apps also became embroiled in well-meaning efforts to stem the spread of the virus through contact tracing. And in a bizarre twist of fate that perhaps highlights how central mobile technologies are in the public consciousness, conspiracy theories around the world strangely claimed that 5G wireless technology was responsible for spreading the novel coronavirus, resulting in vandalism of 5G cellular towers. Mobile telephony has made it into conspiracy theories!

Mobile telephony is also not merely about human communication and human access to knowledge. More *things* than people are already connected to the Internet. These "Internet of Things" objects—from telemedicine devices to delivery robots to connected bikes—require mobile wireless access to function. In many ways, these mobile objects use the same infrastructure over which smartphone communications flow. But they also involve a new wave of proprietary technologies in that they are based on a tangle of competing technical standards, many more closed than the open traditions of the Internet. These devices, in part because of the innovation rush to be first to market, also have largely insufficient security by design, all while collecting even more personal information with heightened privacy consequences even beyond smartphone data collection. They also raise the stakes of outages and security breaches because a disruption is not just about losing access to content but potentially about physical harm to people.

It is worth a reminder that mobile telephony involves far more than the end device such as a phone or a fitness bracelet—99.9 percent of the technical architecture enabling mobile technology is beneath the surface of what is immediately visible to the people that use these technologies. This vast underlying infrastructure includes antennas, switches, technical standards, digital addresses, cloud computing networks, software, cables, and institutions that collectively support the ability of an end user to pick up a phone and access knowledge. Understanding the social and economic implications of mobile telephony—never mind the engineering considerations around broadband penetration, access speeds, and reliability—requires making this technology visible.

The world has indeed cut the cord and so has digital policy. This technical architecture of mobile telephony vital for so much access to knowledge and societal functioning is also a concentrated point of power at which many public interest issues are mediated. Mobile telephony is at the center of all major Internet governance debates of the contemporary era. Who has access? How affordable is it?

What skills are necessary? What public policies and investments are necessary to provide mobile access? Even efforts to provide mobile access for free raise enormous concerns about accompanying tracking and anticompetitive practices that block access to some services and information. What are the market conditions for those wanting to become network operators providing mobile connectivity? Are access providers legally allowed to discriminate against some types of information and traffic? What can be done to circumvent censorship and outages via mobile telephony? With constant data collection the prevailing business model of the digital world, what privacy policies are necessary for human autonomy and to push back against massive human surveillance in authoritarian and democratic societies alike? These are some of the most difficult public policy problems of our generation and answers involve complex and sometimes competing interactions among important values such as privacy, freedom of expression, consumer safety, and law enforcement. The book you are about to read—*Mobile Technology and Social Transformations: Access to Knowledge in Global Contexts*—is a wonderful guide to this new world.

Note

1 From the Supreme Court opinion *Riley v. California*, 134 S. Ct. 2473 (2014), opinion delivered by Chief Justice John Roberts, June 25, 2014, p. 13.

1

INTRODUCTION

Mobile Technologies and Access to Knowledge

Ramesh Subramanian and Stefanie Felsberger

Mobile phones have become nearly ubiquitous both at the margins and the centers of capitalism. Today they are essential means of communicating, accessing and sharing information, navigation, participating in society, organizing social movements, spreading information (and disinformation), and of participating in the digital economy. Mobile phones are used for disparate purposes such as accessing information, downloading movies and music, performing financial transactions, conducting business, education, art, and other creative endeavors. They play a part in rendering humanitarian assistance in disasters, circumventing censorship and information blockades, and in organizing popular revolutions and protests. The use of multifarious applications of mobile phones has contributed to development, democratization, human rights, and financial inclusion. At the same time, this technology has provided many new avenues for tracking and controlling people's communication and movements. Often tracking is even part of the solution to problems these technologies offer. A prominent example is the tracking of the spread of a disease. Mobile technologies have led to the commodification of people's everyday activities and an erosion of privacy rights, the consequences of which are still unfolding. Yet phones have also provided more privacy to people whose life takes place in close quarters which do not allow for privacy in the home. Mobile phones have helped to provide access to information to many people but have also enabled the spread of misinformation and propaganda. Mobile phones have contributed to the empowerment of women yet have also enabled new avenues for control and surveillance of women's activities. In short, mobile phones can be a lifeline but at the same time the information on your phone can put your life at risk.

The Internet revolution that began in the 1990s, and the virtual public spheres that emerged from that, gave a major impetus to the global Access to Knowledge (A2K) movement. With global Internet working, knowledge and information that was until then difficult to access or simply kept away from peoples' reach was suddenly accessible to infinitely more people who had a connection to the Internet. The Internet became a primary carrier for global information exchange. Initially restricted to fixed-line communications networks, within a short time the Internet was extended to wireless networks—a development that vastly improved accessibility, especially in those in countries that did not have mature fixed-line communications infrastructures. Many countries catapulted themselves to the Internet age by leapfrogging over wired onto wireless communications technologies. Some countries, such as India, explored new wireless technologies that were more adaptable to local conditions (Subramanian 2011). These moves, along with an ever-increasing computing power of mobile devices, reductions in costs, as well as innovations in mobile applications development, heralded the mobile communications revolution starting in the late 1990s. Knowledge was accessible through a device that fit into a person's back-pocket or handbag.

Indeed, a case can be made that access to the Internet has only reached such high levels primarily due to Web-enabled mobile phones. Mobile phones with Internet access arrived in 1996 in Finland through the Nokia 9000 Communicator phone (Microsoft Devices Team 2009). This was followed by the Web-enabled i-mode from Japan in 1999 (Mallon 2013). And since 2007, when the first "smartphones" arrived, the world has seen an accelerated shift from fixed-line Internet access to mobile web access. In January 2014, mobile Internet access exceeded desktop Internet access in the United States (McCullough 2014). The 2017 Virtual Network Index (VNI) Report from Cisco forecast that there will be 5.7 billion global mobile users (71 percent of the population) by 2023 (Cisco 2017).

Given these statistics and the many uses of phones, it is not surprising that the mobile phone is so widely accepted and has become indispensable to many—but not all—people. The phone's phenomenal growth is matched only by the growth of global broadband Internet applications. Today's mobile phones have become veritable extensions to the human body. Mobile phones with even minimal broadband capabilities have become a key access points to information for all people around the globe. Especially in the Global South, the mobile phone has become the most important gateway to the Internet for many people. In Sub-Saharan Africa mobile phone penetration rates fluctuate around 75 percent and the African continent shows the fastest growing rate of mobile phone adoption (Archambault 2017, 1). Despite these numbers, large parts of the global population do not have access to mobile technology or the Internet and significant gaps in mobile penetration rates within countries and between different regions remain. These divides between who has access to technology run along gender, class, and race divisions.

The undisputable success story of the spread of mobile phones can also be understood within the context of the promises and hopes for change that are attributed to this technology. The origin of these hopes lies in the "putative link between ICT and socioeconomic development" (Archambault 2017, 2): the phone is believed to be more than a means to vastly improve communication infrastructures. In addition, the mobile technologies are believed to allow developing countries to catapult themselves to the Internet age by leapfrogging over wired onto wireless communications technologies (Muchie and Baskaran 2006, Nielinger 2006, Subramanian 2011). Especially in developmentalist imaginaries but also in Tech4Good narratives situated in the Global North, mobile technologies are imbued with the potential to drive socio-economic development. Mobile technology was cast as panacea to the many problems in developing and developed countries: access to healthcare, economic inequality, tracing diseases, gender inequality, climate change, and lack of democracy. In recent years, more emphasis has been placed on the transformative potential of information rather than mobile phones themselves (Archambault 2017, Robins and Webster 1999). Within this framework, socio-economic development can be fostered through the provision of access to "useful information" which can range from information related to education, health, different markets, or governance (Archambault 2017, Burell 2008, Slater and Kwami 2005). For example, access to health-related information can improve health care provision (Breslauer et al. 2009, Crentsil 2013), and information related to civil rights can support democratization. Better access to market information is said to boost entrepreneurship (Jensen 2007). The latter is part of a larger shift where "entrepreneurship and innovation [are seen] as engines of development" (Irani 2019, 5). Mobile phones here play the key role of the infrastructure through which this information and knowledge is accessed.

As has already been pointed to earlier, mobile phones do not just have the potential to drive socio-economic development but the consequences of their use and adoption are much more complex. Araba Sey (2011) in her study on the adoption of mobile payphones in Ghana shows that the introduction of mobile payphones did not benefit small entrepreneurs and led to an overall decline of the industry. Mobile technologies also allow for tighter controls during elections according to Aker, Collier, and Vicente (2011) and provide means to spread ethnically motivated hatred (Osborn 2008). Governments across the globe have repeatedly shut down entire communication networks in an attempt to undermine people's use of mobile phones to organize protests. What becomes clear from these dichotomies is that mobile technologies and access to information can be invested with all the transformative potential but, in the end, daily practices and encounters of people with this technology as well as the socio-political and economic context ends up shaping use of information and adoption of technology (Archambault 2017, 4). Don Slater and Janet Kwami's study (2005) on the use of mobile phones in Accra, Ghana, provides an important reminder that despite phones' potential to provide useful information, they found that phones were mainly used for everyday mundane conversations.

This leads us to why this book is important: both access to technologies and access to knowledge are imbued with promises for positive social change, but it is important to see how stories in concrete contexts actually unfold. In addition, mobile technologies and the politics of accessing information are part and parcel of many current debates in Internet governance and global debates about economic development, democracy, and inequality. From questions about free speech to debates about the end of privacy, from celebrations of the power of machine learning to warnings about its dangers, from Google, Uber and Facebook's meteoric rise to the erosion of workers' rights, from the Arab Spring to the Snowden revelations and the Cambridge Analytica scandal, mobile phones and Access to Knowledge have played a crucial role. Yet the specifics of the role they play have not been systematically and specifically addressed. Given the powerful and ubiquitous role that mobile telephony plays in today's world, there is an imperative to document its varied roles in multiple contexts. That is our primary aim for bringing out this volume.

The idea for this project was born at the Yale Law School's Information Society Project (ISP) and the Access to Knowledge for Development Center (A2K4D) at the American University in Cairo, both members of Access to Knowledge Global Academy, a network of scholars at institutions in Brazil, China, Egypt, India, South Africa, and the United States dedicated to promoting academic scholarship, research, and policy analysis on access to knowledge issues for information-poor communities. The book explores mobile telephony as the source of opportunities and challenges, especially with respect to access and control. How have the ways in which people access knowledge changed when this access is mediated through mobile technology? What are the consequences for either socio-economic development or democracy as they play out in each context and for each case study?

Framework: access to knowledge

Access to knowledge is essentially the right of an individual to participate in the creation, distribution, and acquisition of raw information, secondary analyses of data, and knowledge-embedded tools and services (ISP, Yale Law School n.d.). A2K focuses on the value of openness—open access to all types of information and hence knowledge. This focus has important ramifications on a variety of policy issues, such as freedom of expression, development, democratization, access to government information, access to education and scholarship, access to products that directly affect the health and well-being of peoples across the world, access to traditional knowledge, open communications standards, as well as issues that pertain to intellectual property, such as patents and copyrights.

Previous books published by the A2K Global Academy have focused on country-specific analyses, i.e. of Brazil (2008), Egypt (2010), and India (2011). These volumes were followed in 2015 by a more global-focused book on global censorship. The current volume continues in this vein by addressing mobile technologies and A2K on a global scale. As explained by Lea Shaver (Shaver 2011, 3), the A2K perspective asks some simple questions, which are: As innovation progresses, who is able to benefit from it and who is not? Who gets in the door and who is left outside? And will barriers to access, and control, actually have a negative impact, not only on those individuals who cannot access such knowledge, but also on economic growth and future innovation? From this perspective, the A2K perspective and its policies fall within the framework of the right to science and culture—a right that is recognized in Article 27 of the Universal Declaration of Human Rights: "Everyone has the right freely to participate in the cultural life of the community, to enjoy the arts and to share in scientific advancement and its benefits" (United Nations 1948).

Nevertheless, this book's framework is not human rights or development, but Access to Knowledge. In our understanding, while not separate, they are different lenses through which different questions come to the fore. For us, A2K speaks to but also goes beyond a strictly rights-based approach, because the framework allows us to analyze who has the material abilities to participate in knowledge creation and the knowledge economy. The question also becomes who can produce knowledge, who has the abilities to use the new technologies–such as mobile phones–to access and produce knowledge that is valuable to their context. This opens our analysis to the structural political, economic, and legal conditions in which knowledge is accessed as well as questions of infrastructures, such as mobile technologies. A2K (and its relationship with development or socio-economic opportunities) brings to the fore questions about power and participation. This book, therefore, explores mobile telephony as a source of opportunities and challenges, especially with respect to access and control: who is allowed to participate, whose access is curtailed for the benefit of whom, does access to knowledge and technology lead to more participation in society?

Practices and power dynamics around mobile technologies and A2K are particular to each location and look different whether one chooses to highlight the legal, social, political, or economic context. The application, regulation, and use of mobile technologies are multi-faceted and this book hopes to shine a light on as many of these aspects as possible. Therefore, this book brings together scholars, journalists, activists, and other subject-matter experts, in a wide-ranging set of chapters that collectively explore Access to Knowledge on the world's mobile phone networks. This book is situated at the intersection of several academic disciplines. Scholars studying development, communications, technology or media, as well as journalists, practitioners in development, and members of civil society fill find this book useful. The authors who have contributed to this book also come from such a diverse background and work from within different assumptions and frameworks: while some focus on the potential for positive socio-economic change, others focus on the potential dangers for control and loss of privacy. But they are all bound together by their focus on access to knowledge. It was important to us as editors to bring together this diversity in approaches to studying mobile technologies in order to reflect the also very different experiences and consequences that unfold across the globe through the use of mobile phones. In this sense, this book is unique in that it provides a very multifaceted picture of mobile technologies that aims to present the contradicting consequences of accessing knowledge through mobile technologies. These tensions and contradictions are explored in more detail in the conclusion of this volume.

Book structure

While soliciting authors, we were keenly aware of the enormous range of topics that fall into the intersection between A2K and mobile technologies. Therefore, we, along with other members of the Access to Knowledge Global Academy, held several discussions and compiled a preliminary list of subjects or themes that the book would cover, namely (I) Access and Control, (II) Political and Social Change, (III) Economic Opportunities and Developments, and (IV) Technological Underpinnings. Our thinking was guided by questions posed within the A2K framework: how do mobile technologies increase the access to knowledge and what are impediments to this access? In what ways does access to and use of mobile technologies spur social change? What economic opportunities do mobile technologies enable and for whom?

As becomes clear from these questions, we had initially planned to explore the dichotomy between access to and control of mobile technologies. Further deliberations led us to realize that within this dichotomy many important issues surfaced that were better addressed as two separate themes. We also received many chapter abstracts that proposed investigations of control and privacy concerns. Therefore, we separated the single theme into two separate themes. We also realized that there was considerable overlap between the theme economic opportunities and social change, which we combined into a single theme. To sharpen the focus of the book we decided to eliminate the fourth theme, "Technological Underpinnings." This book's main objectives were not really about technology as such, rather, to bring to light the ways in which mobile technologies are shaped through legal, economic, social, and political structures and agencies and how this in turn shapes how knowledge is accessed.

The final result of these deliberations is a volume that encompasses three themes, namely (I) Access, (II) Control, and (III) Social Change and Economic Opportunities. All chapters fall into one or more of these themes. Each part of the book also includes a brief introduction which further explains our thinking of how the three themes intersect with the A2K framework:

Access—the proliferation and accessibility of cellular devices and technologies, legal restrictions on access and technologies, intersections between access to knowledge and access to mobile technologies, tradeoffs between access to knowledge and other economic or political concerns

Control— the question of control over personal information, privacy, data protection, and ownership of mobile devices, and surveillance conducted both by state and corporate entities, and censorship

Social Change and Economic Opportunities— mobile technologies and effects on traditional social institutions and the reconstruction of community, the use of mobile telephony in political action, including expression, participation and organizing, positive and negative implications on political culture, mobile technologies and the rise of digital entrepreneurship, innovations in emerging economies, and mobile technologies as sites of innovation

In addition, the chapters in this book investigate A2K and mobile technologies in different countries around the world. Chapters focus on and come from Botswana,

Brazil, Egypt, Hong Kong, South Korea, the United States, and Syria. Many of the issues explored in these chapters do not neatly fit into one category. Often more access can also allow for more control, or economic opportunities for some can mean decreased access to knowledge for others, or the social change that mobile technologies are hoped to bring about are not more access to knowledge but instead increased opportunities for control and less privacy. The conclusion of this volume addresses these seeming contradictions and tensions between access, control and social change and economic opportunities. In the next few sections, we briefly introduce the individual chapters and explain how they fall into these themes.

I Access

The first theme of our book is access. By this we largely mean the politics behind accessing mobile technologies and knowledge as well as the intersections between both. While the theme is titled "Access," the chapters on this theme address underlying issues such as exclusion and marginalization, their implications, and efforts to overcome the digital divide. The first chapter in this part examines the use of mobile technology in language learning. It seems appropriate to position a chapter on language learning before all the other chapters. To paraphrase Noam Chomsky, language can be considered to be "a system that is internalized in the mind/brain, yielding specific cases of propositional knowledge and knowledge how to do so and so" (Chomsky 1997, 12). Thus, one can argue that language is the basis for knowledge. John Bosco Lourdusamy and Rishika Czarzasta take on the interesting concept of language learning in a foreign, non-immersive setting and study its effectiveness when information and communications technologies (ICT), especially mobile technologies, are adopted to aid such learning. Their study consists of field studies on learning the French language in Chennai, a city in South India. They argue that the use of new technologies not only expands access to the knowledge of the language in question, but "also widens the horizons of the learner to knowledge in general."

The next chapter also focuses on the various efforts to provide access to knowledge and technology to villagers in rural South India by giving access to "the last mile" of telecommunications. In this study, Saji Matthew, Arun Kumar, and Ramesh Subramanian take a look at the many efforts to bring Internet access to villagers, and the results that this can bring in increased access to health information, to market resources, women's empowerment and entrepreneurship, as well as democratization. While there have been many studies in this area, the authors of this chapter focus not just on the success stories, but also on the many failures and missteps that have occurred in efforts to provide access to communications infrastructure (and thus the Internet) to rural villages. The authors show, through several case studies, that while enhanced access to communications via mobile telephony has indeed increased Access to Knowledge, there are also several caveats that hinder progress or even impede progress on achieving desirable results. Their case studies provide an excellent template that could be used by access providers and policy makers not only in India but also in several other developing economies.

Another country in the Global South, this time the Sub-Saharan country of Botswana, is the subject of William Lesitaokana. In his chapter, Lesitaokana traces the dramatic increase of mobile telephony over the last twenty years and adds a valuable contribution to the literature on the digital divide which sometimes overlooks developments on the ground attempting to close this divide. He notes that over 80 percent of the adult population in continental Africa own and use mobile phones. The author focuses on Botswana, tracing the diffusion of mobile phones over the past decade, and the way this has significantly facilitated access to mobile communication services, especially among urban youth countrywide. The chapter then goes on to describe, using cases, how the extensive availability of mobile phones and access to the Internet have transformed the lives of the citizens of Botswana. Lesitaokana notes that this is a prime example of how, in a technologically less-advanced country, the use of mobile phones proves to be a significant means to access mobile public services, and thus enhance their socio-economic status. The author also notes how the mobile revolution in Botswana fosters not only extensive knowledge, but also increases civic participation among its citizens. This chapter, along with the earlier chapter on the last mile problem in India, provide a solid base for those interested in seeing how mobile telephony has become indispensable as a communication medium, and as a tool for economic development and well-being.

The next chapter by Celina Bottino, Carlos Affonso Souza, and Beatriz Nunes discusses the attempts by the National Telecommunications Agency (Anatel), the quasi-government agency that regulates the telecommunications sector in Brazil, to block certain mobile phones. In 2014, Anatel announced a measure whereby non-approved cell phones would be blocked in the country. This has obvious ramifications for access to knowledge and freedom of expression. The authors analyze Anatel's measure from an A2K perspective and argue it would result in restricted access to the Internet to millions of Brazilians, especially those in the lower economic strata of society. In addition, this would also impact of the rights of citizens' privacy, as it would require the development of a database containing the "approved" phone-owners' data. Arguing that this measure, enacted presumably to protect and enhance national security, law and order, and public morals is both disproportionate and unnecessary, the authors propose alternate solutions that would not result in citizens' access to the Internet though non-approved phones.

II Control

Part II focuses on the theme of control, surveillance, and privacy. Harry Halpin, former research scientist at MIT, a cybersecurity and social activist, discusses in stark relief the troubles activists face in repressive authoritarian regimes—in this case Syria. His chapter focuses on the attempts of Bassel Safadi, a Syrian activist, who in the wake of the Syrian Uprising sought to establish free Internet access beyond the restrictions placed on the Internet and mobile communication by the Syrian government. Halpin, who works for an organization providing secure and free online communication, was contacted by the activist in search of assistance. The author describes in detail the conversations between the activist and himself, using free software applications and access to the Internet, and how Safadi's efforts eventually led to his death. The chapter shows how difficult it was to provide assistance due to language barriers, as well as lack of local knowledge and preparation, even though Safadi knew exactly what was needed on the ground. Halpin discusses how it is often the case that even well-intentioned restrictions imposed by Western governments often end up aiding such repression. This chapter tells a story that is at once a guide as well as an inspiration to all those who are interested in creating free Internet software applications for mobile phones, which enable users to overcome state controls and censorship in the quest for access to knowledge.

While Syria provides a stark example of state-controlled repression and censorship to mobile telecommunications and the Internet, the next chapter provides an interesting contrast—by focusing on the United States, and efforts by the government to provide high-speed Internet access to citizens. The author Enrique Armijo notes that this effort, while laudable and in line with the A2K movement, nevertheless comes with major caveats, and even threats to freedom of expression. The author discusses three models of Internet access provision: a public utility model (i.e. fully owned and operated by the government), a public–private partnership model (wherein local municipalities work in partnership with some ISPs who provide free high-speed Internet access within a specific area such as a park), and a third model where a city owns the Internet infrastructure, while ISPs utilize the infrastructure to provide access for an agreed-upon fee. While these efforts are laudable and purportedly enhance access to the Internet (and hence knowledge), the author argues, from actual case studies, that they often come with restrictions to free expression, which are enforced through various "terms of service" that come from the government in conjunction with the local network providers. The author ends by projecting a warning about how such "free access" could end up curtailing citizens' free speech and make it easy for governments to surveil and censor citizens.

Moving south to Brazil, in the chapter that follows, we learn of the enormous growth in Internet access that has come to Brazilians through access to cell phones. According to authors Dennys Antonialli and Jacqueline de Souza Abreu, out of the 120 million accesses to Facebook from Brazil, 91.6 percent came just from mobile connections. Thus, we see that an overwhelming number of people access the Internet through mobile telephones. However, the exponential growth of mobile telephony and its use to access the Internet has also provided the state with enhanced surveillance powers, under the guise of criminal investigation. The authors state that despite the 1988 Brazilian Federal Constitution which guarantees secrecy of communications, there is an exception granted for criminal investigations. Interception of communications falls within the scope of such criminal investigations, and there has been a general increase in the number of cases where such exceptions have been granted by the legal wing. The authors show the mismatch between telephone, especially mobile, usage in Brazil and the protections provided under Brazilian law. They also show that the existing interception of mobile communications establishes the lack of a legal framework that establishes limits for law enforcement access to mobile communications content and associated metadata. Their hope, through this exposure, is to provide policy makers a strong direction in which to develop legal frameworks that will afford more privacy protection to Brazilian citizens.

III Economic opportunities and social change

The Internet revolution has spawned multiple communications and media revolutions all over the globe. The explosive growth of social media, accessed often through mobile phones, is a prime example of this. Starting from the Arab Uprisings, social media accessed via mobile phones have played a crucial but widely debated role in protest movements and revolutions. In the next chapter, Colin Agur focuses on the use of mobile telephones and social media in the so-called "Umbrella Movement" of Hong Kong, a semi-autonomous territory of the Republic of China. Agur traces the movement's roots starting from September 1994, when China prevented Hong Kong residents from electing their own chief executive. Protests erupted on the streets. But as Agur notes, these protests were not random. They were planned almost 18 months earlier, when the organizers of "Occupy Central with Love and Peace" (OCLP) began using social media to plan their actions and strategies. Social media was used as a tool for social deliberation, for seeking opinions and strategies, and for generating a civil referendum. The protests then morphed into what is now known as the "Umbrella Movement" named for the use of umbrellas by the protestors as defenses against tear-gas cannons. Agur goes on to describe in detail how mobile social media was used during every aspect of the protests, as well as beyond.

The Hong Kong protests were ultimately unsuccessful for the student protestors, but there were plenty of lessons learned. The efficacy of using social media to engineer social change depends strongly on the local context of certain cultures and societies. We learn new insights by looking at the events in South Korea, where the citizens' use of social media to spread information and organize protests against government corruption led to the eventual impeachment of the nation's president. In the next chapter, Shubha Gokhale takes us to South Korea and discusses the events that led to the impeachment of president Park Geun-Hye, and her eventual sentencing on April 6, 2018, to serve 24 years in prison for corruption. Gokhale traces the scandal as it unfolded in South Korea, noting the government's efforts to curb and censor news and information from its citizens. However, the citizens resorted to using mobile social media in a variety of ways to spread news and awareness, plan protests, and organize logistics for the protests. In doing so they very successfully overcame the state-imposed restrictions and were able to bring the president to trial. Despite the lower status accorded to women in South Korean society, Park Geun-Hye rose to being president, due to a combination of history and lineage, and South Koreans were initially happy to accept her. However, as has happened in many instances during independent South Korea's history, Park

Geun-Hye eventually fell into the web of corruption and cronyism, which led to disenchantment of the citizens. This chapter offers a deep look into South Korean society, the status of women, and the citizens' savvy use of mobile social media to engineer social change. The two chapters show how mobile technologies' potential to affect social change is large, but that the outcome depends on specific circumstances and context.

Another extremely consequential social change that has occurred within the past eight years, and also due to mobile phones, is the advent of the "gig economy" heralded by the ride-sharing service, Uber. Founded in 2009 by Garrett Camp and Travis Kalanick as UberCab, this mobile-based service has expanded to over 600 cities spread over 65 countries and served 75 million passengers in 2018 alone (Iqbal 2018). The business news network CNBC recently rated Uber as the second most disruptive company in the world in 2018 (CNBC 2018). In the final chapter, Nagla Rizk takes us to Cairo, where Egypt's first ride-sharing service was offered by Uber 2014. Within a short time, Uber extended its service to over seven cities in Egypt. As in many other cities around the world, the emergence of Uber initiated responses from traditional taxi services, which necessitated legislative action. The author examines Egypt's new "Ride Hailing Apps Act" from an A2K perspective and discusses the effects of such legalization on the various stakeholders in the ride-sharing and public transport segment in Egypt.

References

Aker, Jenny C., Paul Collier, and Pedro C. Vicente. 2011. "Is Information Power? Using Mobile Phones during an Election in Mozambique." Accessed August 20, 2020. http://pedrovicente.org/cell.pdf.

Archambault, Julie Soleil. 2017. *Mobile Secrets: Youth, Intimacy, and the Politics of Pretense in Mozambique*. Chicago: University of Chicago Press.

Burell, Jenna. 2008. "Problematic Empowerment: West African Internet Scams as Strategic Misrepresentation." *Information Technologies and International Development* 4, no. 4: 15–30.

Breslauer, David N., Robi N. Maamari, Neil A. Switz, Wilbur A. Lam, Daniel A. Fletcher. 2009. "Mobile Phone Based Clinical Microscopy for Global Health Applications." *PLoS ONE* 4, no. 7: e6320. https://doi.org/10.1371/journal.pone.0006320.

Chomsky, Noam. 1997. "Language and Problems of Knowledge." *Teorema* XVI, no. 2: 5–33.

Cisco. 2017. "Cisco Visual Networking Index: Global Mobile Data Traffic Forecast Update, 2016–2021 White Paper." https://www.cisco.com/c/en/us/solutions/collateral/service-provider/visual-networking-index-vni/mobile-white-paper-c11-520862.html.

CNBC. 2018. "Uber – 2018 Disruptor 50." May 22. https://www.cnbc.com/2018/05/22/uber-2018-disruptor-50.html.

Crentsil, Perpetual. 2013. "From Personal to Public Use: Mobile Telephony as Potential Mass Educational Media in HIV/AIDS Strategies in Ghana." *Journal of the Finnish Anthropological Society* 38, no. 1: 83–103.

Iqbal, Mansoor. 2018. "Uber Revenue and Usage Statistics (2018) – Business of Apps." November 28. http://www.businessofapps.com/data/uber-statistics/#1.

Irani, Lilly. 2019. *Chasing Innovation: Making Entrepreneurial Citizens in Modern India*. Princeton, NJ: Princeton University Press.

ISP, Yale Law School. n.d. "Initiatives: Past Initiatives: Access to Knowledge." Accessed December 28, 2020. https://law.yale.edu/isp/about/initiatives/access-knowledge.

Jensen, Robert. 2007. "The Digital Provide: Information (Technology), Market Performance, and Welfare in the South Indian Fisheries Sector." *Quarterly Journal of Economics* 122, no 3: 879–924. https://doi.org/10.1162/qjec.122.3.879.

Mallon, Diarmuid. 2013. "Where Are They Now? I-Mode | ZDNet." October 7. https://www.zdnet.com/article/where-are-they-now-i-mode/.

McCullough, John. 2014. "From FirstSearch to WorldCat Discovery: Cooperative Discovery That Puts You Where Your Users Are." Presented at the ALA Annual Conference, June. https://www.youtube.com/watch?v=MZk_Ufs2eOE (start at minute 4).

Microsoft Devices Team. 2009. "History of Nokia Part One: Nokia Firsts." *Microsoft Devices Blog*. January 19. https://blogs.windows.com/devices/2009/01/19/history-of-nokia-part-one-nokia-firsts/.

Muchie, Mammo and Angathevar Baskaran. 2006. "Introduction." In *Bridging the Digital Divide: Innovation Systems for ICT in Brazil, China, India, Thailand and Southern Africa*, edited by Angathevar Baskaran and Mammo Muchie, 23–50. London: Adonis & Abbey Publishers.

Nielinger, Olaf. 2006. *Information and Communication Technologies (ICT) For Development in Africa*. Frankfurt: Peter Lang.

Osborn, Michelle. 2008. "Fuelling the Flames: Rumour and Politics in Kibera." *Journal of Eastern African Studies* 2, no. 2: 312–327. https://doi.org/10.1080/17531050802094836.

Robins, Kevin and Frank Webster. 1999. *Times of the Technoculture*. London: Routledge.

Sey, Araba. 2011. "'We Use It Different, Different': Making Sense of Trends in Mobile Phone Use in Ghana." *New Media and Society* 13, no. 3: 375–390. https://doi.org/10.1177/1461444810393907.

Shaver, Lea. 2011. "Access to Knowledge: From Development to Human Rights." In *Access to Knowledge in India: New Research on Intellectual Property, Innovation & Development*, edited by Ramesh Subramanian and Lea Shaver, 1–13. London and New York: Bloomsbury Academic.

Slater, John and Janet Kwami. 2005. "Embeddedness and Escape: Internet and Mobile Use as Poverty Reduction Strategies in Ghana." Information Society Research Group, Working Paper No. 4. Accessed August 20, 2020. https://assets.publishing.service.gov.uk/media/57a08c94ed915d622c001431/R8232-ISRGWP4.pdf.

Subramanian, Ramesh. 2011. "ICTs and Access to Knowledge in Rural India: A Comparative Study of Two Models of Deployment." In *Access to Knowledge in India: New Research on Intellectual Property, Innovation and Development*, edited by Ramesh Subramanian and Lea Shaver, 109–147. London: Bloomsbury Academic Publishing.

United Nations. 1948. "Article 27." In *The Universal Declaration of Human Rights*. San Francisco: United Nations. https://www.ohchr.org/EN/UDHR/Documents/UDHR_Translations/eng.pdf.

PART I

Access

Mobile Technologies and A2K

Ramesh Subramanian

A fundamental, elemental, and direct consequence of the emergence of mobile technologies is the direct peer-to-peer communication that it enables. Developments in mobile telephony have enabled people to "cut the cord" and be able to communicate with each other regardless of where they are—be it Sub-Saharan Africa, a village in South India, or a large metropolis that could be located anywhere in the world. And the fact that this medium of communication could be accessible to any and every human on earth, whoever they are, at a fairly nominal cost, is one of the great achievements of modern technology. The chapters in this part showcase three distinct ways by which mobile technologies have been used to further access to knowledge: for teaching and learning, rural inclusivity, and for national infrastructure development. While distinct, these chapters also share two important commonalities: first, each chapter locates itself in the Global South, yet shows how their results are global in scope—all aided by the common thread of mobile telephony; second, each of these chapters, in an important way, is about a particular form of learning, with the aid of mobile telephony.

The first chapter examines the use of mobile technology in language learning. It can be argued that language is the basis for all knowledge. What cannot be expressed is not known. As linguist and philosopher Noam Chomsky noted, language can be considered to be "a system that is internalized in the mind/brain, yielding specific cases of propositional knowledge and knowledge how to do so and so" (Chomsky 1997, 12). John Bosco Lourdusamy and Rishika Czarzasta take on the interesting concept of language learning in a foreign, non-immersive setting and study its effectiveness when information and communications technologies (ICT)—especially mobile technologies are adopted to aid such learning. Their study consists of field studies on learning the French language in Chennai, a large metropolis in India. The scope of this endeavor is interesting as it is far-reaching. An Indian national and Polish national of Indian origin, jointly examining the nuances of French language education using mobile technologies in Tamil-speaking Chennai, show the global reach, range, and potential of the technology.

The second chapter deals with another type of learning. It focuses on the various efforts to give access to knowledge to villagers in rural South India by providing them with the "last mile" of telecommunications connection. This last mile is what separates most rural populations from attaining full (Internet) connectivity. Cellular or mobile telephony helps achieve this last mile connectivity. In this study, Saji Matthew, Arun Kumar, and Ramesh Subramanian take a critical look at the many efforts to bring Internet access to villagers, and the results that this brings in increased access to health information, to market resources, women's empowerment and entrepreneurship, as well as democratization. What is particularly interesting in this research is the emphasis on *learning*, especially from mistakes, that the researchers focus on. There have been many studies in this area that focus on the successes. But in their study, they focus not only on the success stories, but also on the many failures and missteps that have occurred in efforts to provide access to communications infrastructure (and thus the Internet) to rural villages. Their case studies thus provide an excellent template that could be used by access providers and policy makers not only in India but also in several other developing economies.

The third chapter focuses on how access to knowledge through mobile telephony has aided a developing country in Sub-Saharan Africa, namely Botswana, to close the digital divide and transform the lives of its citizens through mobile services. William Lesitaokana's research documents how mobile telephony has enabled over 80 percent of all adults in continental Africa to own and use mobile phones, and how the diffusion of mobile phones in Botswana has significantly facilitated the use of mobile communications services especially among urban youth country wide. The chapter then goes on to describe, using cases, how the extensive availability of mobile phones and access to the Internet have transformed the lives of the citizens of Botswana. Lesitaokana notes that this is a prime example of how, in a technologically less-advanced country, the use of mobile phones proves to be significantly useful to access mobile public services, and thus people use it enhance their socio-economic status. The author also notes how the mobile revolution in Botswana fosters not only extensive knowledge, but also increases civic participation among its citizens.

The final chapter by Celina Bottino, Carlos Affonso Souza, and Beatriz Nunes discusses the attempts by the National Telecommunications Agency (Anatel), the quasi-government agency that regulates the telecommunications sector in Brazil, to block certain mobile phones. In 2014, Anatel announced a measure whereby non-approved cell phones would be blocked in the country. This has obvious ramifications for access to knowledge and freedom of expression. The authors analyze Anatel's measure from an Access to Knowledge perspective and argue it would result in restricted access to the Internet to millions of Brazilians, especially those in the lower economic strata of society. In addition, this would also impact on the citizens' privacy rights, as it would require the development of a database containing the "approved" phone-owners' data. Arguing that this measure, enacted presumably to protect and enhance national security, law and order, and public morals is both disproportionate and unnecessary, the authors propose alternate solutions that would not result in citizens' access to the Internet though non-approved phones.

These four chapters together thus focus on the collective learning that is achieved, and the possibilities that emerge, when access to knowledge is provided though access to mobile technologies.

Reference

Chomsky, Noam. 1997. "Language and Problems of Knowledge." *Teorema* XVI, no. 2: 5–33.

2

INDIA AND FOREIGN LANGUAGE TEACHING

Enhancing A2K through M-Learning

John Lourdusamy and Rishika Czarzasta

Introduction

Foreign language education has been a prominent feature of Indian metropolises. It has particularly been in the ascent in the last couple of decades in the wake of globalization, owing to either greater mobility of personnel or to the significant rise in global trading and other partnerships. Simultaneously, during the past two decades, India has also seen a significant rise in the use of information and communications technologies (ICTs) in socio-economic development, particularly in the field of education. These two factors together are of immense relevance to the goals of the Access to Knowledge (A2K) movement. Introducing ease in language learning opens the space for wider participation and benefit. It enhances access to the knowledge of the language as such, and this newly acquired language in turn further opens vistas to more knowledge through that language. Ease in language learning also expands the world of opportunities in terms of jobs, travel, and acquaintance with the wider world—socially and economically. The use of modern information and communication technology in this domain (as part of the wider universe of "ICTs in Education" or "e-learning") is step towards promoting the goals of A2K, provided that it does not become exclusivist.

ICTs in education can be highly beneficial, yet there are a few challenges that need to be addressed. This chapter discusses the effectiveness and challenges of employing ICTs, specifically in the domain of foreign language education and learning. The challenges in teaching or learning a foreign language are much more complex than the challenges one may face in teaching or learning a second language that is present in the immediate society of the learner. The most obvious reason is the relative absence of the background and culture of the original home of the language. This is a disadvantage to the extent that any language is to a great degree culturally embedded. The other major disadvantage is the limited local use of the language on a daily basis.

Added to this is the fact that language learning requires a lot more motivation and involvement than any other kind of learning and is a particularly time-consuming process. Any method and tool that is sensitive to these special realities is always very welcome, and, correspondingly, the domain of language learning has always been very open to constant innovation and experimentation. This chapter looks at such efforts (or their inadequacy) on the basis of a field study conducted by us in 2015 in Chennai city in southern India.

The aim of this field study was to analyze the effectiveness of employing ICTs, including the hardware and the software, for the purpose of teaching a foreign language to students. It focuses particularly on the teaching of French as a foreign language in the city of Chennai. The field research did not specifically focus on mobile phones alone (though it included them). Nevertheless, it is useful in the context of the theme of this book due to the fact much (if not all) of the blessings and benefits of mobile devices, especially smart-phones, are derived from their belonging to the larger universe of the Internet. It is this aspect of the mobile devices that is of particular relevance to A2K in so far as mobile devices amplify the potentials the Internet provides for knowledge acquisition and dissemination. Based on existing literature, we consider various ideas concerning language learning and examine some of them in relation to the new world of possibilities opened by ICTs. We also underline the particular advantages and disadvantages of mobile devices within the field of language learning.

Key terms

We begin by explaining some of the key terms used here, with a measure of clarity, before going on to examine some of the key ideas concerning language learning and their relation to ICTs and A2K.

For the purposes of our study, we define ICTs as tools (hardware) and applications (software) that are useful for the SPREADD of Information (Storage, Processing, Retrieval, Exchange, Access, Display, and Dissemination of Information). ICTs can be positively utilized in various fields including education, agriculture, governance, healthcare, etc. ICTs for education can facilitate activities such as distance learning, video-conferencing, and asynchronous interactions that may be highly beneficial to the students (Mukerji 2013, 1). The most commonly used ICT tools used in education are computers, smart-boards, speakers, projectors, and mobile devices (like cellular phones, tablets and iPads).

ICTs contribute in a major way to learning both in situations where students are with the teacher and also while the teacher and the student are not physically present in the same place. In addition, ICTs enable the students to learn at their own pace. ICTs open up an abundance of learning materials to the students with the freedom of accessing them whenever they wish to. Using ICTs can facilitate and complement the existing classroom teaching, while they may also be used in a more informal setting for the purpose of learning. Language learning applications (apps) in mobile phones are a good example for learning in an informal manner/setting. Though the use of ICTs (including mobile phones) may not efface the significance of the teacher, they certainly add value to the learning experience and supplement classroom teaching. This is known as *blended learning*.

While looking at ICTs in education and in learning of foreign languages, it is also important to focus on "ICT integration," which connotes a range of learning environments from a stand-alone computer in a classroom to a situation where the teaching is done by the computer through pre-packaged "teacher-proof courseware" (Lloyd 2005, 3–4). In today's context, this may be extended further and naturally to include mobile devices.

A *foreign language* is a language that is not spoken in the native country of the learner. A foreign language is not usually learned by a learner for the purpose of everyday communication, as the usage of that foreign language is minimal in the learner's immediate social context (Saville-Troike 2006, 4). Instead, a foreign language is normally (though not necessarily) learned by a learner with a certain motive, which is usually to work, study, or travel abroad. The learner's knowledge of the foreign language is purely based on the input received through textbooks or any learning material the learner is exposed to. This is where ICTs can help better as they enable the learner to have greater access to an abundance of learning materials. Thus ICTs, particularly mobile devices, are of considerable significance to A2K in terms of both ease and variety because of their greater ease of use and their affordability.

Sarac (2013), while analyzing the role of language teaching software, felt that the purpose of the software would not be satisfied if the user interface is not easy enough for the user to handle. Kan (2011) also argues that for online material to be successful it is important for it to be accessible. In the context of *accessibility*, mobile phones become particularly relevant. The low cost of mobile phones and their small size in comparison to computers make them accessible to a larger audience.

Mobile learning and the use of ICTs is an important advancement in the field of education. In their research on mobile learning, Viberg and Grönlund (2013) also highlight advantages such as the low cost and small size and user-friendliness of mobile technologies as compared to computers. According to Stockwell (2008), the reason for the success of mobile learning is that the learners were able to complete their activities anywhere and anytime at their own pace.

One of the important factors in language learning is *motivation*, and this is also a key area where ICTs and mobile devices in particular can play a vital role. Klimova and Poulova (2014) argue that ICTs could help in achieving some of the motivational aspects such as making the learning more interesting and interactive. With mobile technologies, the focus is more on the learner now than on the teacher (53). The process of learning becomes more effective because, with the aid of ICTs, the materials are up to date and can be customized according to the learner's needs. One of the most important aspects of language learning is learning the culture of the country (of origin of the language), and this can be learnt best with the help of ICTs through audio-visuals. The learning process becomes more and more dynamic with the help of multimedia. According to Tschirner (2001, 318) foreign language learning is a social process as much as it is a psychological process. Through ICTs, an artificial learning environment can be created even though it is not possible for a learner to have natural interactions with the native speakers of the targeted language. The digital classroom makes the classroom atmosphere a learner-friendly one.

ICTs can be used in a variety of other ways to motivate the students. They can be used to facilitate online interaction with native and non-native speakers through video calling software available online. The students can be motivated by getting their work published in the target foreign language on social networking websites, thus giving them recognition as well as probable feedback.

Instrumental motivation is the main kind of motivation when it comes to foreign language learning. There is an immediate short-term goal for which the foreign language is learnt. According to Dettori and Lupi (2010, 2712), ICTs have been used for the purpose of learning and teaching a foreign language ever since they came into existence, which was roughly during the 1970s. There was a shift in the focus of the purpose for which these foreign languages have been learnt. The shift in focus occurred from learning the grammatical and lexical structures to the use of language to communicate. This shift is of particular significance to A2K in terms of the emphasis on the more practical aspects of the learning and its immediate benefits. This obviously has a broader social impact in terms of opportunities and livelihood than the more dominant, scholarly, and technical approach that was more prevalent prior to this shift. Communication has now become the most important purpose of language learning. We can extend this view to argue that such change in focus and motivation makes the field particularly fertile for ICT interventions, especially at the individual level. And nothing can fit the bill better than mobile devices in this regard.

An important factor in language learning where ICTs and especially mobile devices can play fruitful roles is *autonomous learning*. Klimova and Semradova (2012) highlight the importance of autonomous learning experience that ICTs offer. ICTs promote a situation in which the teacher is no longer a teacher but a co-learner along with the student (89). Such a scenario naturally strengthens the concept of blended learning that combines a face-to-face interaction between the students, the teachers, and online teaching materials (90). Blended learning is found to be very efficient as the different methodologies combined together compensate for what is absent in a particular methodology.

Thus, we find that ICTs in general and mobile devices (particularly mobile phones as there are varieties of them which are far more affordable than other mobile devices like the iPad) have huge potential to influence language learning. Apart from theorizing, some of the sources cited above also point to practical studies already undertaken elsewhere. It is in an effort to apply and extend some of these concepts within the specific context of India, choosing a particular location (Chennai) and language (French), that we embarked on our own minor field study.

Methods of data collection

The data for this study has been collected through the following methods from various institutes that teach (using or not using ICTs) French to students in the city of Chennai:

1. Non-participatory classroom observations
2. Personal interviews
3. Online questionnaires

The interviews and the responses for the online questionnaires were collected from the following sites or from students belonging to them (all located in Chennai):

- Alliance Française de Madras
- Indian Institute of Technology Madras (IITM)
- Anna University
- Stella Maris College
- Loyola College
- MOP Vaishnav College
- Justice Basheer Ahmed Sayeed College for Women

The study followed both qualitative and quantitative methods of data collection in order to get subjective and quantitative answers from the respondents. Non-participatory classroom observations were conducted at Alliance Française de Madras and at IITM French classes. At Alliance Française de Madras, we attended French classes of various levels of proficiency to observe how the teacher used ICTs to teach the students. At the end of each class, a personal interview was conducted with the teacher to gather the teacher's views on the advantages and disadvantages of employing ICTs in classrooms. To gather the students' perceptions on the use of ICTs, interviews were taken with a few students at the beginning and at the end of each attended class. Likewise, observations were made at the French classes at IIT Madras where the teacher did not employ ICTs to teach French.

Apart from the interviews, online questionnaires were circulated among teachers and students to elicit their opinion and experiences on teaching or learning with or without the aid of ICTs. The online questionnaires were also circulated to the management of the institutions where these foreign languages are taught to get the management perspectives on the advantages and challenges of employing ICTs for foreign language teaching. Personal interviews were also held with the management personnel of institutions where French was taught.

Sampling method

The institutes were chosen at random with a balance between the institutions that teach French with and without the aid of ICTs. The respondents for this study were chosen by simple random sampling method. The sample size and distribution is shown in Table 2.1.

The collected responses have a bearing upon some of the key concepts discussed in the previous section of this chapter. The following sector-wise sections elaborate on the findings based on the non-participatory classroom observations, interviews conducted at the field sites, and the questionnaire responses.

TABLE 2.1 Sample distribution of different target groups

Method	*Those who use ICTs*		*Not using ICTs*	
	Teachers	*Students*	*Teachers*	*Students*
Online questionnaires	12	127	9	35
Personal interviews	8	10	1	8

Students learning French with the aid of ICTs

The sample size of this segment of respondents is 137 out of which 127 responded through online questionnaires, while the other 10 responses were collected through personal interviews. The most commonly used ICTs in ICT-enabled classrooms are computers, projectors, screens/smart-boards, and speakers. A computer with Internet access is the most common ICT used by the students who are taught French with the aid of technology. Over 95 percent of the respondents said they used computers as the main ICT tool for learning French. Out of these, approximately 90 percent used the Internet along with computers for accessing language-teaching websites. Mobile phones are rarely used in the classroom setting as such. However, the students make use of mobile phones outside the classroom for the purpose of learning French. An application called Duolingo seems to be very popular among the students with about 43 percent using it to improve their French. The application enables the students to undertake short quizzes. With regard to motivation and satisfaction, 71 percent of the respondents gave a rating of "feeling extremely satisfied" (10 out of 10) with using ICTs for learning French.

The high satisfaction level suggests that students relish learning through ICTs and that they are motivated in a positive way. The advantage of *blended learning* was noted and appreciated by a majority of the students: 79 percent of the students found it interesting to learn via ICTs, yet they preferred a combination of teacher-driven and technology-driven method of learning. And of course, both approaches can meet in the classroom itself: 66 percent of the students responded that the use of ICTs in classroom breaks monotony during the class and increases their attention span. There was appreciation among 72 percent of the students for the online grammar exercises given to them and for the projection of videos or pictures to better cultivate their vocabulary. The latter has enabled the students to learn the language with the cultural context. This is quite essential for foreign language learning because learning a foreign language is not only a linguistic phenomenon but also a cultural phenomenon.

With regard to specific aspects of the learning process, 64 percent of the respondents found ICTs to be most helpful for the listening aspect of the language. 57 percent of the respondents felt ICTs helped them improve their speaking skills. The practice exercises provided to the students for listening helped them to appreciate the different accents that native speakers of French have. Overall, the students stated that they found ICTs to be very beneficial because ICTs enabled them to learn at their own pace and even outside the classroom. This last point makes mobile phones (among all the modern ICTs) particularly valuable for language learning. Being able to learn at one's own pace and in informal ways has to be seen as a crucial element in A2K.

There are ways in which the promises and potentials of mobile phones can be better tapped. One of the important areas to pay attention to is customization in order to understand the kind of technology-mix that fits various stakeholders. One kind of technology-mix may work better with a certain group than another. While mobile phones have opened the gates in a big way for individual engagement (in terms of possession and ease of use), it would be a pity if the contents, individual approach or their use are not customized, either in terms of the stand-alone apps or in terms of the technology mix that the mobile will be part of. This is a good example of the need for A2K endeavors to give particular importance to customization. Greater sensitivity to the social and economic situation of the beneficiaries will advance the cause of A2K better. Once sensitivity is in place, mobile phones can be particularly helpful to translate that sensitivity into customized action plan—given the special advantages of mobiles phones pointed out here.

There is the important need to involve all the stakeholders, including students and teachers, while planning the methodologies and technology mixes. It is incumbent on the managers of the institutes and the developers and providers of the Internet content and apps to undertake appropriate preliminary survey/feedback/need-analysis that will help incorporate the expectations, changing attitudes, and problems pertaining to the teachers and learners.

Teachers teaching French with the aid of ICTs

The sample size of this segment of respondents is 20. Of these, 12 responses were collected through online questionnaires, while 8 were through personal interviews. Ninety percent of the teachers use computers extensively in the classroom combined with the computer applications that help them in different ways. The main source for dynamic resources for teaching is the Internet. The teachers use online resources for grammar exercises as there is an abundance of them in contrast to the limited materials available in the prescribed textbooks. Seventy-five percent of the teachers felt that ICTs saved their time in writing on the board as they can prepare presentation slides that can be projected on the smart-board in the classroom repeatedly over different sessions. With regard to the specific aspects in which ICTs are most efficacious in language learning, the listening and speaking aspect comes out on top.

The teachers understand the growing importance of ICTs in a globalized world and the changing trends in language education. Ninety percent of the teachers also responded that they would strongly recommend ICT-aided teaching methods to other teachers of foreign languages. As far as future advancements are concerned, 55 percent of the teachers would like to see tablets replacing notebooks. They also look forward to more software, mobile apps, and web resources, which would help a student to improve the writing aspect of the language.

Students learning French without the aid of ICTs

With regard to students learning without the aid of ICTs, one of our primary aims was to ascertain the reason for the non-use of ICTs. The responses were mostly divided between the lack of infrastructure in their classrooms and the unwillingness of the teacher to use ICTs. Sometimes the teachers are unwilling to employ ICTs even though they have the infrastructure to use them. The unwillingness stems from the fact that they are not trained to use technology. The students did not seem to feel very satisfied with the traditional pedagogical methods. Some felt that they would learn better if they were taught using ICTs. Herein, we need to underline the role of the wider technological context in the particular geographical locality. A significant prevalence of ICTs outside of the classroom (even if they are geared towards other purposes) would spur the interest and demand for ICTs in the classroom. By this logic too, as far as language learning is concerned, one of the important domains where interest would rise is the use of mobile phones, considering their wide prevalence and rapid spread compared to other ICTs.

It is interesting to note that 40 percent of the students felt that the student–teacher interaction might reduce if ICTs are used in class. They felt that ICTs could come (adversely) in between the student and the teacher. This bolsters further the importance of blended learning where classroom teacher is relevant—only that he/she has to become more relevant in a different sense—in relation to the changing scenario i. e., a situation should not arise where the human element in the class room does not dwindle because of excessive and mechanical use of technology. The teacher along with creative use of technology should also maintain congenial conditions of interaction inside the classroom and also try to use the (foreign) language as much as possible in such interaction. This is particularly important where students do not have much opportunity for socializing through that language in day-to-day life outside of the classroom. According to Vygotsky (1978), the learners learn from the outside world much more than they learn inside the classroom through a process of construction on language. Since the level of interaction is very low, this phenomenon never occurred with the students learning through traditional methods. Also, these methods of learning are very teacher-oriented. The students responded that through traditional teaching methods they are still able to learn the writing aspect of the language fairly well but they seem to lag behind when it comes to listening or speaking. Thus, with good use of technology inside the classroom without yet reducing the human interaction, teachers can create situations, which can compensate for the absence of the opportunities for learning in the outside world (through socialization).

Teachers teaching French without the aid of ICTs

Among teachers, the foremost reason stated by them for not using technology in classrooms is that it is a time-consuming process. This is in direct contrast to what the teachers who use technology felt about their method. The primary reason for this is that the teachers who are not trained take a lot of time to control the devices and this in turn causes frustration to the user. So they avoid using ICTs and stick to the traditional methods of teaching. Some teachers did not want to use ICTs although they had the infrastructure to use them. It is hard to tell if training or if lack of infrastructure is a bigger issue. At some level, both are equally important issues that have to be addressed.

Herein, one should take note of the relation between the level of technology (complicated or simple) and A2K. Sometimes the complicated nature of technology leads to alienation with negative impact on access to technology and therefore access to knowledge. Wherever possible, technology needs to be simplified (and in some cases demystified) in order to promote accessibility. It is not enough just to have the technological wherewithal alone.

There are mixed opinions among teachers on the success rate of traditional methods. While 50 percent of them felt traditional methods are more effective, the other 50 percent felt ICT-aided modern methods could help in language learning. The teachers who felt ICTs could help are the ones who desired changes but had infrastructural constraints. A point very specifically relevant to mobile phone is that teachers have a negative opinion of it; they feel that mobile phones are a distraction. This has a discouraging effect on students, even those who sincerely desire to take advantage the possibilities that mobile technology could offer for language learning—especially where the teachers are not using ICTs generally in the classroom.

One has to realize that perceptions about technologies also matter for A2K. Technologies do not operate in and through people impersonally. They are colored by the personal and social preconceptions and perceptions. In this case, we see that the teachers' negative perception about mobile phones (based to some extent on the social perceptions—many of which are not entirely untrue) can have a negative impact on access as it impedes both their usage and that of the students (due to the teacher's hesitation to look at and tap the positive potential of mobile phones for the students' immediate language needs).

Management/institution teaching French

As for the management's view of things, there was a broad consensus about the immense amount of materials available online that would extend the possibilities for the students to learn outside the classroom. The possible disadvantages of using ICTs according to them are: occasional power cuts, Internet connectivity disruptions, and other technological hiccups that can disturb the teachers' lesson plans. The management typically considers the problem from an energy-consumption angle. Since ICT devices require more electricity to run, it results in increased energy consumption. We note that the problems put forward by the management's side require broader reforms related to the cost of power, its regular supply, and robust connectivity. These and their investment-shyness make a further strong case for exploring mobile phone as a viable option at least in the short term. Of course, this would run against the argument for blended learning. But a positive point emerging from the survey is that if the benefits of ICTs become more and more convincing, the managements are ready to bear the associated costs and are even hopeful of running cost-efficient.

Yet another useful lesson for A2K here is that technological efforts cannot be seen or planted outside of wider infrastructural readiness and enabling or impeding policies. In our case some of them may be within the ambit of the management (like internal infrastructure) and some external (like power supply and government policies related to Internet access). But one of the important roles that management can play is with regard to some of the problems highlighted earlier like alienation and perception building. This can particularly be done through appropriate training of all stakeholders. Also, the training should be a periodic and constant process coinciding with the new vistas opening up constantly especially in rapidly advancing realms like mobile technology.

Conclusion

The theories of learning have been evolving over a long period of time. The traditional methods of teaching may have been successful in the past when ICTs were not available. Also, the primary learning objectives were different at that point. There has been a shift in focus from what is expected from foreign language learning. The listening and speaking aspects of the language have gained as much importance as reading and writing. Traditional methods had proven successful when the focus of learning was on reading and writing. Additionally, there is a growing trend towards building a more learner-centric atmosphere. However, in spite of all these potential advantages, it can still be said that ICTs can only supplement a teacher but not replace one. Both the students who learn with and without the aid of ICTs in our survey confirmed this reality. The institutions that teach French are also open to installing and expanding ICTs where absent.

To summarize the advantages of using ICTs in classroom, one can say that ICTs help in motivating the students and increasing their self-confidence. The use of ICTs increases the overall input of the foreign language to the learner and also enables the learner to observe the variations in the language. ICTs also help in creating artificial scenarios to promote natural interactions, hence improving communication skills. This can be achieved only if the instructor uses the target language to communicate with the students during the process of teaching. ICTs provide an outside learning experience to the students and therefore enable them to learn at their own pace. The use of ICTs helps the students in learning the language in a cultural context by the visual and other impacts ICTs create among the learners.

While these are advantages of ICTs in general, many can easily be extrapolated to the context of mobile phones (especially smart-phones) in particular. This is because many of the advantages attached to ICT-based learning (like ample material, dynamic content, exposure to the culture of the country—especially the latest trends in culture and their reflection in the language, etc.) are derived basically from being connected to the Internet. Mobile phones in their own way utilize and extend the possibilities born out of the Internet, especially at the individual level. This extrapolation is also justified as we also underline here the importance of blended learning (and not a pedagogy based on mobile phones exclusively) as the most effective way forward. This is not just because of the vital and useful role played by the teacher, but also because there are other ICTs (like audio and video tapes/CDs) within the classroom which are not internet based but which are useful in their own ways.

On the one hand, learners who have been enchanted by the power of ICTs in the classroom setting may miss some of the benefits of that setting (like the big smart-screen, the computer monitor, and the interactive advantages of group learning). On the other hand, mobile phones can easily take over once the initial enchantment, motivation, convictions about advantages of blended learning, familiarity with various possible exercises, and appropriate sites have all been attained within the classroom. While size of the screen and handling difficulties (in the absence of keyboards, pointers, remote controllers etc.) may be disadvantages with mobile phones, they can nevertheless sustain the spirit and enthusiasm generated in the classroom and even compensate for the disadvantages with advantages of their own: the cheaper costs (of the instruments and data plans), easier connectivity, the sense of possession, the greater intimacy, uncomplicated operability, portability, and use-anywhere/anytime advantage (including such times as waiting in queues or at bus-stops, journeys, or even while lying in bed just before sleep!).

And in the meantime, it is important on the part of social scientists and educationists to research into this area in further depth as the importance of incorporating technology in education is only going to be increasing in the globalized world and a world being increasingly "connected" and animated by ICTs—especially with rapid spread of mobile phones, particularly in countries like India. As mentioned at the very beginning, this is of multiple relevance to A2K as access to new languages opens many other vistas and opportunities.

References

Dettori, Giuliana and Valentina Lupi. 2010. "ICT and New Methodologies in Language Learning." *Procedia – Social and Behavioral Sciences* 2(2): 2712–2716.

Kan, Soh Or. 2011. "Critique of a Language-Learning Website." *US-China Education Review* 8 (5): 675–681.

Klimova, Blanka Frydrychova and Petra Poulova. 2014. "ICT as a Motivational Tool in the Learning of Foreign Languages." In *Proceedings of the 2014 International Conference on Educational Technologies and Education*: 53–56.

Klimova, Blanka Frydrychova and Ilona Semradova. 2012. "The Teaching of Foreign Languages and ICT." *Procedia Technology* 1: 89–93.

Lloyd, Margaret. 2005. "Towards a Definition of the Integration of ICT in the Classroom." In *Proceedings AARE '05 Education Research – Creative Dissent: Constructive Solutions*. Parramatta, New South Wales. Accessed from https://eprints.qut.edu.au/3553/1/3553.pdf.

Mukerji, Maitrayee. 2013. *ICTs and Development: A Study of Telecentres in Rural India*. Basingstoke: Palgrave Macmillan.

Sarac, H. Sezgi. 2013. "Belief, Knowledge and Expectations on Language Instruction." *Procedia – Social and Behavioral Sciences* 70: 696–701.

Saville-Troike, Muriel. 2006. *Introducing Second Language Acquisition*. Cambridge, UK: Cambridge University Press.
Stockwell, Glenn. 2008 "Investigating Learner Preparedness for and Usage Patterns of Mobile Learning." *ReCALL*, 20(3): 253–270.
Tschirner, Erwin. 2001. "Language Acquisition in the Classroom: The Role of Digital Video." *Computer Assisted Language Learning* 14 (3–4): 305–319.
Viberg, Olga and Ake Grönlund. 2013. "Cross-cultural Analysis of Users' Attitudes toward the Use of Mobile Devices in Second and Foreign Language Learning in Higher Education: A Case from Sweden and China." *Computers & Education* 69: 169–180.
Vygotsky, Lev Semenovich. 1978. *Mind on Society*. Boston: Harvard University Press.

3

INDIA AND THE PAIN OF THE LAST MILE

Human-to-Human ICT Interface for the Poor and the Marginalized

Saji Matthew, Arun Kumar and Ramesh Subramanian

Introduction

The International Monetary Fund (IMF) projected India's economy in 2017 to be US $ 2.45 billion (IMF 2017). India's 2017 GDP growth is estimated to be 7.1 percent (Ministry of Finance, Government of India 2017). That makes India the fifth largest (nominal) economy in the world and the third largest if purchasing power parity (PPP) is considered. Much of India's growth in the last two decades has been led by the service and industrial sectors, which include the information technology (IT) sector. In 2016–17, the services and industrial sectors were projected to grow 8.8 percent and 5.2 percent respectively (ibid.). The Indian Information Technology-Business Process Management (IT-BPM) industry was projected to grow at a rate of 8.6 percent and reach over US$ 155 billion by 2017 (Venkatesh 2017).

Despite these impressive growth figures, India still lags far behind in the sphere of human development. India's population, which is around 1.2 billion, is expected to surpass China's by the year 2030. The 2007–2008 Human Development Report published by the United Nations Development Program (UNDP) gave India a Human Development Index (HDI) score of 0.619, which placed it in the 128th position among 177 countries (UNDP 2007). In 2016, this situation seems to have worsened, with the HDI placing India at the 131st position among the 188 countries ranked (UNDP 2016). Since 1984, developmental efforts have gained much stronger focus, coinciding with the gradual liberalization of India's economy coupled with the above-mentioned growth of India's IT sector.

For the last decade, there has been increasing emphasis on narrowing the "digital divide" by bringing IT developments, especially telecommunications and the Internet, to rural areas. Information and communications technologies (ICTs) are considered to be the vehicles to bring economic and human development to rural India. Rural development through telecommunications is being addressed at several levels: the governmental level, non-governmental level (NGOs), private-enterprise level, and the scientific/research level (at academic and research institutions). In this chapter, we discuss key efforts undertaken in India over the last decade to use ICTs to enhance rural development. It is important to note, in the context of this book, that "ICT" is a generic term that we use to refer to all types of telecommunications systems, including mobile telecommunications. We look at successes and failures of these efforts. We then situate the results of these efforts within the context of established theories in information systems implementation and acceptance pertaining to the "bottom of the pyramid" or BoP segment (Prahalad and Hammond 2002). Finally, we summarize and analyze our findings and provide directions for new research in this area. The main directions and objectives of the chapter are set forth in the next section.

ICT for rural development

The potential of ICTs to provide the rural poor access to healthcare, education, government, and financial services and help them find markets has been well established (Cecchini and Scott 2003). These, in turn, empower the poor to gain freedom from exploitation and improve their livelihood. For example, Jensen (2007) reported that the adoption of mobile phones by marginalized fishermen of Kerala in Southern India increased the welfare of both producers and consumers. Whereas large-scale adoption of ICTs supports the notion of technological determinism (MacKenzie and Wajcman 1999), where the attractiveness of a technology alone causes its large-scale adoption, other factors also come into play. Rural ICT initiatives have relied on the "Village Level Entrepreneur" (VLE) as a human-to-human ICT interface to make ICTs acceptable to the rural poor (Prahalad and Hammond 2002; Dass and Bhattacherjee 2011). However, the "shared services center" (telecenter) initiative by the Government of India where the VLE is the last mile interface with the rural service receivers has shown mixed results (Dass and Bhattacherjee 2011).

The rural telecenter, which is essentially a rural Internet kiosk that is used to disseminate relevant information regarding farming, education, health, weather, governmental news, job, loans, and aid opportunities has been globally attempted as a way of connecting government and rural citizens (Grace, Kenny, and Qiang 2004). In the Indian context, the village-level telecenter is usually connected to a district-level headquarters via mobile transmission towers using adaptations of the Digital Enhanced Cordless Telecommunications (DECT) mobile technology standard or through satellite communications. However, this concept has faced huge implementation challenges in different countries, including India, especially where the readiness for electronic forms of exchange by communities is low. There are also other implementation challenges, which also include infrastructure and social issues. Because of these challenges, telecenters did not accrue the intended benefits in several countries as noted in prior studies (Ernberg 1998; Dass and Bhattacherjee 2011). For example, in Bangladesh, rural women were denied access to the Internet, accessed through telecenters, as the community felt that it was being used for pornography (Mahmood 2005). In India, there have been both successes and challenges in the results of these efforts.

In the backdrop of ICTs pivotal role in providing opportunities, empowering, and providing security to the rural poor (Cecchini and Scott 2003), this chapter has the following specific objectives:

1. Describe insightful cases on ICT-based initiatives in India for the poor and the marginalized and elicit lessons learned
2. Understand and map user segments and their defining characteristics with respect to ICT characteristics implemented for rural poor

We discuss some of the ICT-based Indian initiatives below.

ICT for "bottom of the pyramid" and women: stakeholders and impacts

The "bottom of the pyramid" as popularized by C. K. Prahalad (2004) is a socio-economic concept that groups a vast number of people around the world, in excess of four billion, who live in under US$ 2.50 a day. This group has been generally excluded from the modernity of present-day societies. This exclusion has led to exploitation. This group does not have consumption choices, access to financial services, or freedom to produce and sell services and goods. In India, many women, especially in rural areas, have been traditionally exploited and fall well within this group. ICTs have the potential to empower the poor to get freedom from being exploited and improve their livelihood, as explained in the previous section. The use of ICT in the rural context, especially for people or enterprises at the lower end of the economic spectrum, varies from providing simple text messaging services to using higher-level technology for assessing the competition and pricing. There have been efforts by non-governmental, governmental, para-statal, and private entrepreneurial agencies in this regard in India. This section discusses some of the ways in which ICTs have been deployed specifically towards enhancing the lives of those at the bottom of the pyramid.

Non-governmental efforts

ITC, a large Indian corporation, created the *eChoupal,* [1] an electronic meeting place that functions as a human-to-human ICT interface that allows for the implementation of an e-procurement system connecting farmers. Before the advent of eChoupal a farmer could sell their produce (only) to the nearby market, and wait for payment, often for the whole day, thus losing potential earning for a day. The eChoupal kiosks operate through a human-to-human interface called *Sanchalak* (facilitator) who acts as a mediator between the farmer and the kiosk. A *Sanchalak* is a person from the same area but selected and trained by ITC to own and run the kiosk as an entrepreneur with support from ITC. The farmers are included in the implementation process and receive training that helps them to realize benefits from the system. This project has spread to 15 states of India, connecting about 1.6 million farmers through the eChoupal interface. The project has delivered huge benefits to farmers by providing them with information on soil conditions, weather forecasts, and farming practices. The eChoupal also enables farmers to sell their products with up-to-date market information and thus reducing transaction costs. Similar positive outcomes have been reported on the *eKutir* project where a microentrepreneur from the rural community provides nutrient analysis of the soil (using ICT's technology) to local farmers. This project is also an example of a successful project that was received positively by the community (Jha, Pinsonneault, and Dubé 2016).

There are also NGOs which focus on establishing "business to business" (b2b) marketplaces in rural areas. The b2b efforts aim to enhance the capability of rural entrepreneurs to use technology to grow their businesses. This is done by improving their familiarity with mobile devices such as smartphones and encouraging them to use the Internet and online market places. The entrepreneurs are given training on government regulations and compliance, as well as how to enhance the quality of their products and market them. The b2b marketplace typically uses an SMS-based alert system that is gradually evolving into an e-commerce app and eventually into an e-commerce portal for transacting business. By providing dedicated and exclusive virtual marketplaces, it is hoped that the products of entrepreneurs would get adequate visibility and will be sold easily. It would also enable entrepreneurs to enhance their managerial ability. As they transact with other members of the portal, they become aware of effective sales and marketing techniques, build business networks, learn manufacturing techniques, and optimize their business to reduce costs (Ghosh 2011).

Governmental efforts

The Indian government adopted the telecenter model while rolling out its National eGovernment Plan (NeGP) in 2006. The objective was to set up 100,000 Common Service Centers (CSC) across the country at a cost of US$ 1.2 billion. The model included a VLE (Village Level Entrepreneur) to cover the last mile of delivery of government services to rural citizens through ICT with a Service Centre Agency (CSA) and a State Designated Agency (SDA) for further coordination. However, the results failed to meet the intended objectives. Many centers became non-operational due to inadequate support services for the VLE, poor VLE motivation, as well as training-related issues (Dass and Bhattacherjee 2011). While it has been reported that some CSCs were successful where the necessary infrastructure such as electricity and Internet was in place, many CSCs were unsuccessful even where the infrastructure was sufficient. Therefore, we infer that while ICT infrastructure is a necessary requirement to operate a CSC, it does not ensure that a telecenter will be successful or that services will reach the poor (Ernberg 1998; Dass and Bhattacherjee 2011).

One of the initial initiatives by the Indian government was intended to "bridge the digital gender divide" by familiarizing or exposing rural women to computers with the hope that they would use them for their entrepreneurial activity. The ability to access information and establish communication with customers, business networks, and local business bodies enabled their income earning process. The target beneficiaries revealed that the sustained use and exposure to ICT opened up the possibility of earning additional income. The women's groups were exposed to word processing software, especially in the vernacular language, followed by e-mail, helping them access their emails and communicate. The benefits of such exposure go beyond income generation. Rather, it has helped rural women gain social status and also become aware of current developments, especially those affecting them directly or their region.

Such governmental initiatives have yielded multiple innovative revenue generating opportunities for the rural population as a whole. Through ICT exposure, some of them have availed loans from banks to purchase computers and set up desktop publishing facilities in their villages. The initiatives have also helped some of the rural populace to become service providers, like operating an Internet kiosk to help other people in the village with travel booking, posting job applications, availing online matrimonial services, filing PAN (Permanent Account Number—used for Income Tax filing) card applications, selling online insurance products, etc. (Subramanian 2011).

Rural citizens have been quite innovative in finding newer ways to generate income through computers. A kiosk owner who was part of the digital divide intervention initiative used the Internet to access public high school examination results, which are published by the State Examination Board on their website. The kiosk owner then charged RS 10 for checking the results of any student interested in knowing their results before they were published by the school, which had a time lag of 24 hours. Kiosk owners also help rural citizens to access online copies of birth and death certificates. Again, the owner was able to charge a fee for accessing and printing these certificates. The kiosk also helps the rural citizens in accessing the basic entitlements such as their land records and government-provided amenity services (Subramanian and Arivanandan 2009).[2]

ICT and rural women

Some rural women have become particularly enterprising. Armed with their knowledge of the Web, they have been able to help their family and husbands identify the government's "calls for tenders"[3] with regard to infrastructure development in their village. This has enabled them to bid for tenders and win contracts thereby augmenting their income. Access to the Internet has also spawned some unintended results. One of the most popular "entrepreneurial" activities in rural India is illegal "music downloading" in various languages and from different websites. The music is then sold to the locals for a nominal fee that varies based on the timing and usage. Though this practice is illegal, the rural people involved in this activity seem to be unaware of the legality and consequences of such activity.

Rural women's exposure to basic ICT has generated sufficient interest that they have begun to encourage their children to learn computers in a formal manner. Some of them have gone a step further, augmenting their knowledge using a formal source and in turn providing formal training to other children in their village. A few enterprising individuals have been able to use this exposure to get advanced training in accounting software like Tally to provide outsourced accounting services for the enterprises in and around their village. A good example of women's empowerment through ICT involves a woman entrepreneur who operates a beauty salon in a remote village in Tamil Nadu in Southern India. The woman uses the Internet to search and order beauty care products that are less expensive when purchased online. Purchasing online also ensures that she gets the products that she requires in the remote rural setting. The beautician also browses the web for accessing good designs and learning about newer techniques in the market. Another woman uses a computer in her microenterprise for ordering goods online based on customer needs. She charges an extra RS 10 per order which is paid by the customer. There are other microentrepreneurs who use computers and Internet facilities, not to start any new venture but to augment their income by providing value-added services such as photo editing, etc.[4]

In summary, ICT systems intended for use by the uneducated poor have reported successes as noted above. However, there have been several failures in large-scale projects, most notably in the government-initiated telecenters or CSCs. Given this limitation, important questions arise as to why some of these efforts have met with success and others have not. What are the antecedents of success and failure? What pre-conditions exist that result in success? To answer these, we look at theories available in information systems literature.

ICT for the "bottom of the pyramid": motivation and intermediated co-creation

Developing ICTs for the BoP has several challenges. It differs from systems development for other settings. The best practices that lead to successful system use and delivery of benefits to the poor remain underexplored. ICT differs with respect to characteristics such as difficulty of use, familiarity, acceptance by peers, affordability, availability, etc. Similarly, users vary in terms of their familiarity, habit, motivation, efficacy, etc. in relation to ICTs. In other words, more understanding is required on (a) the mental costs of using a new system alongside the benefits claimed by the service providers and (b) mapping of ICT attributes and user segments among the rural poor. Some of the challenging questions are: What works in interfacing ICT with the rural poor to deliver services? What factors must be considered while designing user interfaces for this group of users who lack basic literacy and computer literacy in particular? What are the nuances of acceptance behavior for the VLE and the rural poor that will ensure system use? How can the technology be designed so that they have ownership over technology?

As noted above, some of these issues have been addressed in different settings including business and government. For example, user acceptance of technology has been analyzed for employees (Venkatesh et al. 2003), households (Brown and Venkatesh 2005), and individual consumers (Venkatesh, Thong, and Xu 2012). However, the rural poor as a segment does not fall into any of these categories, as there are contextual factors that are markedly different, such as awareness, education, and social background.

Although information systems research has highlighted key factors that influence acceptance of new technology by consumers, it is not clear how these factors are relevant to the BoP segment. Further, only a few studies have highlighted certain behavioral traits of this segment, while throwing light on the misconceptions about the segment's adoption behavior towards new technology innovations. Our review of ICT for the poor in India shows that many technology solutions developed for emerging markets have failed owing to "design-reality gaps—there have been too great a difference between design expectations built into the IT and the developing world realities in which the IT is to be used" (Heeks 2012). In this section, we analyze studies pertaining to users of technology in the BoP by developing a framework based on insights from key studies by Prahalad and Hammond (2002), Heeks (2012), and Venkatesh, Thong, and Xu (2012) in this area.

While proposing a framework for the consumer acceptance of technology, Venkatesh, Thong, and Xu (2012) identified performance expectancy, effort expectancy, social influence, facilitating conditions, hedonic motivation, price value, and habit as the determinates of intention to accept a new technology. Since this model is an extension of the corporate user's rationale for using technology, we expect that this set of variables would have a different impact on the BoP segment. As evidenced from the study of Prahalad and Hammond (2002), the BoP segment differs from the rest of the world as they:

a Often lack prior use of technology
b Lack basic things in life like shelter or access to drinking water
c Have little or no formal education
d Do not know English

Heeks (2012) argues that the major differences between technology innovators and BoP technology users arise because of cultural, psychological, and linguistic differences. Therefore, it is important to understand the acceptance and usage behavior of this segment separately.

In a seminal study exploring the potential of the BoP market, Prahalad and Hammond (2002) observed that 65 percent of the world's population (i.e. about four billion people) earned below US$ 2,000 per year. Unfortunately, the low-income status of this segment gets often mistaken as having a lower appetite for new technology and technology products. However, the fortune at the bottom of the pyramid as identified by Prahalad and Hammond (2002, 6) brought out a different behavioral pattern of this segment:

> Conventional wisdom says that people in BoP markets cannot use such advanced technologies, but that's just another misconception. Poor and rural women in Bangladesh have had no difficulty using GSM cell phones, despite never before using phones of any type. In Kenya, teenagers from slums are being successfully trained as web page designers. Poor farmers in El Salvador use telecenters to negotiate the sale of their crops over the Internet. And women in Indian coastal villages have in less than a week learned to use PCs to interpret satellite images showing concentrations of schools of fish in the Arabian Sea so they can direct their husbands to the best fishing areas.

In other words, poor communities are ready to accept technologies that obviously improve their economic opportunities or quality of life. The perception about a technology as having the potential to improve their economic wellbeing could serve as a strong motivation for poor communities to accept that technology. This is further corroborated by the acceptance of eChoupal and eKutir technology by farmers despite the BoP segment characteristics previously discussed such as lack of prior experience in use of technology, lack of basic things in life like shelter or access to drinking water, and little or no formal education. In both cases, the technology acted as a channel to access services that would enable their economic activity and livelihood.

Prahalad and Hammond (2002) also argue that it is wrong to assume that poor communities are too preoccupied with their concern for fulfilling basic needs and that they do not waste money on non-essential and luxury technological products. The authors highlighted that in Mumbai's Dharavi slum, 85 percent of the households owned a TV set, although they did not have proper housing or access to drinking water. This observation provides support for certain seemingly hedonic motivational factors acting in a different way and having a strong influence on the acceptance of technology by the BoP segment (Venkatesh, Thong, and Xu 2012). They tend to accept the reality of life and, within the constraints of their environment, try to improve their quality of life.

Intermediated co-creation

Facilitating conditions as proposed by Venkatesh, Thong, and Xu (2012) translate into a different meaning in the case of the BoP segment. Help available to use a technology for the BoP must be in the local language and from their own trusted community. This notion of self-help at the community level is at the core of A2K, as noted by Lea Shaver (2007). The implementation of eChoupal provides a powerful example of facilitating technology beyond helplines (Bhatnagar and Dewan 2004). The case history of eChoupal shows that it was co-created with farmers, who were to be the end users of the kiosk-based agricultural products procurement system (Prahalad and Ramaswamy 2004).

Table 3.1 provides a list of variables (motivation variables) along with the human–machine interface (HMI) that various researchers on the subject have shown to be successful when used in designing technology for the BoP segment.

TABLE 3.1 Motivation variables for technology for the BoP segment

No.	*Variable*	*Human HMI*[a] *(H2MI)*	*Direct HMI*	*References*	*Key Evidences*
1	Livelihood opportunity	×	×	Jensen (2007), Jha et al. (2016), Bhatnagar and Dewan (2004)	eChoupal's *Sanchalak* and eKutir's micro-entrepreneurs acted as H2MIs, fishermen used mobile phones directly
2	Quality of life oppor-tunity		×	Prahalad and Hammond (2002)	85% of Dharavi slum in Mumbai own TV sets
3	Co-creation	×		Bhatnagar and Dewan (2004)	Farmers involved from design to implementa-tion of the eChoupal system, given access to data
4	Price value			Bhatnagar and Dewan (2004)	Perceived reduction in transaction costs of sell-ing farm produce by farmers
5	Peer influence	×	×	Bhatnagar and Dewan (2004), Jensen (2007)	Use by peers and the perceived benefits they draw act as motivation

a Human–machine interface.

The eChoupal training programs deliberately involved the farmers. The benefits of the system were explained clearly, the interface was developed in the local language, and pricing data pertaining to buyers other than ITC was made transparent and accessible. Acceptance by peers and the perception of reduced transaction costs acted as motivation for farmers to use eChoupal. Moreover, a *Sanchalak* selected by ITC from the same locality acted as a human interface between the machine and another human. A *Sanchalak* (facilitator) here is a *son of the soil*—someone belonging to the same location and who understands the cultural ethos—and is also an entrepreneur who owns and operates the kiosk, acting as a human interface to the kiosk. This is similar to the human–human-machine interface (H2MI) implemented in the case of eKutir for farmers (Jha, Pinsonneault, and Dubé 2016). Figure 3.1 summarizes the above discussion and lists the drivers for using a technology by BoP and how it acts: HMI or H2MI as the last mile.

It is interesting to note that technology and its success in the BoP segment follows a slightly different trajectory as compared to the urban, educated, and middle/upper class segment in India. Certain technologies like the cell phones have been owned and used by the BoP segment when they found it useful for their livelihood. There was little training or need for an H2MI arrangement for the acceptance of the technology in such cases. However, even technologies that improved the livelihood of farmers were implemented successfully through H2MI in the case of eKutir and

Motivation	Livelihood	HUMAN-HUMAN-MACHINE INTERFACE *(H2MI)* [eChoupal's Sanchalak, eKutir's Micro Entrepreneur]	HUMAN- MACHINE- INTERFACE (HMI) [adoption of mobile phones by marginalized fishermen
	Quality of Life	HMI & H2MI [Age, gender, education, etc. likely to influence preferences]	HUMAN- MACHINE -INTERFACE (HMI) [TV owners in Dharavi slums]
		High	Low
		Task Complexity	

FIGURE 3.1 HMI and H2MI preferences of BoP based on task complexity and motivation.

eChoupal. These interfaces were sources of information for the farmers and not just points of connectivity as in a mobile phone. The task of comparing prices and interpreting them and applying them required a *Choupal* or advisor. Therefore, task complexity could be playing a significant role in deciding between HMI and H2MI in the case of technology for the poor. Figure 3.1 provides a visualization of BoP preferences for HMI and H2MI based on task complexity and motivation.

Analysis and conclusion

As noted in the introduction, the Indian economy has made great strides in economic development over the last two decades. However, this growth has not been matched in its human development. It still lags behind most countries with respect to the UN's HDI. In the last two decades, there have been various initiatives undertaken by different actors and stakeholders to leverage India's information technology prowess for rural development in India. There have been several projects using information technologies, especially mobile technologies, and the Internet. These efforts have yielded mixed results. In general, initiatives by NGOs and corporates seem to have yielded better results, whereas the telecenters approach promoted by the government has only had partial success. Thus, we attempted to identify if the factors that enhance user acceptance in other non-BoP segments also work for the BoP segment. The answer, quite predictably, is negative. Then the chapter looked into the BoP literature and noted that the best predictor of success was to understand and engage the beneficiaries of the system (i.e. the rural poor or the BoP segment) in the design of the system—a process termed as "intermediated co-creation." Starting from that idea, certain "motivation variables" that needed to be addressed in this process were identified. These were then mapped to the projects and initiatives that have been met with success, along with the theories that they are based on.

What becomes clear is that these motivational variables may be different across different contexts and may not work across different BoP segments. What may work in one part of rural India may not work in another, primarily because the contextual needs may be entirely different across regions and even cultures. Thus, initiatives to enhance human development through technology must clearly be aware of these aspects and appropriately study the environment without using a "one size fits all" approach. Another point to note is that the list of motivational variables is just a starting point and is still incomplete. Further qualitative studies should be conducted in the future that could considerably add to this list of variables. In addition, technologies, especially mobile technologies, may change over time, which may add new factors to be considered.

There are also additional concerns. When the ICT mobile infrastructure is developed and operated by the government, there is always a chance that the government could block or censor certain transmissions that it considers to be inappropriate. This could potentially lead to serious violations of the concept of freedom of expression. Thus, there should be enough legal safeguards that would preserve the individual's rights to freedom of expression, while providing opportunities for rural development. Another potentially serious issue is security. As the rural population becomes comfortable with ICT and mobile technologies for all types of applications, there is the serious issue of security breaches that could compromise the entire system or at least an individual's private data (such as financial data and medical data). While the initial emphasis of the ICT4Poor initiatives should obviously focus on bringing technology to the rural poor to enhance their development, adequate policy and security considerations should be incorporated within the technologies to avoid potential security breaches that could arise in the future. But despite these challenges, there are enough successes evident in this literature that can be used as starting points in replicating successful initiatives not only in India, but also the BoP segments in other developing and emerging economies.

Notes

1 A *Choupal* is a Hindi word denoting a community meeting place in rural areas of North India.
2 In addition to this reference, it should be noted that similar observations were made by the other authors during various field visits to rural locations. This section as well as the sections that follow reference these observations.
3 "Calls for tenders" are invitations for open bidding for government contracts in official Indian government parlance.
4 Based on observations made by at least one of the authors during field visits to villages around Kancheepuram, Gingee, Melmalayanur, Tindivanam, Cuddalore, and Pondichery, during the period between February and April, 2016. The NGO associated with the projects is "Hand in Hand India."

References

Bhatnagar, Subhash, and Ankita Dewan. 2004. "E-Choupal: ICT's Rural Networking Project." Accessed December 18, 2020. http://siteresources.worldbank.org/INTEMPOWERMENT/Resources/14647_E-choupalweb.pdf.

Brown, Susan A., and Viswanath Venkatesh. 2005. "Model of Adoption of Technology in Households: A Baseline Model Test and Extension Incorporating Household Life Cycle." *MIS Quarterly* 29, no. 3: 399–426.

Cecchini, Simone, and Christopher Scott. 2003. "Can Information and Communications Technology Applications Contribute to Poverty Reduction? Lessons from Rural India." *Information Technology for Development* 10, no. 2: 73–84.

Dass, Rajanish, and Atashi Bhattacherjee. 2011. *Status of Common Service Center Program in India: Issues, Challenges and Emerging Practices for Rollout* (No. WP2011–2002–03). Indian Institute of Management Ahmedabad, Research and Publication Department.

Ernberg, Johan. 1998. "Universal Access for Rural Development: From Action to Strategies." In *Proceedings of IRST International Conference on Rural Telecommunication*, Washington, DC, November 30–December 2.

Ghosh, Arijit. 2011. "Initiatives in ICT for Rural Development: An Indian Perspective." *Gobal Media Journal*, December. Accessed May 4, 2018. http://www.caluniv.ac.in/global-mdia-journal/Winter%20Issue%20December%202011%20Commentaries/C7%20-%20Ghosh.pdf.

Grace, Jeremy, Charles Kenny, and Christine Zhen-Wei Qiang. 2004. *Information and Communication Technologies and Broad-Based Development: A Partial Review of the Evidence*. Washington, DC: World Bank Publications.

Heeks, Richard. 2012. "IT Innovation for the Bottom of the Pyramid." *Communications of the ACM* 55, no. 12: 24–27.

IMF (International Monetary Fund). 2017. "World Economic Outlook Database, April 2017 – Report for Selected Countries and Subjects." Accessed July 3, 2017. https://www.imf.org/external/pubs/ft/weo/2017/01/weodata/weorept.aspx.

Jensen, Robert. 2007. "The Digital Provide: Information (Technology), Market Performance, and Welfare in the South Indian Fisheries Sector." *The Quarterly Journal of Economics* 122, no. 2: 879–924.

Jha, Srivardhini K., Alain Pinsonneault, and Laurette Dubé. 2016. "The Evolution of an ICT Platform-Enabled Ecosystem for Poverty Alleviation: The Case of eKutir." *MIS Quarterly* 40, no. 2: 431–445. MacKenzie, Donald, and Judy Wajcman. 1999. *The Social Shaping of Technology*. Maidenhead: Open University Press.

Mahmood, Khalid. 2005. "Multipurpose Community Telecenters for Rural Development in Pakistan." *The Electronic Library* 23, no. 2: 204–220.

Ministry of Finance, Government of India. 2017. "Union Budget Highlights 2017–18." February 1. http://indiabudget.nic.in/ub2017-18/frbm/frbm1.pdf.

Prahalad, Coimbatore Krishnarao. 2004. *The Fortune at the Bottom of the Pyramid: Eradicating Poverty through Profits*. Philadelphia: Wharton School Publishing.

Prahalad, Coimbatore Krishnarao, and Allen Hammond. 2002. "Serving the World's Poor, Profitably." *Harvard Business Review* 80, no. 9: 48–59.

Prahalad, Coimbatore Krishnarao, and Venkat Ramaswamy. 2004. "Co-Creating Unique Value with Customers." *Strategy & Leadership* 32, no. 3: 4–9. https://doi.org/10.1108/10878570410699249.

Subramanian, Ramesh. 2011. "ICTs and Access to Knowledge in Rural India: A Comparative Study of Two Models of Development." In *Access to Knowledge in India*, edited by Ramesh Subramanian and Lea Shaver, 109–147. London: Bloomsbury Academic Publishing.

Subramanian, Ramesh and Masilamani Arivanandan. 2009. "Rural Development through Village Knowledge Centers in India." *Communications of the International Information Management Association (CIIMA)* 9, no. 2: 101–120.

Shaver, Lea. 2007. "Defining and Measuring Access to Knowledge: Towards an A2K Index." Faculty Scholarship Series, paper 22. http://digitalcommons.law.yale.edu/fss_papers/22.

UNDP (United Nations Development Programme). 2007. "*Human Development Report 2007–2008.*" http://hdr.undp.org/sites/default/files/reports/268/hdr_20072008_en_ complete.pdf

UNDP (United Nations Development Programme). 2016. "*Human Development Report 2016.*" http://hdr.undp.org/sites/default/files/2016_human_development_report.pdf.

Venkatesh, Shruti. 2017. "Indian IT-BPM Industry Clocks Growth Rate of 8.6 Percent in FY2017: NASSCOM." *Forbes India*, February 15. http://www.forbesindia.com/article/nasscom-ilf-2017/indian-itbpm-industry-clocks-growth-rate-of-8.6-percent-in-fy2017-nasscom/45951/1.

Venkatesh, Viswanath, Michael G. Morris, Gordon B. Davis, and Fred D. Davis. 2003. "User Acceptance of Information Technology: Toward a Unified View." *MIS Quarterly* 27, no. 3: 425–478.

Venkatesh, Viswanath, James Y. L. Thong, and Xin Xu. 2012. "Consumer Acceptance and Use of Information Technology: Extending the Unified Theory of Acceptance and Use of Technology." *MIS Quarterly* 36, no. 1: 157–178.

4

BOTSWANA AND A2K

The Diffusion and Civic Application of Mobile Telephony

William O. Lesitaokana

Introduction

The advent of mobile telephony has prompted much interest from many scholars across the globe. Amongst the related research are studies from developing countries that focus specifically on the diffusion of mobile phones, user accessibility, and the use of mobile devices to improve human lives (Horst 2006; Chabossou et al. 2008; Duncombe and Boateng 2009; Kreutzer 2009; Sey 2011). According to James (2012), many developing countries have taken significant steps to close the digital divide by ensuring that citizens have access to mobile phones and related services. For instance, in countries such as Jamaica, El Salvador (James 2012), and Thailand (Srinuan, Srinuan, and Bohlin 2012), governments have privatized mobile telephony sectors, liberalized mobile markets to allow for the licensing of mobile operators, and permitted foreign investors to establish mobile telephony networks in their countries. Srinuan, Srinuan and Bohlin (2012) reported that, due to efforts made by both the government and private networks in Thailand, mobile telephony has diffused considerably throughout the country including to areas where fixed telephony has been inadequate. As a result, youth used mobile phones to access the Internet.

An exception to this trend is Sub-Saharan Africa, which continues to be classified as information poor (Gebremichael and Jackson 2006) and as having a serious digital divide (Fuchs and Horak 2008). The concept of the digital divide is referred to as the gap between rich and poor countries with regard to access to and use of information and communication technologies (James 2009). It is the gap that exists between those who have access to information and communication technologies (ICTs) and those who do not. The digital divide is particularly relevant in the contemporary context because ICTs are useful to promote economic growth, deliver public services, and enhance development at various levels: communal, national, or international (Loo and Ngan 2012; Manohar 2005; Srinuan, Srinuan, and Bohlin 2012). Rice (2002, p. 106) refers to the digital divide as inequalities that exist regarding access to and use of the Internet in view of the demographic characteristics of gender, income level, race, and setting. Nonetheless, Gandy (2002) argues that within new media, research about the digital divide should not only focus on inequalities of access but also opportunities to engage information services. Whereas the computer, Internet, fax, and fixed telephones have received much reference in previous studies of the digital divide (Gyamfi 2005; Nwagwu 2006), it has been only recently that the mobile phone has received some attention. In 2005, many countries in Sub-Saharan Africa were still lagging behind with regard to citizens' access to and use of ICTs (Gyamfi 2005). According to Gyamfi (2005), this was because these countries lacked strategic policies that guided the implementation of approaches for facilitating access to technologies needed for information services. Gebremichael and Jackson (2006, 276) suggest that "while economic factors and various levels of governmental instability have traditionally served as a hindrance to technology adoption in the region, there are several viable possibilities for providing low-cost ICT access in the short term."

The purpose of this chapter is two-fold. First, it considers the efforts of the Botswana government to facilitate citizens' access to mobile phones and mobile communication services, while adding to the literature on the diffusion of mobile phones. It is worthwhile to establish the commonalities and varied experiences of citizens regarding the diffusion and access to mobile phones in different countries. Second, this chapter examines citizens' uses of mobile phones to enhance social lives in order to contribute the case of Botswana to the global literature on mobile phone use. Research from the Global South, where citizens' access to mobile phones has dramatically increased in the past few years, will help inform on the trends associated with the latest use of the devices. Moreover, previous studies have demonstrated that the socio-economic challenges of mobile phone users in each society influence the impact of the devices. Therefore, it is necessary that related research is extended to many diverse societies with distinct cultures.

The data presented throughout the chapter was obtained using two sets of qualitative, in-depth semi-structured interviews. Semi-structured interviews are those that are undertaken in a flexible manner and, thus, are interactive conversations between the researcher and an informant (Byrne 2004). Silverman (2006) also notes that semi-structured interviews involve asking questions, sharing ideas, and recording the conversations. Addressing the first objective, the first set of interviews involved a total of seven officials working in the mobile telephony sector in Botswana and one representative from each of the following local mobile telephone service providers: beMobile, Mascom, and Orange. Their selection to participate in this study was based on their knowledge and experiences they gained while working in the mobile telephony sector. To contact these, formal requests were first sent to their workplaces through their superiors, and then after they agreed to participate in the study they were visited and interviewed at their workplaces. To address the second objective, interviews were conducted with a total of 28 randomly selected young people aged between 18 and 35 from the cities of Francistown and Gaborone in Botswana. The two places are Botswana's main cities, and it is here where the mobile telephony signal is adequate and where many people using mobile phones can be found. The young people who participated in this study were recruited from colleges and universities through poster advertisements and were then randomly selected for interviews. Interviews with these sought to solicit information regarding their accessibility, adoption, and use of mobile phones for civic, social, and economic purposes. All interviews were audio recorded and later transcribed for analysis.

Mobile phone application—a global overview

Goggin (2009), Middleton (2008), and Christensen and Prax (2012) acknowledge that both the significance and consumption of mobile phones have surpassed that of landline telephones. For instance, mobile phone users have access to important applications through which they can perform multimedia activities, networking, and information exchange as part of their contemporary lifestyles. The mobile phone is also useful as a gaming device (Christensen and Prax 2012) and as a personal device that provides users with access to mobile media (Watkins, Hjorth, and Koskinen 2012) and online public services (Duncombe and Boateng 2009; Kushchu and Kuscu 2003). This is because mobile phones, especially smartphones, converge ICT and multimedia features that include audio and video recording devices, FM radio, telephone, camera, watch, calculator, the Internet, social network applications, caller ID, and digital games (Christensen and Prax 2012).

There is a large set of literature discussing the role of mobile phones in different countries. In Malaysia (Karim et al. 2009) and Pakistan (Kamran 2010), the mobile phone is considered an additional communication tool that facilitates mobile connection with families, friends, and classmates through emails and online social networks among college students. The students made significant use of mobile phones because the devices offered them access to mobile Internet from anywhere as long as network coverage was accessible. In addition, access to the Internet on their mobile phones was affordable and easily manageable, especially when acquired through a prepaid subscription.

In India, a study by Watkins, Kitner, and Mehta (2012) indicates that mobile phones afforded users opportunities to exchange information and consume services that were previously inaccessible in the region (although it was considered that both income and digital literacy implicated the adoption of mobile phones, especially smartphones among rural participants in India). For example, the radio reporters in rural locations who were provided with Nokia N97 handsets as part of the above-mentioned study used the devices to facilitate production of new programming and innovative engagements in their community radio station. This included recording audio interviews for the radio programs using the Nokia N97 phones. As a result of their innovative approach, two advantages of adopting smartphones for use in community radio stations were explored in that study. First, the reporters who participated in that study mentioned that the quality of audio recorded on the Nokia N97 was much better than the previous audio recorded on the community radio station's consumer audio equipment. Second, the villagers, including youth who were interviewed for the radio broadcasts, concurred that unlike earlier recordings, which were done with microphones and tape recorders, the use of the Nokia N97 made them feel more at ease to participate in radio programs. This is because with smartphone devices villagers were not compelled to travel to the radio station and could telephonically reach the studio personal.

The use of mobile phones in civic, social, and economic matters has also been recorded in the literature. For instance, in a study conducted in Sub-Saharan Africa, Duncombe and Boateng (2009) describe how the financial institutions in the region had made use of the high uptake of mobile phones and introduced mobile banking to the poor who did not previously have access to banking services. Some of these mobile banking services, which are also commonly used by young adults, include access to financial information and the ability to make mobile payments and monetary transfers. Also, in Finland, Helsinki City Transport offers mobile payment services for tram and subway tickets, through which customers send text messages to service numbers to order one-hour SMS tickets (Mallat, Rossi and Tuunainen 2004). According to Mallat et al. (2004), this service has been declared significant in two closely related ways. On the part of customers, it has helped increase access to tickets for travel on subway. It has also reduced the problem of people travelling without a ticket, thus increasing financial returns for Helsinki City Transport.

Indeed, the mobile phone has in some cases become the only device that has made the Internet accessible to citizens in many economically developing countries. Watkins, Kitner, and Mehta (2012, 695) note that the "mobile and the smartphone are supplanting the personal computer as the standard online access point." During their Internet consumption on their mobile phones, users are open to a world of opportunities through which they can enhance their day-to-day living. In particular, the above-mentioned studies indicated the role of mobile phones in enhancing the social lives of their users in countries such as Malaysia, Pakistan, India, and some parts of Sub-Saharan Africa.

Despite the success of mobile phones in general, Botswana remains classified among developing nations in Sub-Saharan Africa where both access and use of ICTs such as telephone landlines, the Internet, and computers remain a challenge (Sebusang and Masupe 2003; Nkwe 2012). Other factors associated with these challenges, which also characterize citizens in many developing countries, include poverty, gender inequality, costs of ICTs, and a lack of skills to use ICT devices (Paterson 2007; Nkwe 2012; Oladokun and Aina 2011).

Basic education is provided free to all youth in public schools in Botswana. Despite acquiring basic education and with the exception of mobile phones, many people in Botswana, including youth, do not have access to ICTs. Although in some cases young people in Botswana are introduced to computers in secondary schools, they only have limited access to ICTs in the form of computers and the Internet in colleges and universities and sometimes in workplaces countrywide. In fact, many people outside of these places do not have an opportunity to use computers nor to access the Internet. Other limited access to ICTs, especially computers and the Internet in Botswana is possible at the Post Offices in large villages countrywide.

This scenario of limited access to computers and the Internet demonstrates to some degree the digital divide in Botswana. However, considering that mobile phones are widely accessible to many people countrywide, it is therefore necessary to establish if and how the introduction and consumption of the devices have helped to bridge this gap. Furthermore, it is therefore worthwhile to critically consider how despite these challenges, Botswana has been able to initiate and facilitate mobile telephony diffusion and how citizens subsequently adopted and use mobile phones in their everyday lives to enhance their social lives.

The history and diffusion of mobile telephony in Botswana

The rise in literacy levels among the people in Botswana over the first three decades after Botswana's independence in 1966 significantly propelled demands to expand information and communication systems across the country (Rantao 1996). The Botswana Telecommunications Cooperation (BTC) was established as a quasi-governmental organization in 1980 to facilitate and manage telecommunication services within the country (Botswana Telecommunications Corporation n.d.). The services under the BTC included provision of telephone landlines and fax, and the establishment of information and communication infrastructure, which facilitated telephonic communication locally, regionally, and internationally. Mobile telephony was first introduced in Botswana in 1998 after the development of a telecommunications policy that provided recommendations for the licensing of private network operators to lessen the monopoly of the BTC, which provided fixed telephones countrywide. The first two of the current three network operators to be licensed were Mascom Wireless and Vista Cellular (rebranded Orange Botswana). Both these networks have been operating mainly from Gaborone, the capital city, from which they have spread their coverage to other towns and large villages across the country. After realizing that fixed landlines were not able to withstand fierce competition from mobile operators, in 2008 BTC introduced BTC beMobile, the third and latest mobile network operator in Botswana. Following this, competition for subscribers intensified so much that each local network operator was forced to extend its transmission network to many villages.

Once mobile telephony was introduced in Botswana in 1998, the process of diffusing mobile telephony throughout the country started off slowly (Lesitaokana 2014). The participants in this study pointed out three explicit reasons for this. After being licensed, Mascom and Orange first took their markets to larger populated areas, such as towns and large villages, which strategically guaranteed them quick business. Thus, their transmission signals were restricted to those places. Despite this, a large part of the population which lived in these towns and large villages were unemployed and did not have money to purchase mobile phones and related services. Consequently, many people considered the expense of acquiring a mobile phone device and mobile telephony services costly, whereas fixed landline telephones provided by the BTC were comparatively cheaper. Also, potential subscribers were reluctant to adopt mobile phones because fixed landline telephone services and public pay phones, which were installed by the BTC in various public places across the country such as in shopping centers, public clinics, and hospitals, were a guaranteed alternative.

Consequently, the Botswana Government took it upon itself to facilitate the installation of network technologies, while the local network operators focused on increasing access to mobile telephony products and services and extending signal coverage to many underserved communities. For instance, in 2006 the then Minister of Communications, Science and Technology (MCST)[1] liberalized the mobile telephony market by introducing new developments such as allowing the self-provision of transmission equipment by network operators, permitting local network operators to find their own international gateways, and also providing value-added services. Indeed, these developments by the Minister of MCST favored the network operators as they started to expand their businesses and offer more mobile telephony services to their subscribers, including wireless and mobile Internet and international roaming. Through their international gateway licenses, the local network operators managed to establish interconnection agreements with other international mobile network operators, and this simplified the transmission of international calls made within the interconnected mobile networks. Additionally, by building their own transmission networks, both Mascom and Orange were able to extend their transmission signals to many other places in Botswana and consequently gained more subscribers from those places. Moreover, once the local network operators started to provide mobile Internet and more opportunities for mobile phone use, mobile phone subscription increased further. The licensing of BTC beMobile, the third mobile network operator in Botswana in 2008, also boosted the uptake of mobile phones and related services, since the three mobile operators (Mascom, Orange and BTC beMobile) competed for subscribers.

These advances were also facilitated through the *Maitlamo* [2] policy of 2007. Among others, the policy recommended that citizens in remote, rural, and urban communities be provided with affordable access to computers and the Internet. Referring to the government's efforts in this regard the former Minister of Ministry of Transport and Communications through which telecommunications and postal services falls under, noted:

> Despite facing budgetary constraints, our government has committed itself to ensuring that by 2016[3] [fifty years after Botswana's independence in 1966], the whole population of Botswana is widely connected. We want to provide telecommunications [including mobile communication] in all towns, large and small villages countrywide so that by the target year no one would be left out.
>
> *(Hon. Nonofho Molefhi, interview)*

As evidence to the viewpoint suggested by the MTC Minister, the Botswana Government engaged with the local network operators to make continuous efforts to install transmission infrastructure in many parts of Botswana, with plans to advance transmission signals countrywide, thus, also promoting the adoption of mobile phones in those places.

Undoubtedly, the efforts of the Botswana Government and mobile operators to facilitate the diffusion of mobile telephony countrywide produced significant results. As indicated in the 2012 annual report of the Botswana Communications Regulatory Authority (BOCRA),[4] the total number of mobile phone subscribers across Botswana's network operators increased dramatically from 332,264 in March 2002 to 2,953,116 by March 2012 in a population of around 2.1 million (Botswana Telecommunications Authority 2012). Also, by March 2012, the market share among the three operators stood at 54 percent for Mascom, 35 percent for Orange, and 11 percent for BTC beMobile (Botswana Telecommunications Authority 2012). The high number of subscribers for Mascom is a result of its demonstrated higher level of commitment through the *Nteletsa* project to extending its transmission networks to many large and some small villages across Botswana in comparison to Orange and BTC beMobile. Moreover, the low number of subscribers for BTC beMobile has been caused by it being the latest entrant into the Botswana mobile telephony market.

The public's access to mobile phone enabled services

As researchers have pointed out, ICTs are useful to promote economies, deliver public services, and enhance development at community, national, or international levels (Manohar 2005; Srinuan, Srinuan, and Bohlin 2012; Loo and Ngan 2012). However, Kaba et al. (2009) decry failures by many developing countries to efficiently utilize new technologies. In the case of Botswana, the mobile telephone service providers (Mascom, Orange, and BTC beMobile) endeavor to extend transmission signals to many parts of the country. They also sell mobile phone handsets and provide opportunities for mobile phone enabled services that users could take advantage of to maximize the functionality of mobile phones in their lives.

Interestingly, upon realizing the potential of mobile phones to deliver social and public services, many government departments and private businesses in Botswana have introduced mobile phone enabled services, which are considerably useful to many mobile phone users countrywide. For instance, from time to time the Department of Road Transport and Safety (DRTS) under the MTC in Botswana sends text messages to owners of motor vehicles to remind them about the expiry dates of their vehicle licensing and the need to re-register their cars annually before the due dates. Likewise, the Department of National Disaster Management under the Office of the President in Botswana often sends text messages to mobile phone users in Botswana warning them about expected weather disasters such as heavy rains and possible floods during the rainy seasons. Similarly, doctors in private clinics and hospitals connect with their patients through the use of mobile phones, and from time to time they send them text messages about their next visits and appointments. In addition, the Ministry of Tertiary Education, Research, Science, and Technology (MTRST) has also embarked on sending text messages to secondary school students in Botswana informing them about examination results and sponsorship opportunities for tertiary education. Also, the universities and colleges in Botswana sometimes send text messages to young people informing them about admission and registration issues. As the participants in the study concurred, the need to access these services continues to be a significant motivation for adopting mobile phone devices, particularly for those who did not already own such a device.

Moreover, the local commercial banks in Botswana, such as Barclays Bank Botswana, First National Bank Botswana (FNBB), Standard Chartered, Capital Bank, Bank of Baroda, and the Botswana Building Society (BBS) have also taken advantage of mobile telephony and strategically introduced online and mobile banking services. Through mobile banking services, mobile phone users who have bank accounts in local banks can transfer money in and out of their accounts on their mobile phones without having to go to the bank. FNBB has also introduced *E-wallet* [5] services to assist mobile phone subscribers who do not have bank accounts, thus, prompting many young people who want to use this service to adopt mobile phone devices. The local mobile network operators have also introduced mobile money services that are possible through the use of mobile phones. These include Mascom *MyZaka* and Orange *Money*.[6] In view of this, a representative from one of the local network operators mentioned, "With mobile phones, there is so much that subscribers can do. Mobile money and online banking are some of those services provided by Mascom which demonstrate the convenience of owning a mobile phone."

In addition to adopting mobile phones to undertake mobile enabled services, young people have also bought for themselves smartphone devices that afford them opportunities for accessing the Internet and undertaking online social networking with their family, relatives, and friends in Botswana and in the Diaspora. The most popular social networks include Facebook, Twitter, Skype, Messenger, and LinkedIn, most of which are accessible on smartphones.

Through the availability of mobile enabled services, many mobile phone users in Botswana are provided with information and access to social and economic services. In addition, ownership of mobile phones and the use of mobile devices continue to increase nationwide among youth and adults. Perhaps, this is due to the ubiquity of mobile phones and devices and their user friendliness. As is the case in Botswana, the introduction of mobile enabled services makes it possible for citizens, who do not have other means of communication such as the internet and expensive landline calls, to access these services. Thus, whereas diffusion of mobile phones boosts national wide coverage of network signals and uptake of mobile devices, the introduction of mobile enabled services has been a significant incentive that has yielded an increase in the use of mobile phone among citizens of Botswana.

Mobile phone applications to enhance social lives

Generally, the accessibility of mobile phones has helped transform the lives of the people in Botswana in three distinct ways. First, and as stated above, there is certainty that with mobile phones users have access to advanced mobile communication through voice calls, SMS, emails, and social networks such as Facebook, WhatsApp, and Skype. Young people interviewed in this study concurred that mobile phones afford them opportunities to link up with their parents through text messages and calls to relate issues that are difficult to discuss face-to-face. This is widely common in situations that require young adults in Botswana to discuss matters of manhood and womanhood with their adult relatives, such as sexual relationships, parenting, and marriage. For other young people, especially students who left their family and friends in their home villages to either take up employment or attend colleges and universities in towns and major villages in Botswana, the mobile phone serves as a communication link between them.

Second, due to their multimodal features, mobile phones provide many people in Botswana access to mobile services such as mobile money, mobile news, and FM radio. For example, many participants interviewed in this study confirmed that they had registered for mobile banking with the local commercial banks. As these participants explained, since they carry their mobile phones with them all the time, they can easily undertake their monetary transactions without having to go to the bank. As a result, many people in Botswana have bank accounts with the local commercial banks such as First National, Botswana Building Society, Barclays, Standard, and Stanbic Banks, even though they spend much of their livelihoods in rural areas where banking facilities are not available. In addition, others who dwell in towns and large villages but often travel to the countryside or settlements where there are no banks during weekends and school vacations can also use their mobile phones to make financial transactions. Advantageously for mobile phone users in Botswana, mobile banking does not require the use of the Internet, suggesting that everyone in Botswana who has all of the following can register for and use such a service: a bank account at any of the local commercial banks, a basic mobile phone handset, and a subscription to any of the local networks. Other participants in the study pointed out that they use their mobile phones to access news headlines and blurbs through services such as Mascom *MyNews*[7] on a weekly basis. Moreover, young people who use FM-ready mobile phone handsets are able to access radio broadcasts from local radio stations while in transit. Mobile phone users in Botswana also use FM radio features on their mobile phones to access music broadcasts from the local radio stations especially during the night and at times when they are bored (Lesitaokana 2013). In addition, the participants mentioned that they also access MP3 music and play it while on the go on their handsets.

Third, many locals have access to public services which were previously impossible to access without mobile phones. A number of participants in this study confirmed that they have benefited significantly from this development, citing that it has improved their lives. For instance, two adults praised the mobile phone for its ability to link them up with the Department of Road Transport and Safety (DRTS) annually with regard to renewal of their drivers' licenses and car registration. Below are extracts from separate interviews I conducted with them during which I asked them to comment on the significance of the mobile phone to relay information about public services:

> Since the DRTS introduced text-messaging services to their clients, I rest assured knowing that they will contact me when the due date for my car registration arrives. As far as I can remember, this has been going on over the past three years.
>
> *(Katlo, 48, male, Gaborone)*

> Just this year, DRTS contacted me through my mobile phone reminding me that I should go to their offices to renew my driver's license.
>
> *(Gaone, female, 43, Francistown)*

In another related example, Tau, a 23-year-old who lives in the large village of Mochudi, about 40 kilometers from Gaborone, had this to say.

> Last year, after I applied for a new passport, I received a text message from the Department of Immigration and Citizenship in Gaborone that it was ready for collection. Since I do not have a fixed telephone line, they had promised to contact me on my mobile, and so they did.
>
> *(Tau, 25, male, Gaborone)*

For Katlo, Gaone, and Tau, the mobile phone provided an assuring link between them and government departments. Specifically for Katlo and Gaone, text messages from DRTS served as reminders that helped them to avoid penalties associated with non-renewal of drivers' licenses and car registration. For Tau, the information from the Department of Immigration and Citizenship was helpful for him since he did not have to be under any pressure to frequently travel long distances between his home village and Gaborone to find out if his passport application had been processed. Moreover, college and university students indicated that the mobile phone became significantly relevant during their search for college and university sponsorships with the Ministry of Education and Skills Development (MOESD). At that time, once they submitted their applications for sponsorships, including their mobile contact details, the mobile phone served as a convenient link between them and the ministry officials.

According to many of these young people, before they started attending colleges and university in Gaborone, they lived in their home villages far away from the places where they could access national services such as information for college and university scholarships. Prior to adopting and using the mobile phone for communication, these youth would be required to travel long distances to visit offices where they were provided with services, and this was often expensive for some of them. Therefore, communication through the mobile phone, which often included text messages and calls about the decisions taken by the MOESD regarding sponsorship offers, was considerably convenient.

Further discussion and conclusion

This chapter provides the starting point to demonstrate how in Botswana, which in 2005 was categorized as an "information-poor" country, the government and local network operators have facilitated diffusion and access to mobile phones and mobile enabled services, thereby laying the foundation for increased access to mobile enabled services for its citizens. Local network operators continue to sell mobile phone products, extend mobile phone signals, and provide mobile enabled services throughout the country, and, as a result of this increased access to mobile telephony, citizens have adopted mobile phones. The Botswana government has also licensed privately owned network operators (Mascom and Orange) and BTC beMobile, which extended their services countrywide due to competition for subscribers. Furthermore, despite its status as a developing country, the Botswana Government through the MTC committed itself to establishing the necessary infrastructure in order to provide access to telecommunications services to many under-served communities in Botswana by 2016. Even though more empirical studies are yet to be undertaken to establish whether this has been achieved, indications are that significant milestones regarding this goal have been achieved. For instance, the significant increase in the number of subscribers reported by BOCRA, and evidences that almost every household has at least one member connected through a mobile phone. This endorses the viewpoints of Donner (2008) who proposed that it is the responsibility of governments in developing countries to promote the diffusion of mobile telephony.

Indeed, some of the accomplishments regarding the diffusion of mobile telephony in Botswana are analogous to those that have taken place in other developing countries, such as Vietnam (Hwang, Cho, and Viet Long 2009), El Salvador, and Jamaica (James 2012). Considering that Botswana, like the rest of Sub-Saharan Africa, is an information-poor country, what has been achieved by both the government and the local network operators so far has generated an impetus on the majority of citizens to adopt and use mobile phones. For those who did not have the devices, these services have encouraged ownership of mobile phones, so that they can avail themselves of these services. As for those who already own mobile phones, the availability of mobile enabled services in Botswana encourages them to continue adopting new mobile phone devices (smartphones) that function efficiently to perform these services. Significantly then, the Botswana situation is an example for other developing countries that if diffusion of mobile phones is adequately facilitated, access to mobile phones and mobile enabled services, citizens will undoubtedly adopt and use mobile phones in large numbers.

The chapter has also shown a nuanced demonstration of the uses of mobile phones by citizens of Botswana to improve their social lives, thus bridging the digital divide. As is the case with citizens in some developing countries such as Ghana (Sey 2011), South Africa (Kreutzer 2009), India (Biancini 2011; Watkins, Kitner, and Mehta 2012), and Pakistan (Ahmed and Qazi 2011), the challenges of poverty and the digital divide have led many people in Botswana to depend mainly on mobile phones to access mobile Internet and social services from their government. Indeed, because of the lack of technical resources and infrastructure to reach the people and provide them with services, both the government and private companies have sought mobile communication technologies as alternatives due to their wide penetration, ubiquity, and multi-modality. In this regard, the mobile device is convenient for local use because it allows access to information, online news, online public services, and online social networks. It is also a tool that helps to enhance students' opportunities for learning and processing information services, such as mobile and online banking. Using the example of Botswana, it is clear that mobile telephony has the potential to economically transform the citizens in developing countries by providing them with opportunities for accessing government services and global information through the Internet and also promoting self-entrepreneurship. Clearly then, because the mobile phone is a low-cost device that is easily accessible, portable, and comes with multimedia features, such as the Internet and text-messaging services, it is well suited to bridge the digital divide in developing countries, such as Botswana.

This study has also revealed that mobile telephony has spread across Botswana. It is therefore worth noting that more in-depth research should be carried out far from urban areas, such as in rural areas and settlements in Botswana, to explore the extent to which citizens put the devices to use. Conceivably, such a study would consider how access to mobile phone and mobile phone services has helped to better the lives of citizens in those places.

Notes

1 MCST used to be the Botswana Government ministry under which all telecommunications including mobile telephony falls. It was dissolved into two ministries in 2008, one being the Ministry of Transport and Communications (MTC); the other is the Ministry of Infrastructure, Science and Technology (MIST).
2 Maitlamo translates to "Commitment."
3 Vision 2016 was the long-term vision for Botswana. This marked 50 years since Botswana's independence from Britain. It proposed that by 2016 Botswana would be a prosperous, educated and informed nation.
4 BOCRA is a quasi-governmental corporation that regulates the communications sector, including mobile communication in Botswana.
5 When FNBB customers send money to non-FNBB customers using e-wallet services, an SMS (short messaging services) code will be sent to the recipient's mobile phone. The recipient will then use the SMS code as a PIN to withdraw money from any FNBB ATM.
6 Mascom *MyZaka* is a mobile money service provided by Mascom networks and Orange *Money* is for Orange networks.
7 *MyNews* is a mobile enabled service that allows complete access to several local online newspapers in Botswana. Mascom prepaid customers should first register and pay for this service for them to access these newspapers.

References

Ahmed, Ishfaq, and Tehmina Fiaz Qazi. 2011. "Mobile Phone Adoption and Consumption Patterns of University Students in Pakistan." *International Journal of Business and Social Science* 2: 205–213.

Biancini, Sara. 2011. "Behind the Scenes of the Telecommunications Miracle: An Empirical Analysis of the Indian Market." *Telecommunications Policy* 35: 238–249.

Botswana Telecommunications Authority. 2012. *Annual Report*. Gaborone.

Botswana Telecommunications Corporation. n.d. "About Us: About BTS." Accessed December 17, 2020. http://www.btc.bw/about

Byrne, Bridget. 2004. "Qualitative Interviewing." In *Researching Society and Culture*, edited by Clive Seale, 179–192. London: Sage Publications.

Chabossou, Augustin, Christoph Stork, Matthias Stork, and Pam Zahongo. 2008. "Mobile Telephony Access and Usage in Africa." *African Journal of Information and Communication*: 17–41.

Christensen, Christian, and Patrick Prax. 2012. "Assemblage, Adaptation and Apps: Smartphones and Mobile Gaming." *Continuum: Journal of Media and Cultural Studies* 26(5): 731–739.

Donner, Jonathan. 2008. "Research Approaches to Mobile Use in the Developing World: A Review of the Literature." *The Information Society* 24(3): 140–159.

Duncombe, Richard, and Richard Boateng. 2009. "Mobile phones and Financial Services in Developing Countries: A Review of Concepts, Methods, Issues, Evidence and Future Research Directions." *Third World Quarterly* 30(7): 1237–1258.

Fuchs, Christian, and Eva Horak. 2008. "Africa and the Digital Divide." *Telematics and. Information* 25(2): 99–116.

Gandy, Oscar. 2002. "The Real Digital Divide: Citizens Versus Consumers". In *Handbook of New Media*, edited by Leah A. Lievrouw and Sonia M. Livingstone, 448–460. London: Sage.

Gebremichael, Meseret D., and Jackson W. Jackson. 2006. "Bridging the Gap in Sub-Saharan Africa: A Holistic Look at Information Poverty and the Region's Digital Divide." *Government Information Quarterly* 23(2): 267–280.

Goggin, Gerard. 2009. "Adapting the Mobile Phone: The iPhone and its Consumption." *Continuum: Journal of Media & Cultural Studies* 23(2): 231–244.

Gyamfi, Alexander. 2005. "Closing the Digital Divide in Sub-Saharan Africa: Meeting the Challenges of the Information Age." *Information Development* 21(1): 22–30.

Horst, Heather A. 2006. "The Blessings and Burdens of Communication: Cell Phones in Jamaican Transnational Social Fields." *Global Networks* 6(2): 143–159.

Hwang, Junseok, Youngsang Cho, and Nguyen Viet Long. 2009. "Investigation of Factors Affecting the Diffusion of Mobile Telephone Services: An Empirical Analysis for Vietnam." *Telecommunications. Policy* 33(9): 534–543.

James, Jeffrey. 2009. "From the Relative to the Absolute Digital Divide in Developing Countries." *Technological Forecasting and Social Change*, 76(8), 1124–1129.

James, Jeffrey. 2012. "Which Developing Countries Have Done the Most to Close the Digital Divide?" *Telematics and Informatics* 29(1): 2–10.

Kaba, Bangaly, Koffi N'Da, Peter Meso, and Victor Wacham A. Mbarika. 2009. "Micro Factors Influencing the Attitudes Toward and the Use of a Mobile Technology: A Model of Cell-Phone Use in Guinea." *IEEE Transactions on Professional Communication* 52(3): 272–290.

Kamran, Sohail. 2010. "Mobile Phone: Calling and Texting Patterns of College Students in Pakistan." *International Journal of Business and Management* 5(4): 26–36.

Karim, Nor ShahrizaAbdul, Rose AlindaAlias, Shamsul AnuarMokhtar, and Zairah Abdul Rahim. 2009. "Mobile Phone Adoption and Appropriation in Malaysia and the Contribution of Age and Gender." In *ICIMT '09. International Conference on Information and Multimedia Technology*, 485–490.

Kreutzer, Tino. 2009. "*Internet and Online Media Usage on Mobile Phones Among Low-Income Urban Youth in Cape Town.*" Paper presented at "Mobile 2.0: Beyond Voice?" Pre-Conference Workshop at the International Communication Association. Chicago, IL, May 20–21.

Kushchu, Ibrahim, and M. Halid Kuscu. 2003. "*From e-Government to M-Government: Facing the Inevitable.*" The 3rd European Conference on e-Government.

Lesitaokana, William Ofentse. 2013. "Radio in Botswana: A Critical Examination of its Growth and Dominance Across Botswana's Mass Media Landscape." *Journal of Radio and Audio Media* 20: 197–211.

Lesitaokana, William Ofentse. 2014. "Key Issues in the Development of Mobile Telephony in Botswana (1998–2011): An Empirical Investigation." *New Media & Society* 16: 840–855.

Loo, Becky P.Y., and Y. L. Ngan. 2012. "Developing Mobile Communications to Narrow Digital Divide in Developing Countries? Some Lessons from China." *Telecommunications Policy* 36: 888–900.

Mallat, Niina, Matti Rossi, and Virpi Kristiina Tuunainen. 2004. "Mobile Banking Services: Adopting New and Innovative Mobile Financial Applications and Service Provisioning Methods." *Communications of the ACM* 47: 42–46.

Manohar, B. Murali. 2005. "Information and Communication Technology Applications in Development: India as a Role Model for Other Developing Countries." *Information Development* 21: 47–52.

Middleton, Catherine A. 2008. "Illusions of Balance and Control in an Always-on Environment: A Case Study of Blackberry Users." In *Mobile Phone Cultures*, edited by Gerard Goggin, 28–41. London: Routledge.

Nkwe, Nugi. 2012. "E-Government: Challenges and Opportunities in Botswana." *International Journal of Humanities and Social Science* 2(17): 39–48.

Nwagwu, Williams Ezinwa. 2006. "Integrating ICTs into the Globalization of the Poor Developing Countries." *Information Development* 22(3): 167–179.

Oladokun, Olugbade, and Lenrie Aina. 2011. "ODL and the Impact of Digital Divide on Information Access in Botswana." *Home* 12(6): 157–177.

Paterson, Andrew. 2007. "Costs of Information and Communication Technology in Developing Country School Systems: The Experience of Botswana, Namibia and Seychelles." *International Journal of Education Development using ICT* 3 (4): 89–101.

Rantao, Paul. 1996. "The Role of the Media in Promoting Participatory Politics in Botswana." In *Botswana's Media and Democracy*, edited by Methaetsile Leepile, 3–20. Gaborone: Mmegi Publishing House.

Rice, Ronald E. 2002. "Primary Issues in Internet Use: Access, Civic and Community Involvement, and Social Interaction and Expression." In *Handbook of New Media*, edited by Leah A. Lievrouw and Sonia M. Livingstone, 105–129. London: Sage.

Sebusang, Enele Sebusang and Shedden Masupe. 2003. "ICT Development in Botswana: Connectivity for Rural Communities." *African Journal of Information and Communication* 2003(4): 41–51.

Sey, Araba. 2011. "'We Use it Different': Making Sense of Trends in Mobile Phone Use in Ghana." *New Media & Society* 13(3): 375–390.

Silverman, David. 2006. *Interpreting Qualitative Data: Methods for Analyzing Talk, Text and Interaction*. London: Sage Publications.

Srinuan, Chalita, Pratompong Srinuan, and Erik Bohlin. 2012. "An Analysis of Mobile Internet Access in Thailand: Implications for Bridging the Digital Divide." *Telematics and Informatics* 29(3): 254–262.

Watkins, Jerry, Kathi Kitner, and Dina Mehta. 2012. "Mobile and Smartphone Use in Urban and Rural India." *Continuum: Journal of Media & Cultural Studies* 26(5): 685–697.

Watkins, Jerry, Larissa Hjorth, and Ilpo Koskinen. 2012. "Wising Up: Revising Mobile Media in an Age of Smartphones." *Continuum: Journal of Media & Cultural Studies* 26(5): 665–668.

5

BRAZIL AND THE BLOCKING OF NON-APPROVED CELL PHONES

An A2K Perspective

Celina M.A. Bottino, Carlos Affonso Souza and Beatriz L.M. Nunes

Introduction

Knowledge can come in many different forms, such as ideas, inventions, and information. Having more access to it means that more people will be able to learn and pass along this knowledge, influencing how doctors treat patients, how artists create their work, and ultimately how new opportunities in life are discovered (Subramanian and Shaver 2011, 2). The Internet has come to play a significant role in the pursuit of knowledge; serving as a major source of information, it provides users with access to an unprecedented tool for communication. Access to the Internet can come in many different forms as well, such as computers, tablets, cell phones, and other devices. However, access to such devices is far from being equally distributed. Due to their low cost, cell phones are quickly becoming the main gateway for people, especially those from low-resource communities, to connect and access the Internet. Nonetheless, the use of certain cell phones by Brazilians has been endangered by a measure first announced by the Brazilian Telecommunications Agency (Anatel) back in 2014.

Since 2014, Anatel has been issuing announcements that it would be unilaterally blocking non-approved cell phones—those not in compliance with Anatel's regulations—by means of technical measures (Anatel 2014). To achieve this, the Agency would make use of the fact that each handset has a unique identifying number, an IMEI (International Mobile Equipment Identity), that functions as the digital fingerprint of the handset. When it comes to devices that have passed Anatel's approval process,[1] this number is stored in a database called the Equipment Identity Register.

Non-approved handsets, although they have an IMEI number, are not recorded in this database. According to Anatel's announcement, the first stage of blocking of non-approved devices was supposed to begin back in January 2014. It would have consisted in the implementation of the Handset Management Integrated System (hereafter referred to as SIGA, from the Portuguese acronym for *Sistema Integrado de Gestão de Aparelhos*)

(Anatel 2014). Anatel's explanatory note on SIGA was the only form of manifestation on the measure announced in 2014.[2] The IMEIs collected would allow for an assessment of the legality of the devices connected to the Internet. Secondly, to the best of our knowledge, the handsets considered unauthorized and without a recognized IMEI would be unilaterally disconnected from the network, with the support of the telecommunications service providers.[3]

In a recent publication (Martello 2017), however, it has been announced that Anatel will begin the implementation of said measures—unilaterally blocking non-approved cell phones, i.e. counterfeit handsets—starting on May 9, 2018, implicating, in an initial phase, only the irregular handsets in Brasília and Goiás. In other regions of Brazil, the blocking will begin in December/2018 (first phase) and March/2019 (second phase). One of the main goals of this measure, according to Anatel, is to inhibit the sale of stolen phones and tablets.

The use of cell phones in Brazil is so widespread that there are more cell phones in operation than people using them. Currently, the estimated Brazilian population is 207 million people (IBGE 2017), and, in January 2017, there were 243.4 million cell phones (TELECO 2017a), which is equivalent to 117.65 cell phones per 100 inhabitants. The use of cell phones has been responsible for an increase in the number of people connected to the Internet in Brazil, a common trend observed throughout the world. According to a 2014 survey conducted by the International Telecommunications Union (ITU), approximately 32 percent of the world's population accesses the Internet through cell phones (ITU 2014b). In 2016, the same survey was conducted, concluding that mobile-broadband networks (3G or above) reached 84 percent of the global population (ITU 2016). In Brazil, access to mobile broadband services was the sector that grew fastest in recent years, from 10 percent in 2010 to 22 percent in 2015 (TELECO 2016). In 2014, 43 million people in Brazil accessed the Internet through their cell phones, and 3.8 million Brazilians had their first contact with the Internet through the cell phone (FNazca and Data Folha 2013/2014).

According to the latest Household Analysis National Research (PNAD)[4] released by the IBGE (Brazil's Statistics and Census Institute), the northern region presented the highest percentage of households using cell phones to access the Internet at 96.7 percent, surpassing access through personal computers at 43.4 percent (IBGE 2016, 43). In Sergipe, for example, a state located in the northeast region of Brazil, 57.4 percent of connections were obtained through cell phones or tablets whereas only 1.2 percent through computers. In the more sparsely populated northern states of Pará, Roraima, Amapá, and Amazonas, the ratio of access via cell phones to personal computers was 66.1 to 1.6 percent, 52.4 to 1.4 percent, 55.9 to 0.7 percent, and 52.4 to 1.6 percent respectively (IBGE 2016, 44). See Table 5.1.

TABLE 5.1 Ratio of access via cell phones to personal computers

	Pará	*Roraima*	*Amapá*	*Amazonas*
Only computers	1.6%	1.4%	0.7%	1.6%
Only cell phones or tablets	66.1%	52.4%	55.9%	52.4%

Thus, cell phone technology has been a major gateway to connectivity for Brazilians. This massive use of cell phones has benefitted especially the impoverished part of the population and those living in more remote areas, as cell phones are more affordable than computers or tablets and are an alternative in areas with no available landlines. The Internet is an essential tool for accessing and sharing ideas and information and these devices have become crucial to the widespread dissemination of knowledge, affecting economic growth and human development.

If cell phones have led to an increase in connectivity for the Brazilian population, non-approved devices, known in Brazil pejoratively as *xing ling,* are an important factor in this growth due to their affordability. While the price of cell phones (smartphones) ranges between R$500 and R$4.000 (Lojas Americanas 2017), *xing ling* devices cost around R$200.[5] Moreover, these devices often allow the simultaneous use of more than one SIM card, enabling the user to take advantage of promotions by different carriers and, therefore, allowing users to pay a minimum price to communicate. These devices are referred to as *xing ling* because many of them, though not all, are manufactured in China and in other Asian countries and often fail to comply with regular customs procedures (Fusco and Wiziack 2011). However, once these devices come into the country, they are sold at popular stores, where consumers buy them legally. Thus, if there is any regulatory failure with respect to the entry of these devices and their non-approval, these failures should not be attributed to the consumer, but to other actors in the chain that ultimately failed to act before the consumer acquired the unit in good faith.

The measure announced by Anatel began to be implemented in February 2018 in the state of Goiás and in the Federal District and in September 2018 it was implemented in the states of Acre, Espírito Santo, Rio de Janeiro, Rondônia and Tocantins, and the third and final phase was planned to be in effect early 2019, affecting the northern states of Brazil. The implementation that was taken in effect was modified, since the users of non-approved phones were not disconnected overnight, as was initially announced. The users of non-approved phones received messages alerting them that they had 75 days to change their phone number to a certified handset, otherwise they would be disconnected. In addition, Anatel also created a website to inform users about the implementation process. If the users did not take action, millions would be disconnected overnight from the telephone network and Internet access. Such a measure would not only have a direct impact on the right of these users to communication but would also directly affect their right to freedom of expression and interfere with their access to knowledge, since such an act would remove the necessary infrastructure for those rights to be fully exercised. Furthermore, the measure would violate the good faith of those users who had purchased non-approved devices unaware of that fact. In other words, the disconnection would render purchased handsets useless. It would be tantamount to a real expropriation of private property without any previous compensation and outside of constitutional procedures. Even though Anatel has not disclosed the number of people who use non-approved cell phones, available data suggests that this number varies between 34 and 40 million sets. According to a 2011 survey conducted by the *Folha de São Paulo* newspaper, 20 percent of 202.9 million sets at the time did not have certification by Anatel, which amounts to about 40 million sets (Fusco and Wiziack 2011). Accounts shows that in the first phase of the measure more than 100 thousand handsets were disconnected.

This chapter will examine the measures announced by Anatel to implement the blocking of the so-called non-approved cell phones in Brazil from an Access to Knowledge (A2K) and human rights perspective. The A2K movement unites several civil society groups, governments, and individuals converging on the idea that A2K and fundamental principles of justice, freedom of expression, economic development, and human rights are intertwined. This is especially important considering that the Internet, as a channel for communication, has become an essential tool for accessing and sharing ideas and information. The A2K movement roughly dates back to 2004. In October of that same year, in Geneva, a declaration on the future of the World Intellectual Property Organization (WIPO) emerged from a call from Brazil and Argentina for the development of an agenda that focused on the creation of a Treaty on Access to Knowledge and Technology. The movement initially emerged as a way of responding to and rejecting the main justifications for intellectual property (IP) law, seeking an alternative for emphasizing the importance of information, knowledge, creativity, and innovation in modern society (Krikonian and Kapczynski 2010, 9). It challenged the ability of IP law to efficiently promote access to knowledge as it had been traditionally conceived.

Amy Kaczynski conceptualizes the movement in its initial phase as both a reaction to the trends in technologies of information processing and in law but also as a critique of the idea that IP rights and protection should be expanded (Krikonian and Kapczynski 2010, 17). The aforementioned trend showed that, over the past few years, exclusive rights over information have increased exponentially. That situation ended up providing IP owners with even more exclusionary rights and increased the severity of penalties imposed on infringers (Kapczynski 2008, 821). In a second phase, the A2K movement expanded to other areas outside of intellectual property and the traditional access to knowledge debate, building capacity for researchers, educators, and policy makers to promote A2K in different areas. Since its initial bearings, the A2K network has continuously strived to expand its focus to include concerns in connection to the ample enjoyment of freedom of expression and related rights, as is the case with the right to information and communication (Prakash, Souza, and Rizk 2015, VII). In this sense, it is important to acknowledge the connection to human rights analysis when addressing A2K concerns (Subramanian and Shaver 2011, 2).

After having already introduced the Brazilian context and providing information on Anatel's measure to block non-approved devices, the first of three sections presents A2K and human rights concerns regarding the blocking of non-approved cell phones. This section focuses on how the implementation of this measure would not only hinder access to information and communication but would also violate fundamental rights such as the right to freedom of expression and the right to citizenship. It covers the Brazilian Internet Bill of Rights and the disproportionality of Anatel's measure considering the arguments provided for the ban, further analyzed in the second section. The third and final section covers the certification standards that are necessary for approving devices in Brazil. The conclusion, in short, sets out that while there is a need for observing fundamental rights, such as Internet access and access to knowledge, there is also a need for the Brazilian state to address the use of non-approved products that were marketed and acquired in good faith. Any measure taken by the Brazilian state to deal with this issue should be done through the human rights and A2K framework in order to expand the opportunities for more people to be connected and, therefore, have access to knowledge.

A2K and human rights concerns in the blocking of non-authorized cell phones

As mentioned, mobile phones have become one of the main means of communication and a gateway to Internet access. These devices allow the exercise of freedom of expression by a considerable part of disadvantaged portions of the Brazilian population. The Internet, more than any other means of communication, has had a relevant impact on the sharing and means of accessing ideas and information. Not by chance, Article 7 of the Brazilian Internet Bill of Rights (Law no. 12.965/2014) establishes that "Internet access is essential to the exercise of citizenship." Furthermore, Internet access has become essential not only for the exercise of the right to freedom of expression but also for the enjoyment of other rights. These rights include: the right to participate in cultural life and to enjoy the benefits of scientific and technological progress,[6] the right to education,[7] the right to assembly and association,[8] political rights,[9] and the right to health,[10] among others (IACHR 2013, 16–17).

According to the A2K framework, the right to freedom of expression goes beyond information and data. The concept of A2K embraces "the right to both receive and to participate in the creation, modification, and extension of information, tools, inventions, literature, art, popular media and other expressions of human inquiry and understanding" (Prakash, Souza, and Rizk 2015, VII). One way to understand how developing and new technologies affect access to knowledge is to look at how censorship may use the very same technologies to hinder speech. Censorship often works by reinforcing existing power imbalances and may occur in different forms or through different means. Regardless of the form by which it takes place, knowledge, invariably, is negatively affected. What the A2K movement aims to achieve is not only the means to access content but also the means to enable participation in the creation of content (Prakash, Souza, and Rizk 2015, IX). Ultimately, these tools will make it possible for individuals to exercise their right to freedom of expression (which, evidently, encompasses the right to communication) and democratic participation.

Therefore, in order for there to be a system of free speech, there must not only be an absence of censorship but also what Jack Balkin refers to as an "infrastructure of free expression" (Balkin 2009, 36).[11] As pointed out by Balkin, the infrastructure of free expression includes the Internet in all of its aspects: domain name system, broadband services for storing and hardware platforms such as computers, tablets, but especially smartphones, which have become an all-purpose information and communication devices. To illustrate this assertion, in 2016 alone, Brazil had more than 248 million handset sign-ups and 26 million broadband plan registrations, placing Brazil as the country with the largest online population in Latin America (TELECO 2016).

Access to knowledge depends on such an infrastructure. In his article "Old-School/New-School Speech Regulation," Balkin (2014) refers to censorship as speech regulation and divides it into two types: old-school and new-school. The distinction and understanding of such concepts are especially relevant when considering the Anatel decision concerning unregulated cell phone devices and the necessary technology involved for distinguishing between regulated and unregulated devices.

Old-school speech censorship or regulation has characteristics of direct and salient use of state power to detain, block, or destroy information. These techniques generally employ criminal penalties or civil damages for the purposes of regulating individual speakers (Balkin 2014, 2298). In contrast, new-school speech censorship is not performed by the state itself but rather is outsourced through third parties, such as Internet service providers or is undertaken by private actors to exert control over digital networks and auxiliary services. In new-school censorship, speech is controlled through digital networks, including targets such as ISPs, broadband providers, search engines, hosting services, among others.

Anatel's announced measure would arguably fall under both categories of speech regulation, considering how uncertified cell phones would be identified and the consequence of being an uncertified and unregulated device. Disconnecting millions of users from their cell phones and, consequently, from the Internet will limit their access to information, to freedom of expression, and to other fundamental rights such as the right to exercise citizenship as provided by the Brazilian Internet Bill of Rights (Law no. 12.965/2014). This action will also negatively hinder the integration process of the affected users to the social fabric and their relationship with the state itself.

To the extent that information and communication technologies increasingly pervade every person's life, the simple blocking of a certain technology may be regarded as a real act of censorship. In this particular scenario, the blocking of the technology may also be analogous to the expropriation of assets or even confiscation if there is not a correct balance between the rights and the interests involved in the implementation of this measure. Additionally, the collection and storage of IMEIs would be for accessing the handset and asserting whether it would fall under the category of certified or uncertified. This process is an example of both categories of speech regulation or censorship. By implementing technological and digital measures, a regulation undertaken by an independent agency would unilaterally curb the access to the Internet, information, communication, and ultimately, to knowledge of individuals who happen to have acquired unregulated devices.

In this regard, the report published by the Special Rapporteur for Freedom of Expression of the Inter-American Commission on Human Rights explicitly affirms that the right to freedom of expression has two dimensions: an individual and a collective or social one. Therefore, freedom of expression is an instrument for the exchange of information and ideas between people and for mass communication between humans. This includes both the right to communicate one's own point of view, information, or opinions to others and everyone's right to receive and get to know such views, information, opinions, reports, and news freely without any interference that may distort or obstruct them (IACHR 2013, 15–16).

Disconnecting users would be a violation of the fundamental right to freedom of expression and international law, which would subject Brazil to international accountability based on the international legal system. Article 19 of the Covenant on Civil and Political rights, of which Brazil is a signatory, states that the right to freedom of expression includes "the freedom to seek, receive and impart information and ideas of all kinds, … in printed or artistic form, or by any other means of their choice." Cell phones have been instrumental to the exercise and enjoyment of that right, especially considering the Brazilian context where many people depend on apps such as WhatsApp on a daily basis for work-related issues. That is true for those who work autonomously, for example, and relate to their clients via the app. In this regard, the UN Special Rapporteur for Freedom of Expression expressly recognized that mobile technology is crucial for connectivity, especially in remote areas and in developing countries, becoming a means of exercising other rights.[12]

Additionally, the Rapporteur for Freedom of Expression of the Inter-American system states that the positive obligation of countries to provide universal access to the Internet should include measures to ensure that vulnerable individuals may acquire computers and similar equipment at affordable prices (IACHR 2013, 22). Additionally, the UN Special Rapporteur on Protection of the Right to Freedom of Opinion and Expression recommends that countries support policies and programs that facilitate the connection to the Internet with mobile technology.[13]

The measure announced by Anatel seems to go the opposite way to the recommendations of several international bodies, to which Brazil has a binding relationship, including the UN. Anatel was created by the general law on Telecommunications (Law no. 9.472/1997), establishing it as the first regulatory agency in Brazil. It is part of the Federal Public Administration and is linked to the Ministry of Communications. As such, it is administratively independent and financially autonomous. As part of its measures, Anatel should take the necessary measures in order to answer and fulfill public interest as well as develop the telecommunications sector in Brazil, acting independently, impartially, and under its legal restrictions (Anatel 2015). However, with the discussed measure, instead of supporting and facilitating network connections, the Brazilian government would be doing the opposite: disconnecting the very people who rely on this type of equipment for the exercise of their citizenship, allowing minimum levels of communication and Internet access.

It is worth highlighting that another report by the UN's Rapporteur on Protection of the Right to Freedom of Opinion and Expression, published in May 2015, emphasized the importance of keeping communication through mobile handsets anonymous, as well as free from state interference, allowing the full exercise of freedom of opinion and expression in contemporary communication. The report pointed out some governmental practices that would represent an obstacle to the implementation of these rights. One of the practices specifically mentioned in the report, among others, is the required record of cell phone SIM cards, which would allow governments the ability to monitor the users of those lines.[14]

If the mandatory SIM card identification poses risks to the exercise of freedom of expression, the IMEI identification of all handsets is cause for even more serious concern, especially because a SIM card can be easily changed. With respect to a mobile device, which has a unique IMEI, such a change comes up against prohibitive economic barriers, especially for the most vulnerable part of the population. Thus, the mere control and registration of IMEIs in Brazil, even if being used for legitimate purposes, is an action with damaging effects for the fundamental right of privacy and, consequently, for freedom of expression. The report even recommends that countries should not adopt measures to identify users and their communication media,[15] as would be the case if obligatory SIM and IMEI identification were required.

Internet access and the Brazilian Internet Bill of Rights

As briefly mentioned above, the Brazilian Internet Bill of Rights (Law no. 12.965/ 2014) has asserted some of the civil rights that ensure freedom of expression, defended by special rapporteurs representing both the OAS (Organization of American States) and the UN. They include the right to have access to the Internet, to information, to knowledge, and to participation in cultural life and in the conduct of public affairs.[16]

Furthermore, the Brazilian Internet Bill of Rights determines that Internet access is fundamental to the exercise of citizenship and that there must be "no suspension of Internet connection, save for debt directly resulting from its use."[17] Therefore, the right to Internet access should be guaranteed by the state. Ensuring the necessary conditions for people to have effective access is one of the many measures the state should embrace, which does not include taking steps to prevent or hinder Internet access, especially in relation to the most vulnerable sectors of the population as they use cell phones as their only or main means of communicating. Additionally, the blocking of these non-approved devices would be an unreasonable and disproportionate measure affecting a precondition to the exercise of citizenship and in violation of the Brazilian legal system.

Disproportionality of the measure

Any restriction of the right to freedom of expression must observe the parameters stipulated by international law and the restriction must not put the right itself in jeopardy.[18] Article 19 §3° of the International Covenant on Civil and Political

Rights states that the exercise of the rights provided for in this document implies duties and responsibilities. Therefore, it may be subject to certain restrictions, which must be expressively provided for in the law in order to ensure the respect of the rights and reputation of others as well as to protect national security, order, health, or public morals. The measure announced by Anatel goes far beyond simply putting that right at risk. The blocking of these devices would increase the digital divide, placing the economically underprivileged classes at a distinct disadvantage. It would affect consumers who, in good faith, acquired their non-approved devices because they could not afford to purchase other equipment and without any knowledge of their lack of approval.

Anatel's measure will most likely have a significant impact on those who belong to a low social income class. A study conducted by the ITU on counterfeit devices found it relevant to take into consideration the fact that in developing countries, such as Brazil, with low social and economic conditions, mobile phones are the main source of communication and means of participating in society (ITU 2014a, 23). Considering that this layer of society is dependent on this type of device, as it is cheaper and therefore more accessible, to communicate, be informed, work, and relate to others, it would be a violation to their fundamental rights such as freedom of expression and the right to be informed.

Telecommunications networks should not be used to remedy failures in other parts of the governmental system that allowed the widespread use of devices not approved by Anatel. The effort to prevent the use of these cell phones should be made at the entry point of such devices in Brazil[19] by halting smuggling, introducing a crackdown on tax avoidance, and inspecting retail stores. Attacking the consumer at the end of the chain seems to be an alternative that only hurts those who bought the device in good faith. Although Article 156 of Law 9472/97 establishes that the connection of non-certified equipment may be blocked, this provision should be analyzed in conjunction with Article. 7, III of Anatel's Resolution that provides that, in the absence of a certification standard, one must take into consideration the impact of the product on the universalization of telecommunications. In fact, non-approved handsets play an important role in the universalization of telecommunications[20] and the spread of knowledge in Brazil. This simple fact should be taken into account before defining the scope of the decision to block non-approved cell phones.

The ITU recommends that any practice related to the disconnection of cell phones be taken gradually and that transitional measures be adopted, such as blocking only new devices that have just been connected to the network instead of disconnecting devices in use (ITU 2014a, 23). Any adopted measure must be preceded by a major communication campaign, in conjunction with consumer defense entities, to guide and inform people about the changes, presenting alternatives. Finally, the complete blockage of these devices alone, without the implementation of measures that will meet the connectivity needs of this part of the population is also discriminatory, as only the poorest will suffer the consequences of being disconnected.

Privacy and IMEI database

In addition to the violation of freedom of expression, Anatel's measure raises serious questions regarding users' privacy. As mentioned above, a database of the IMEIs of the devices connected to the Brazilian network is being compiled and will be used to create a cell phone "black list" of non-approved, illegal devices so that they can be later blocked. This measure alone is already in violation of the referred UN reports. Furthermore, the creation of this database in itself, even before any cell phone shutdown, presents risks for the violation of users' privacy. As mass surveillance concerns grow, the creation of such a database is met with a peculiar situation in Brazil considering that Brazil has no general data protection law. Privacy and data protection are guaranteed by the Constitution, but more detailed protection concerning liability for data leaks, rules for the commercialization of personal data, and regulations for the international transfer of data are still lacking in the Brazilian framework. The absence of such provisions makes the creation of a large-scale database a worrisome move. In this scenario, once the database is created, the potential for the improper usage of the acquired data is significant. The Brazilian government could potentially promote the temporary blockage of any device for any given reason, which would be contrary to acting as an agent of citizenship.

Therefore, the creation of such a database can lead to several possibilities for violating human rights, for example, the right to privacy. Hence, it is paramount that the Brazilian state act as an agent of citizenship, to establish parameters, checks, and counterbalances to prevent the monitoring and surveillance of its citizens. In addition to this, when it comes to any possible requests for blocking, there must always be prior judicial control as a way to ensure the constitutional guarantees of privacy and proper legal proceedings to these cell phone holders, including at the administrative level, since the decision to block these devices produces effects in the sphere of private interests.[21]

Anatel's arguments for the ban on non-approved devices

To support its measure, Anatel has consistently argued that the disconnection of non-approved cell phones is necessary considering they have not gone through the necessary certification process and this may cause accidents, such as affecting the aircraft communications network. Anatel claims that such devices pose health risks to users in relation to the level of noise and emission of radio frequencies (Swerdlow et al. 2011, 119)[22] in addition to exposing the user to the risk of shocks during the use of the device or while charging the cell phone batteries and to halt the commercialization of counterfeit handsets (Anatel n.d.). Furthermore, the use of non-approved devices constitutes a violation punishable by a fine or seizure of the device.[23] Concerns about network interference and possible risks to the health of users are legitimate and important. However, it turns out that Anatel, so far, has not presented any technical study that supports these claims and that justifies the adoption of such a radical measure. These devices have already been in use for years and have not caused any noticeable disruption in the aircraft communications network. Any measure that restricts or, in this case, makes it impossible for users to enjoy a fundamental right must be widely justified, especially by empirical data. Studies conducted by the ITU indicate that non-approved devices do affect the telecommunications network (ITU 2014a). Still, the Brazilian state must adopt the principle of proportionality and seek measures that prove to be less harmful to the fundamental right to freedom of expression, privacy, individual rights, and access to knowledge and communication.

If, on one hand, one of Anatel's concerns is to ensure that consumers have access to safe products, on the other hand, it cannot fail to protect consumers who have purchased products in good faith. Many of the non-approved devices are purchased at stores without the consumer knowing of the need for government approval. So, if their devices are blocked, they should be indemnified for their loss, especially since the purchase of the unit occurred due to the failure of the state itself to monitor these devices and prevent them from being sold. Furthermore, it would be the responsibility of the government to supervise marketed products effectively in order to avoid harm to consumers. If cell phones really expose people to danger, agencies with enforcement power should act effectively to withdraw them from the market and not just interfere with the telecommunications network to block the cell phones that were bought, to the detriment of their purchasers in good faith, as announced by Anatel.

Certification standards

In addition to the scenario described above, the process of certification and approval of devices in Brazil is complex and bureaucratic (TELECO 2017b). This is unavoidably a piece of the puzzle that must be addressed in order to come to a solution that is more adequate than the direct blocking of non-approved devices. Anatel's Resolution 242/2000 provides that when there are no certification standards issued by the Agency it should "decide on the desirability and feasibility of conformity assessment and approval," considering some principles. Among such principles are the "contribution of the use of the product or equipment to the compliance with the goals of universalization and modernization of telecommunication services"[24] and "the international experience in the use of the product or equipment."[25] Anatel itself acknowledges that the products used must also be considered in view of the fulfilment of the goals of universalization of telecommunication services and that these devices have indeed played a very important role in order to achieve this goal. Disconnecting them from the network would represent a backward step on the path towards the complex goal of universalizing telecommunications services.

The Agency must also consider the international experience in the use of non-approved cell phones. Because these devices are also used in other countries, before carrying out the disconnection, Anatel should present a risk study of the use of non-approved devices and possible damage caused by them. In these cases of lack of formal regulations, Anatel could also use other globally recognized international standards,[26] loosening somewhat the current rigid certification system and ensuring that people are connected, following the guidance of Article 7, III, of the 242/2000 Resolution.

Conclusion

The act of permanent blocking of non-approved devices, as it was initially announced by Anatel would affect fundamental rights of millions of Brazilians, especially those who belong to low-resource communities and find themselves in a most vulnerable situation, given that the cell phone is their primary means of communication. It will also affect their access to knowledge, hindering economic and social development. Banning low-resource communities from having access to their mobile phones will exclude them from the array of opportunities that internet connection and access to information provides them. When the government and its public agents can decide who will have access to the Internet, and, therefore, to knowledge and who will become excluded from such an access, its role becomes that of a censor. The act of banning these devices is *unnecessary and disproportionate* in relation to the problems it aims to fight.

Dealing with this issue is not simple, and a solution should be worked out not only by Anatel; it should be a joint effort of several government agencies. Following the recommendations of the UN Special Rapporteur for Freedom of Expression, Brazil should implement positive measures to ensure that people have access not only to the Internet but also to low-cost terminals and equipment, adopting, if necessary, subsidizing measures.[27] It is worth noting that the actual implementation of the measure was adapted, taking some of these considerations into account. First, users were previously notified and had the opportunity to change their number so that their handsets were not disconnected overnight as originally planned. Second, Anatel created a special website page with more information about the measure, informing consumers how they should proceed.[28]

There are two conflicting issues at stake: (i) the right to freedom of expression, privacy, Internet access, and access to knowledge and (ii) the need of the State to combat the use of non-approved products, but which have been freely marketed and acquired in good faith. Considering the human rights and access to knowledge framework, the respect for the fundamental rights to freedom of expression, privacy, and access to knowledge should guide the governmental action in this case. Disconnection of non-approved devices, as announced by Anatel, would only aggravate the digital gap in the country and it fails to comply with basic A2K and human rights concerns. These concerns were raised by civil society organizations and Anatel adjusted the measure, making it more compliant with human rights concerns.

Notes

1 According to Anatel's Article 3, VIII, Resolution 242/2000, "approval by Anatel is a private act, whereby, in the manner and in the cases provided for in this Resolution, the Agency recognizes the certificates of compliance or accepts the declarations of conformity for telecommunication products". Available at: http://legislacao.anatel.gov.br/resolucoes/15-2000/129-resolucao-242. According to Resolution 242/2000, the certification ceases to be issued by Anatel, and begins to be given by independent bodies, Designated Certification Bodies (OCD in Portuguese), which issue certificates of conformity to be approved by Anatel.

2 Anatel clarified that the system, managed by the telecommunications providers, is in an experimental phase and that during the first phase, the system would allow a diagnosis of the legality of the devices connected to the network providers. From this information, the next measures would be announced in order to ensure access of only approved devices to the networks. When the explanatory note was issued, there was no decision as to the period of implementation of the measures or whether the of devices currently in operation would be blocked. Any measures to adopt will be object of broad dissemination to users in a timely manner. Anatel recommended that consumers do not buy handsets, landlines or cell phones, without the seal of the Agency. Equipment without the seal may show connection failures, for they are often made with low-quality material, and they may cause interference (Anatel 2014).

3 "At present, there is no decision as to the period of implementation of the measures or whether there will be blocking of devices currently in operation. Any measures to be adopted will be object of broad dissemination to users in a timely manner" (Anatel 2014).

4 PNAD stands for the Portuguese acronym "Pesquisa Nacional de Análise de Domicílio."

5 Price survey made at the popular market Saara (stands for Sociedade de Amigos da Rua da Alfândega e Adjacências, a series of popular stores on Rua da Alfândega and nearby streets downtown) in Rio de Janeiro in June 2014.

6 OAS (Organization of American States), "Protocol of San Salvador," November 17, 1998, Article 14. https://www.cidh.oas.org/basicos/english/basic5.prot.sn%20salv.htm

7 Ibid., Article 13.

8 OAS, "American Convention on Human Rights 'Pact of San Jose,'" Articles 15 and 16. http://www.oas.org/dil/treaties_B-32_American_Convention_on_Human_Rights.pdf.

9 Ibid., Article 23.

10 OAS, "Protocol of San Salvador," Article 10.

11 "A system of free speech depends not only on the mere absence of state censorship, but also on an infrastructure of free expression. The infrastructure of free expression includes the kinds of media and institutions for knowledge, creation, and dissemination that are available at any point in time." (Balkin 2009, 52–54, n9); see also Yochai Benkler, "Property, Commons, and the First Amendment: Towards a Core Common Infrastructure," 3 (White Paper for the First Amendment Program, Brennan Ctr. for Justice at NYU Law Sch., 2001), archived at http://perma.cc/5DDR-WU5M.

12 UN General Assembly, "Report of the Special Rapporteur on the Promotion and Protection of the Right to Freedom of Opinion and Expression," August 10, 2011, UN Doc A/66/290, 21, http://www.ohchr.org/Documents/Issues/Opinion/A.66.290.pdf.

13 Ibid.

14 UN Human Rights Council, "Report of the Special Rapporteur on the Promotion and Protection of the Right to Freedom of Opinion and Expression, David Kaye," May 22, 2015, UN Doc. A/HRC/29/32, 23, https://documents-dds-ny.un.org/doc/UNDOC/GEN/G15/095/85/PDF/G1509585.pdf.

15 Ibid., 25.

16 Ibid.

17 Brazilian Internet Bill of Rights, Law no.12.965/2014, http://www.planalto.gov.br/ccivil_03/_ato2011–2014/2014/lei/l12965.htm.

18 UN General Assembly, "Report of the Special Rapporteur," 7.

19 Decree no. 6759/2009: Article 605: "Customs may retain, by official request or at the request of the person concerned, during customs conference, those products of counterfeit, altered or cloned brands, or with false indication of origin." Available at: http://www.planalto.gov.br/ccivil_03/_ato2007-2010/2009/decreto/d6759.htm. Accessed on September 4, 2015.
20 Anatel, Resolution 242/2000, Article 7.
21 Federal Superior Court. 1995. Resolution no.158.543, Rapporteur was Minister Marco Aurélio, Judiciary Journal of 6 Oct. 1995.
22 There are studies pointing to the contrary, in the sense that there is no hard and fast evidence that using cell phones causes cancer.
23 Anatel, Resolution 242/2000, Article 55.
24 Ibid., Article 7, III.
25 Ibid., Article 7, IV.
26 Examples of international standards:

- ITU Recommendations on each specific technology. Available at: http://www.itu.int/dms_pubrec/itu-r/rec/m/R-REC-M.1073-3-201203-I!PDF-E.pdf. Accessed on April 10, 2017.
- Information Technology Equipment Safety Standards. Available at: http://www.itesafety.com/standards.htm. Accessed on April 10, 2017.
- International Commission on Non-Ionizing Radiation Protection, which stipulates standards of radiation emission for mobile phones. Available at: http://www.icnirp.org. Accessed on April 24, 2017.
- International safety standards: http://www.itesafety.com/standards.htm
- IEEE-Standards for rechargeable cell phone batteries: https://standards.ieee.org/findstds/standard/1725-2011.html

27 UN General Assembly, "Report of the Special Rapporteur," 24.
28 See http://www.anatel.gov.br/celularlegal/o-que-muda-com-o-projeto.

References

Anatel. 2014. "Note on SIGA." Accessed on April 19, 2017. http://www.anatel.gov.br/Portal/exibirPortalNoticias.do?acao=carregaNoticia&codigo=3294.

Anatel. 2015. "Institutional. "Accessed on August 10, 2017. http://www.anatel.gov.br/institucional/institucional-menu.

Anatel. n.d. "Brochure on the Use of Non-Approved Equipment." Accessed on April 9, 2017. http://www.anatel.gov.br/Portal/verificaDocumentos/documento.asp?numeroPublicacao=239888&assuntoPublicacao=Certificao%20Tcnica&caminhoRel=Cidadao-Informaes%20e%20Consultas-Cartilhas&filtro=1&documentoPath= 239888.pdf.

Balkin, Jack M. 2009. "The Future of Free Expression in a Digital Age." Faculty Scholarship Series. http://digitalcommons.law.yale.edu/fss_papers/223.

Balkin, Jack M. 2014. "Old-School/New-School Speech Regulation". Faculty Scholarship Series. http://digitalcommons.law.yale. edu/fss_papers/4877.

FNazca and Data Folha. 2013/2014. "Survey." Accessed on June 26, 2017. http://pt.slideshare.net/2acesconteudo/pesquisa-fradar-13-fnazca-e-datafolha-20132014.

Fusco, Camila, and Julio Wiziack. 2011. "Celulares Clandestinos já são 20% do total." *Folha de São Paulo*. February, 2. Accessed on April 10, 2017. http://www1.folha.uol.com.br/mercado/2011/02/875189-celulares-clandestinos-ja-sao-20-do-total.shtml.

IACHR (Inter-American Commission on Human Rights). 2013. "Freedom of Expression and the Internet." Accessed on April 24, 2017. http://www.oas.org/en/iachr/ expression/docs/reports/2014_04_08_internet_eng%20_web.pdf.

IBGE (Instituto Brasileiro de Geografia e Estatística). 2016. *Acesso à Internet e à televisão e posse de telefone móvel celular para uso pessoal, 2015: Pesquisa Nacional por Amostra de Domicílios*. Rio de Janeiro: IBGE.

IBGE (Instituto Brasileiro de Geografia e Estatística). 2017. "IBGE Data on Brazil's Current Population." Last modified on June 26, 2017. Accessed on April 19, 2017. http://www.ibge.gov.br/apps/populacao/ projecao/.

ITU (International Telecommunication Union). 2014a. "Counterfeit ICT Equipment." Accessed on April 25, 2018. http://handle.itu.int/11.1002/pub/80ba364f-en.

ITU (International Telecommunication Union). 2014b. "The World in 2014: ICT Facts and Figures." Accessed on June 26, 2017. https://www.itu.int/en/ITU-D/Statistics/Documents/facts/ICTFactsFigures2014-e.pdf.

ITU (International Telecommunication Union). 2016. "The World in 2016: ICT Facts and Figures." Accessed on October 03, 2017. https://www.itu.int/en/ITU-D/Statistics/Documents/facts/ICTFactsFigures2016.pdf.

Kapczynski, Amy. 2008. "The Access to Knowledge Mobilization and the New Politics of Intellectual Property." *Yale Law Journal* 117 (5): 804–885.

Krikonian, Gaëlle and Amy Kapczynski. 2010. *Access to Knowledge: A Conceptual Genealogy*. New York: Zone Books.

Lojas Americanas. 2017. "Price Examples from Lojas Americanas". Last modified August 2017. http://www.americanas.com.br/categoria/350392.

Martello, Alexandre. 2017. "Anatel começa a bloquear celular pirata a partir de maio de 2018." *G1*, Brasília. November 24. Accessed on April 25, 2018. https://g1.globo.com/economia/noticia/anatel-comeca-a-bloquear-celular-pirata-a-partir-de-maio-de-2018.ghtml.

Prakash, Pranesh, Carlos Affonso Souza, and Nagla Rizk. 2015. *Global Censorship Shifting Modes, Persisting Paradigms*. Information Society Project, Yale Law School.

Subramanian, Ramesh, and Lea Shaver. 2011. *Access to Knowledge in India: New Research on Intellectual Property, Innovation and Development*. New York: Bloomsbury Academic.

Swerdlow, Anthony J., Maria Feychting, Adele C. Green, Leeka Kheifets, and David A. Savitz. 2011. "Mobile Phones, Brain Tumours, and the Interphone Study: Where Are We Now?." *Environmental Health Perspectives* 119 (11). http://www.icnirporg/cms/upload/publications/ICNIRPSCIreview2011.pdf.

TELECO. 2016. "Subscribed Cell Phones." Accessed on April 20, 2017. http://www.teleco.com.br/pais/celular.asp.

TELECO. 2017a. "Statistics on Cell Phones in Brazil." Accessed on June 26, 2017. http://www.teleco.com.br/ncel.asp.

TELECO. 2017b. "Certification and Approval." Accessed on June 27, 2017. http://www.teleco.com.br/tutoriais/tutorialhomolog/pagina_1.asp.

PART II

Control

Mobile Technologies and A2K

Stefanie Felsberger

The second part of this book is centered upon questions of the control of mobile infrastructures and control of access to knowledge. Part I, focused on access, has explored how mobile technologies have (re)shaped access to knowledge and how mobile technologies and knowledge are accessed in the first place. Part II focuses on the flipside of access. The three chapters in this part address different restrictions to access, blockages, surveillance of access, and censorship—in short, control. They investigate how this control undermines people's rights to privacy, to access to knowledge, and freedom.

Questions of control over technologies, privacy rights, and surveillance are often added as almost an afterthought to discussing the possibilities of technologies. When we developed the call for chapters for this book, we initially imagined one larger part that would address how access and control are two sides of mobile technologies. This framing was chosen to avoid a framing of privacy as secondary matter. We encouraged authors to send us chapters that would investigate legal frameworks and infrastructural set-ups of mobile technologies to demonstrate how mobile devices enable both access and control. We received so many chapters situated at the intersection between access and control that we ultimately decided to split one part into two.

Concerns over privacy, censorship, data protection, and corporate control over communication are no longer an afterthought. Questions about the control of technologies and control by technologies have become front and center in public debates across the globe as people become increasingly disenchanted by and critical of big technology companies: Who is in control of and who is controlled by technologies? How are technologies controlled? What are the consequences for access to knowledge and participation in public life when mobile technologies can be controlled so easily? How can the control of technology infrastructures by so few be changed? These are some of questions addressed by the authors in this part.

The first of the three chapters delves into the theme of control from the viewpoint of people involved in social movements. Harry Halpin, a cybersecurity and social activist, discusses the massive challenges of Syrian activists faced in trying to use mobile technologies safely and securely. His chapter focuses on the efforts of Bassel Safadi, an activist involved in Syria's revolution, to use mobile technologies and the Internet to communicate between activists and the population in the early days of the Syrian revolution despite the control measures imposed by the Syrian regime. While Syria provides a stark example of state repression and control, Chapter 7 provides an interesting contrast: it focuses on the United States and efforts by state governments to provide high speed Internet access to citizens. On the surface these efforts have little to do with control, but author Enrique Armijo notes that such projects, while laudable and in line with the access to knowledge movement, nevertheless come with major caveats and potential to control freedom of expression. Moving south to Brazil, in Chapter 8, we learn of the enormous growth in Internet access that has come to Brazilians through access to cell phones. According to Dennys Antonialli and Jacqueline de Souza Abreu, out of the 120 million accesses to Facebook from Brazil, 91.6 percent comes just from mobile connections. Thus, the Internet is predominantly accessed through mobile telephones. However, this exponential growth has been accompanied by enhanced state surveillance powers, under the guise of criminal investigation.

Each chapter approaches the question of control from a different angle and interrogates this dichotomy of freedom versus control in a different way. The different chapters in this part focus more on states' control over mobile technologies and infrastructures than on corporate control, but each chapter introduces the reader to a different way in which access to knowledge is foreclosed, limited, restricted, and controlled. Antonialli and de Souza Abreu focus on the ways in which Brazilian police are able to routinely access and take control over people's private communication under the guise of fighting crime. They investigate a legal loophole which enables this control: despite the 1988 Brazilian Federal Constitution guaranteeing secrecy of communications, exceptions are granted for criminal investigations. Interception of communications falls within the scope of such investigations, and there has been a general increase in the number of cases where such exceptions have been granted. Armijo's intervention is also situated in the legal sphere. His chapter is a warning that control over infrastructures of communications can be implemented at a moment's notice, unless careful steps are taken to enshrine constitutional rights into the provision of access to the internet. Halpin takes a step back from the legal sphere and brings questions of technology ownership and production into the conversation about control. By outlining the expansive control of the Syrian government over Syrian activists and citizens who wanted to use mobile technologies to organize and communicate during the early days, he argues that mobile infrastructure is not built in a way that ensures people's freedom.

Based on their different interventions, each chapter also makes different suggestions for how to overcome the control sketched out in the different chapters. Antonialli and de Souza Abreu develop suggestions for policy makers to develop legal frameworks that will afford more protection to Brazilian citizens. Armijo makes a strong case for ensuring that constitutional rights and principles need to be part of any governmental or public–private project in the United States even if or rather especially when these projects might promote access to knowledge. Halpin instead proposes a more long-term approach to tackling the problem of control: extending the argument that access to knowledge entails also people's rights to create and share knowledge that is specific to their context, Halpin argues that people need to be part of building and shaping the infrastructures on which their access to knowledge depends.

6

SYRIA AND THE TRAGIC DREAM OF AUTONOMOUS INTERNET ACCESS

The Case of Bassel Safadi and the Syrian Revolution

Harry Halpin

This chapter is dedicated to all those who perished in the struggle for free communication and knowledge in Syria, including Bassel Khartabil.[1]

Introduction

No-one expected the Syrian revolution: an e-mail in my inbox from a programmer there, Bassel Safadi, asking for an account on the secure riseup.net server, in the early days of the outbreak of the Syrian revolution came as a surprise. Bassel was a friend of a friend, who had put Bassel directly in touch with me when Syrian activists needed access to a VPN (virtual private network). Bassel was a thoughtful, idealistic, and remarkably intelligent advocate of free software and access to knowledge, who had worked for years contributing to projects such as Mozilla and a 3-D model of the ancient city of Palmyra. Overnight, he had become dedicated to social movements as his people began their own uprising for dignity. At that time, we at the LEAP Encryption Access Project (2019) had been working on a highly secure VPN for activists over a year that was free both as in "free beer" and at no cost, but also free as in free software, allowing anyone access to and the ability to edit the source code (Sparrow et al. 2016). With Bassel imprisoned and then murdered by the al-Assad regime, and war in Syria continuing to unfold like a nightmare wherein our agency seems to have been reduced to negligibility, I can only look back in sorrow for not acting faster and having the software we were working on more prepared for deployment by ordinary people, who in this most extraordinary of times, have been unexpectedly transformed into revolutionaries. Bassel also had a clear plan with objectives to create autonomous Internet access to facilitate access to knowledge and across the globe we can learn from his ambitious plan and the wider Syrian experience of censorship and repression.

The term "revolution" is itself contentious in the context of Syria, but the Syrian uprising transformed into a revolution insofar as the uprising eventually adopted as its aim and result the overthrow of the government, and so irrevocably transforming the political order initiated by Hafez al-Assad's 1970 coup. Although the original Facebook page put up to call for the "Days of Rage" in Syria was called "Syrian Revolution 2011" (Ghattas 2011), many participants in the initial series of uprisings in Syria may have not intend to overthrow the government: the initial focus was more on demands for the release of prisoners, the support of human rights, and a measure of increased institutional democracy that Bashar al-Assad himself thought the government could accommodate via reforms. This was even demonstrated by al-Assad's withdrawal of the "state of emergency" that had been in place in Syria for nearly half a century, but this gesture was not enough to quell the uprisings. While the initial popular uprisings in 2011 were not in any way armed, factions ranging from the Free Syrian Army to various Islamic groups, took up arms against the government with revolution as an explicit goal.[2] Whether or not what unfolded in Syria was or an intentional revolution is up for debate, but what is clear is that the uprising eventually became a revolution regardless of whether or not the participants considered themselves revolutionaries. Even though many of the original participants in the civilian uprisings in 2011 considered themselves simply citizens and activists, not standard-bearers of revolution, objectively these voices were treated by the regime as revolutionaries. As the uprisings led to civil war in Syria, and the intended end-result of what should replace al-Assad varied between an imagined representative democracy or the nightmare of Daesh, it became also clear that a revolution does not have to be successful (such as 1905 in Russia) to be a revolution. At the present moment, the Syrian revolution in 2011 has led to devastation and not changed the government in the majority of the country. It is with this critical understanding of the "Syrian Revolution" that we wish to explore how access to knowledge becomes crucial when what starts as a popular "non-violent" demand for dignity becomes, even without conscious intention, a political revolution with human lives at stake.

The power of access to knowledge has always been a political question, as put forward by the Access to Knowledge (A2K) movement:

> the coordination of public policy … to ensure that the potential for knowledge-based development is maximized through programs, technologies and business models that enable knowledge to be shared widely and to flourish in conditions of freedom. In this way, knowledge resources can be leveraged for the benefit of all, rather than be constrained or monopolized for the benefit of a few.
>
> *(Rizk and Shaver 2010)*

This movement has grown throughout the last few years, demanding and often succeeding in opening up forms of closed knowledge so that these new "knowledge commodities" can be used throughout the world. In terms of being able to open up the valuable knowledge needed to run mobile telephony, a vast range of proprietary cell phone tower technology and closed- source software has hampered this development in terms of open mobile telephony. Indeed, open-source software such as OpenBTS and OpenBSC attempts to "reverse engineer" often closed specifications and technologies, and thus it is no surprise that this effort has for the most part proven to be a failure with a few exceptions.

Opening up the knowledge of how to run a mobile telephony network must be a priority, given the foundational role mobile telephony plays in access to knowledge. Rather than opening up any particular knowledge ranging from agricultural to medical knowledge, in the long term, it is more important to open up general methods of transmitting knowledge as given by networking and mobile telephony. Strangely enough, the situation around fundamental rights such as the right to housing, food, health services and even freedom of thought can realistically only be established at this present moment by enabling free and open access to knowledge to the Internet. If the Internet can be accessed, humanity can at least feasibly self-organize around these rights, but if the Internet via control of a few telephone operators can be turned off at a whim, the situation is much grimmer.

To return to the global viewpoint, can programmers in the era of the Internet serve the people rather than their own narrow individual self-interest? Ultimately, programmers are not divorced from the historical, social realities of the rest of the world and cannot isolate themselves from the wider social struggles around them, even by encasing themselves in virtual worlds and safe suburbs in Silicon Valley. These struggles decide the fate of their friends, family, and governments. Programmers should put themselves at the service of the people. Programmers have no choice but to program for unpredictable *future revolutions* without the knowledge of when and where these future moments of rupture will unfold.

Problems similar to those of programmers in the Middle East confronted protesters in the United States of America. A lack of coverage by a tightly controlled "official" news media led to the development of Indymedia, the first web software for independent journalism, where any person could post a news story with photos. Indymedia was created in 1999 before the Seattle WTO protests in order to prevent the press from censoring the street protests in the United States (Coleman 2005). Years later, Indymedia programmers started a Twitter feed based on the same core concepts, and so it should come ultimately as no surprise that these technologies also were useful in the hands of protesters in the Arab world.

As programmers serve a people yet to come, the question facing programmers is *what is to be programmed?* Programming is laborious and methodical slow-going work, requiring months and years of intense concentration and boring debugging. To program in the service of future social movements requires both unyielding patience and radical hope. It cannot be done easily in the middle of the chaos of a protest, much less a revolution. Therefore, the best way to determine what is to be programmed and what wider technological infrastructure is needed is by empirically determining the needs of concrete social struggle rather than idly daydreaming up a technological fantasy, be that a new secure messaging protocol or blockchain system. And what better guide could there be than the ghost of Bassel Safadi, the Syrian hacker that became a freedom fighter and died for the dignity of his people?

Technical needs of social movements

Revolutions are as unpredictable as the falling of a star, and it is precisely this unpredictability that has been accelerated by the widespread access to the Internet. Take the Tunisian revolution: despite all the analysis that all uprisings and revolutions can be predicted by economic factors (Lagi, Bertrand, and Bar-Yam 2011), the first of the Arab Uprisings started after the self-immolation of Mohamed Bouazizi, a humiliated shopkeeper. Despite the crisis of 2008, Tunisia and much of the Arab world has been in crisis since the post-colonial Arab nationalist movements descended into kleptocracies run by inherited despots in the 1980s. The underlying economic and political conditions have been intolerable in Tunisia for decades, so what triggered the spread of the Tunisian revolution? Although it has become fashionable to denounce the role of the Internet in popular uprisings (Morozov 2011), what cannot be doubted is that the Internet allowed the news of the Tunisian revolution in rural Kasserine to bypass the official censorship of Ben Ali and—at least at the onset—the Western corporate press. This in turn led the protests against police brutality to go viral across Tunisia. Due to the divisions in the elite and army as well as the lack of NATO (North Atlantic Treaty Organization) support for Ben Ali—as revealed by WikiLeaks—the army did not fire on protesters in Tunis. As a result, Ben Ali was deposed by his own people. On a larger scale, the good tidings of the success of the Tunisian revolution spread throughout the Arab World, including via social media in countries where the ruling class had censored the press, sparking uprising after uprising: Egypt, Libya, Bahrain, Yemen, and Syria. It is the tragic trajectory of Syria—and the role of access to knowledge via the Internet—that must be understood so that future generations will not make the error of the old.

As 2011 dawned, while witnessing the failure of the "alter-globalization" movement in Europe and the United States, I had been caught unaware by the Arab Uprisings. I found myself re-energized by visits to Avenue Bourguiba in Tunis and Tahrir Square in Egypt. In this regard, I will always owe the courageous people of the Arab Uprisings for their ability to host a strange American like myself, and the knowledge I have learned has been incalculable, and these hard-fought lessons continue to inspire me after so many hard-fought victories and tragic failures. Strangely, it is in a well-intentioned failure that we can learn more from than a superficial success. As the Arab Uprisings spread like a prairie fire throughout the world, they took off in Syria in early 2011 after the arrests of children in Deraa for street graffiti—"The people want to overthrow the regime" and "It's your turn, Dr. al-Assad" (Anonymous 2016). The Syrian protests bore similarities to #BlackLivesMatter protests in the United States, with a protest against police brutality: the parents of the arrested children went to the police to demand their release, and the police threatened to rape them "if they still needed children." Thereafter, on March 18, 2011, people took to the street demanding dignity and freedom in

Deraa, which immediately provoked live gunfire from the police. The protests spread, and the earlier demands for reform spiraled into large scale civil unrest with demands for the overthrow of the President of Syria, Bashar al-Assad. Al-Assad at first seemed caught by surprise but, determined to avoid the fate of the Egyptian President Hosni Mubarak or the Libyan leader Muammar Gaddafi, he began a brutal campaign of military repression. Interestingly enough, one of the first acts he took was to destroy the hackerspace, Aiki Lab, in Damascus (Syrian Observatory for Human Rights 2019). To those in Damascus this was not a surprise, as a number of programmers had taken important roles in the Syrian revolution. One of these was open-source contributor Bassel Khartabil who co-founded Aiki Lab in 2010. In order to protect his identity, he worked under the assumed name Bassel Safadi, including when communicating with me. The emails from Bassel, which I received from him from February 20, 2012 to March 2, 2012, are included in this piece unedited as quoted texts. This means that the text from Bassel generally lacks capitalization and often verges on telegraphic. In order to convey the spirit of the communication I leave the grammar of the e-mail unchanged.

Bassel reached out to me to discuss how to improve the communication of Syrian activists given the centralized telecommunication network in Syria. At the time, activists were spread out in local coordination committees throughout Syria and communicated primarily via online tools like Skype, as there was no central Tahrir Square for protests in Syria. Syria has a highly restricted nationalized telecommunications system, as is normal in many countries (even in Europe until recently). Mobile and Internet communications are mostly governed by Syriatel, a company controlled indirectly by the Syrian government as it was owned by Rami Makhlouf, cousin of al-Assad. MTN Syria is the other main telecommunication provider, which also co-operates with the al-Assad regime. Al-Assad had banned social media sites such as Facebook since 2007 as social media was seen as accelerating subversion, although the sites remained easily accessible via various proxies. After the initial "days of rage" in 2011, al-Assad attempted to placate the protests by removing the ban on Facebook and Twitter by passing new laws, but that particular fig leaf was too little too late (Preston 2011).

Even with the opening up of the Internet in 2011, access to knowledge in Syria was shrouded under possible control and surveillance. A government identity card is required to get a SIM card that is capable of Internet access, and the Syrian government can easily control all fiber- optic and landline Internet access. Indeed, when the mosque in Daraa was occupied and the Syrian protest song *ya hef* ("What a shame") was blared out to the city, the Syrian government cut the Internet and telephone lines before attacking and killing the protesters occupying the mosque on March 23, 2011 (Anonymous 2016). So, one of the most pressing problems facing any protest movement in Syria was how to communicate. As telephone access was entirely controlled by the government and, thus, likely to be spied upon, using the Internet for communications was the only alternative, but the government could also easily capture any unencrypted network traffic. In response, Syrian activists ended up using corporate American services that provided encryption by default, with Gmail for email communication and Skype for replacing voice communication over landlines. Indeed, the initial Syrian revolution spread its new via YouTube channels such as Ugarit and organized primarily via Skype groups. "At that moment we were using Skype, but we were using fake names and closed chat rooms, to get to know each other" (Anonymous 2016).

Paradoxically, the most damaging act of censorship to Syrian Internet access was provoked not by al-Assad but by the United States government: the sanctions imposed by the United States government on Syria prevented Syrian activists from accessing Google and Skype, harming precisely the ordinary people of Syria who were organizing against the regime. The Syrian government already had access to all the secure communication tools they needed via Iran, but sanctions prevented Syrians from accessing the Google Play Store on their Android phone (and for the minority of Syrians with iPhones, the Apple Store), which was the primary way of installing Skype. The first priority for Bassel was to get access to a free VPN for Syrian activists that would let them bypass the sanctions and regime spying in order to obtain free access to the Internet and install the corporate tools like Skype needed for communication. A VPN provided an encrypted tunnel for Internet traffic from a phone or client server, who then provided access to the Internet through its server. For Syrians, it was important that this VPN server be in a jurisdiction outside the US sanctions. Therefore, a VPN could allow someone in Syria to dial into a server in a country like Germany, install Skype, and communicate quickly and securely via encrypted Internet traffic that would be safe from the surveillance of the Syrian regime.

In February 2012, Bassel e-mailed me asking about access to our VPN that worked with free software, introducing himself as a programmer who "develop software under AGPL as well."[3] In particular, he was excited that it might work to bypass the censorship of both the al-Assad regime and the US sanctions, giving them unfettered access to the Internet. Bassel was worried, as the "vpn never worked on any android" and even if it did work on Android, it could not be installed by Google Play. Luckily, the Bitmask VPN that was deployed by Riseup[4] allowed people to download the VPN and install it without Google Play using an APK[5] on Android. Bassel was successful in getting it to work after I gave him the access codes to set-up a riseup.net account. Thanks to quick work by one of the system administrators of Riseup, I managed to pass "super-user" access codes to Bassel that allowed him to create accounts for hundreds of high-risk Syrians.

While Bassel could get the VPN working, what was needed was "an apk with vpn working that doesn't require rooting the device that would be excellent." Bassel personally had to install the VPN on the phones of his friends in the Syrian social movement by obtaining root access, and he noted that "rooting every different taste of android is pain." This led to Bassel having the following idea, "so what would be ideal solution is to have some NGO funding some phones with good cameras … then installing all the stuff on them including vpn." When I offered to help root the phones at my house in France, as I was already training citizen journalists there and pre-installing their phones and laptops with secure software, Bassel said—perhaps jokingly—that "maybe next time when someone wants to donate some phones should send them to you first." Of course, how I would then proceed to ship the phones safely from Paris to Beirut was beyond me, and personally freighting them over would likely only get them seized at the airport. Therefore, the only option we had was to send them over with Syrian citizen journalists.

Another concern I brought up to Bassel was that phones inherently revealed both the geolocation of their users and the pattern of communication of who is talking to whom—a phenomena called "metadata." Metadata is not trivial matter, for as famously put by CIA (Central Intelligence Agency) director Michael Hayden in 2014,[6] "We kill people based on metadata." In detail, I noted to Bassel that "the VPN should work for data over 3G but you still will have all the geolocation problems inherent in mobile triangulation, so your content will be protected but your location will be revealed." Bassel was undeterred by this possible threat, as "it's not a big deal of triangulation since the syrian gov still very busy and don't have enough experience to do that." To summarize, by being thrown off by the revolt, the Syrian government did not have the technical prowess to use geolocation via mobile phone records to target individuals. In order to provide better anonymity than a VPN, I recommended the use of Tor via the Tails operating system, the same system used by WikiLeaks and Edward Snowden, but Bassel said he had not used it and "didn't test yet."

Access to the Internet was only the first step in establishing the knowledge needed by the revolution. One common problem was to hide files on laptops that would be seized by the Syrian police. There were even stories of police storming into houses, demanding access to "Facebook," and taking laptops, believing that the contents of Facebook were stored on the laptop. Though this lack of computer knowledge by the Syrian police was humorous, unfortunately, the contents of Skype address books are stored locally on laptops. At the time, the more technically adept Syrians used mostly Truecrypt, a now discontinued open-source tool, to encrypt files on a computer or laptop, but many did not. The use of advanced security tools on the ground was not widespread, as most people continued to simply use the methods of communication that they had deployed before the Syrian revolution. When I offered Bassel links to information, I recommended Riseup's security information page to Bassel, which includes information about threat models and advanced security measures.[7] Bassel agreed that it was "pretty useful thanks" but that without having a translation in Arabic, it would be of limited utility: "I don't have time to translate even this should be priority." Interestingly, due to Internet censorship, simply having the Arabic translation on a website was not enough. During the early stages of the Syrian protests in 2011, printing digital security information on paper to distribute directly to those involved in social movements was the preferred method of knowledge dissemination. As explained by Bassel, "if you ever get those stuff in arabic. will be glad to print and distribute here. since so far this is the best way to reach people here even if the topic is about the Internet." Although access to a VPN and Skype helped get the Syrian protests off the ground, it would tragically not be enough to let the Syrian social movements endure or even for Bassel himself to survive the coming months.

Like any knowledgeable hacker, Bassel had a strong distrust for corporate tools and so was looking for free software alternatives to the corporate tools used by Syrian activists. However, he understood that people would only use software that was easy to use and install, regardless of whether it was backed by a major corporation. Importantly, Bassel's time was limited, for as the uprising started to take off in earnest, he had to concentrate on organizing protests and coordinating medical supplies for the self-organized hospitals (going into a state-run hospital was quite dangerous for activists, due to the propensity of the doctors to turn their own patients accused of being revolutionaries in). After all, secure communications were useless, if the protests were a catastrophe and the people involved dead. Yet Bassel demonstrated a clear understanding of the different tools that a revolution would need, from collaborative document editing to an Internet infrastructure that could survive attempted government shutdowns.

The common alternative at the time for encrypted text-messaging and voice calls was TextSecure and Redphone, which were later in 2015 merged into the well-known Signal application (Greenberg 2014). In 2013, these applications only worked on newer Android phones such as the Nexus, but Bassel pointed out that "nexus and above is not that common here ... the other problem is that everyone should install this in order for it to work. which is hard to do." Also, group voice teleconferences were necessary, and the soon-to-be Signal application did not support encrypted group voice calls like Skype. By 2019, Signal had millions of users and millions of dollars in funding and still did not support group communication. Groups are the fundamental unit of popular organization, not one-to-one organization. More importantly, software aimed at usage for social change needs to be aimed at popular usage, and software that is only designed for newer or more expensive hardware will fail to be used.

One of the still unsolved problems that becomes exceptionally important for organizers is an alternative to Facebook and other mainstream social media that lets them easily share and edit documents like Google Docs. Although decentralization is of interest, even more important is security and tools for self-organization. Bassel was very excited when I showed him the software Crabgrass[8] by Riseup that serves as a "Facebook for activists" featuring a "task manager, collaborative document editing, comments, and other neat features." Bassel said it was "too early for Syrians to use" the Crabgrass software "but totally worth checking" out, and he asked for the "road map for this project" and offered to help as "I develop software under AGPL as well. it's called www.aikiframework.org just a side note." However, he was worried about the ability of people to create new accounts and the loss of the network effect of Facebook, so he wanted to "find ways to import data from facebook to it." The tragedy of this situation is that even today, when now there is widespread concern over Facebook and well-established standards for decentralizing social data, Crabgrass still struggles to find funding and open-source contributors and still does not have a way to import Facebook contacts. Despite billions being put into blockchain technology and millions being put into "Internet Freedom" funds, people across the world are still beholden to Facebook, Google, and other centralized platforms with no security and tools aimed more at corporate organization than the organization. Indeed, it seems that over the last five to six years, very little progress has been made to create an alternative to the Silicon Valley monopolies for ordinary people. The only tools aimed at activists that are significantly used are Signal and Tor.

Wireless and mobile networking in Syria

The last question Bassel asked to hackers outside Syria before his arrest was "do you want to help the syrian people to connect?" One of the most essential components of Internet access is the physical infrastructure itself: the cables, the towers, the wi-fi routers. In Syria, these are all controlled by forces allied to the regime, and, while encrypted communications such as VPNs allow Internet traffic to be shipped across these enemy lines of communication, the regime could still simply turn them off at any time, as shown even by the initial invasion of Daraa in the first few months of the Syrian revolution. As put by Bassel, "in many cities of syria the gov shutdown the Internet and by that I mean: ADSL, dial up, 3G and so on." One possible solution would be satellite Internet that could directly connect to the outside world, but as Bassel put it, "we can overcome such problem by using sat [satellite] Internet but it's very slow and expensive." However, while satellite could provide autonomous Internet access, the problem facing Syrian activists was how to communicate not only with the wider world but with each other.

Community wireless was a solution put forward by the Guifi network in Catalonia, free software advocates, with whom I put Bassel in touch. These kinds of networks used *mesh networking*, where each node in the network can autonomously and directly connect to other nodes to pass traffic in a decentralized manner. Bassel was quite negative about community wireless networks being effective in Syria, as he explained that "even if we say have wifi mesh network. all Internet gateways are down. this mesh network will be isolated since none of its nodes is actually connected to the Internet." Ruthlessly practical, Bassel continued to note that satellite "can't be used as Internet sources for ad-hoc networks" due to their high latency and cost. Any usable autonomous infrastructure needed to work on whatever hardware was ubiquitous. And in Syria, the only kind of hardware that was ubiquitous was the mobile phone.

What would an autonomous network look like on the ground in Syria? Given that most people in Syria used GSM-capable phones,[9] Bassel reasoned that autonomous communications based on GSM would be the best solution for supporting the revolution as it would seamlessly work with existing mobile phones. Typically, mesh networks were set up using wireless networking based on routers by companies like Ubiquiti, but Bassel thought setting up an autonomous cell-phone network would be possible, as a "a standalone GSM network doesn't even need any service that the gov provide when we have our own 'towers' and infrastructure." Erecting this autonomous Internet for the Syrian revolution was Bassel's master-plan: "I'm planning to do is to build a mobile mesh network to provide free GSM to those areas where the gov shut down the communications." He would then connect it via a satellite link to provide autonomous access to the Internet, although the primary use of the network would be intra-Syria communication that would be free of easy access and control by the regime: A "GSM network at least doesn't need to be connected with the outside world, or can be connected with slow sat links to enable one or two persons to talk outside at a time, but the main idea is to provide a way for people inside to communicate with each other."

Bassel envisaged that such a "network can be built using free software like http://openbts.sourceforge.net/ and asterisk with battery powered high gain antennas." To unpack this, OpenBTS (n.d.) is a free software project that lets off-the-shelf GSM mobile phones serve as end-points for voice-over-IP networks by running an open-source base transceiver station (BTS). OpenBTS implements only the minimal needed portion of the GSM standard in order to get the network off the ground, and then does the rest using digital technologies. This base station in turn delivers calls to an open-source digital version of a telephone private branch exchange (PBX) or mobile switching center (MSC). Asterisk is free software that provides the infrastructure to allow calls to be forwarded to each other locally using Voice-over-IP or even the "backhaul" to traditional phones via the public switched telephone network, as well as providing many features that would be useful to Syrian activists, such as voice teleconferencing.

While the project of building an open-source communication system compatible with GSM may seem impossible, it has already been done at hacker events such as Burning Man in 2008 (OpenBTS 2008). Today, autonomous mobile phone networks based on open-source software serve thousands of people on a scale close to the size of Rojava in the rebellious province of Oaxaca in Mexico, where for decades the indigenous were deprived of mobile phone access by Mexico's corrupt government-aligned telephone companies. Using the "GSM network in a box" OpenBSC[10] and the Linux Call Router as a private branch exchange, the grassroots Rhizomatica collective created the software that knit together an autonomous GSM network for Oaxaca (Myers 2016). Over the years, the software has allowed previously non-technical indigenous villagers to train themselves in running the open-source tools behind the autonomous network, and today the network has finally been accepted even by the Mexican telephone companies. Importantly, Rhizomatica and its users recognize their open-source telephony project as explicitly radically democratic and, therefore, see the struggles of the people in Syria as parallel to their own.

In the last emails he sent before his capture by the al-Assad regime, Bassel ardently desired this autonomous mobile communication network but noted that "we don't have enough infrastructure to build this and this is something we totally need help on." On March 1, 2012, Bassel went silent. I argued over design decisions with various hacker groups, pushing the line that "Bassel is right via the need for an alternative GSM network" but that I "believe we are waiting for news from Bassel about what is wanted." The news never came. Two weeks after our last communication, on March 15, Bassel was arrested by the military intelligence services of al-Assad while leaving his workplace in Damascus. Later, we found out that he had been tortured for five days and sent to the most infamous prison in

Syria, Sidnaya. His computers and documents were seized, including the archive of Skype chats and likely our e-mail conversations. The truth of how exactly Bassel was identified and captured still remains elusive. There was an unsubstantiated rumor that the Syrian government purchased a "backdoor" into the proprietary closed-source Skype software from the Iraqi government, which had originally obtained this backdoor from the United States as a way of tracking down "terrorists." Regardless, the intentional spread via Skype of malware like "remote access tools" by the Syrian Electronic Army let the al-Assad regime seize files and even control of the computers of Syrian activists (Kaspersky 2014). These digital backdoors were used to identify, track, and eliminate democratic dissents, including Bassel Khartabil.

The people must control their own means of communications

For years, I knew Bassel was alive, but I lost touch one by one with the remaining activists and revolutionaries on the ground. Bassel was transferred originally to the Adra jail in 2012, and he managed to maintain communication with his wife and supporters who helped him to post tweets up until 2015. Bassel was present but not freed when the jail was stormed by the armed jihadi group Jaysh al-Islam, and then he was transferred to an unknown location. His name was removed from the registry of prisoners, and in 2017 we discovered that he had been executed by the al-Assad regime. Although he may have been martyred for the cause of democracy in Syria, his dream of autonomous mobile network lives on. If anything, the tragedy in Syria demonstrates that autonomous access to the Internet is a necessary need of democracy not just in Syria, but throughout the world.

The Syrian revolution, which started as a democratic revolution, was taken over by an Islamist counter-revolution when the Free Syrian Army (FSA) took control from the populist citizen councils. Given that the destruction of the initial civilian wave that engulfed activists like Bassel, only the armed struggle of the FSA seemed to be able to resist the militarization of the struggle by the al-Assad regime. However, the FSA itself has been overrun and hijacked by groups ranging from the explicitly jihadist Jaysh al-Islam to the Turkish-backed Jaysh al-Nasr, and the chances of these groups supporting an open culture, much less an autonomous open internet for free expression, are slim at best.

Yet the dream of a decentralized and democratic federation Syria lives on far from Damascus in Northern Syria. Even though the Kurds in Northern Syria served as bystanders to the initial phase of the Syrian revolution, after years of war with Daesh by the YPG/YPG (People's Protection Units), the multi-ethnic Autonomous Administration of North-Eastern Syria (AANES) have established a large swathe of northern Syria, commonly known outside Syria by its Kurdish name "Rojava," that is under control of popular, directly democratic councils with equal participation of men and women. This form of political organization has been heavily inspired by the turn of Abdullah Öcalan, the imprisoned leader of the Kurdistan Workers' Party (PKK), towards democratic autonomy in 1999. The goal of democratic autonomy is to build a parallel social structure that fulfills the needs of society rather than aiming at the revolutionary overthrow of the state.

This democratic revolution in northeastern Syria stands out like a beacon of hope as the rest of Syria descends into chaos, but it is under threat from both the al-Assad regime and Turkey. Caught between these deadly pincers, the people living in Northeastern Syria are in a terrifyingly perilous situation, as all of its access to knowledge via the Internet and communication in general may be cut at literally any moment by either al-Assad or Erdogan. This is no mere hypothetical situation, as Turkcell provides mobile data in the north, while Syriatel still provides internet coverage as well. When Turkey invaded the canton of Afrin that was under the control of the PYD, one of Erdogan's first actions was to cut off all Internet access and telephone communications in Afrin (SMEX 2018). Even journalists could not communicate, and thus news of the bombings of civilians, looting, and torture could barely get out. The very forces that had led the fight against Daesh in Syria were utterly isolated. Although Bassel may be dead, the dream of a democratic, secular, and decentralized Syria becomes real again—yet will it be destroyed in part due to the lack of communications infrastructure that was predicted by Bassel before his death?

There have been different attempts to build a free community-based Internet similar to what Bassel imagined throughout the world. The technical barriers to knowledge that exist in terms of mobile telephony do not hold in the development of community wireless networks, originally envisaged as an alternative to municipal networks that would be politically driven by the local community and economically more efficient. Yet why has community wireless not taken off? Unlike mobile telephony, as community wireless is built ground-up based on open-source, it was expected by theorists such as Benkler (1998) that these networks would eventually become the dominant form of Internet provisioning, only relying on fiber-optic to connect to the "backbone" of the Internet.

There has been some limited success throughout the world, ranging from the aforementioned Guifi.net to the Freifunk network in Germany. The open-source software and hardware that drives these networks are mature, but they face up against antagonistic policy decisions. Usually, these decisions make sharing wifi access spots illegal via contracts by the large broadband providers that control cable and fiber-optic line installation; together they have defeated the wide-scale deployment of community wireless. Instead, community wireless networks have only succeeded in either privileged areas with a large amateur base of open-source enthusiasts, such as urban Germany, or areas like rural Catalonia where separatist community-driven politics and the inefficiency and corruption of large-scale providers like Telefonica simply made community wireless nearly necessary to access to the Internet. These networks have a sound and completely open technical foundation that can be deployed at no cost. Instead, in the developing world where it was imagined these community wireless networks would spring forth, large and often nationalized telecommunications companies have crushed them.

This shows the limits of the idea that is common enough in hackers that simply creating open-source software (and even provisioning hardware such as routers) would be enough to enable something to become a widespread practice. The real struggle in providing open access to knowledge has little to do with the availability of open-source but is derived from both antagonistic politics from existing entrenched oligopolies and a local lack of social self-organization.

The importance of communication and access to knowledge based on technology for human liberation far pre-dates the Internet. Take for example the case of the radio. In an exegesis by Franz Fanon (1994), the radio was first viewed as a tool of oppression brought to the country by foreign colonization, and so the locals had no interest in this tool. Yet, when the Voice of Algeria started broadcasting the news of the Algerian revolution, "the purchase of a radio in Algeria has meant, not the adoption of a modern technique for getting news, but the obtaining of access to the only means of entering into communication with the Revolution, of living with it" (Fanon 1994, 83). With the help of this method of communication, the various factions of the revolution were united throughout Algeria, and the reaction of the French secret services was to systematically jam the Voice of Algeria. Indeed, Franz Fanon attributes to the radio the ability to form an anti-colonial struggle across otherwise fragmented people such as the Kabyles: "Having a radio meant paying one's taxes to the nation, buying the right of entry into the struggle of an assembled people" (Fanon 1994, 84).

Similar to aborted Internet shutdowns throughout the Arab world in 2011, the French radio censorship was ultimately unsuccessful, and the anti-colonial movement for liberation succeeded in Algeria, with similar situations occurring across the world in the 1950s and 1960s. The situation is strangely parallel at this present moment, and, as recognized by the Access to Knowledge movement, the control of communication infrastructure and technological knowledge via closed source and patents is a new form of colonialism in the information economy. Opening up these secrets is needed for genuine liberation, and what is at stake is not technical or economic, but a question of the political creation of a new kind of assembled people that crosses all national boundaries in the same post-Westphalian manner as the Internet itself.

Unfinished conclusions

While imprisoned by al-Assad, Bassel sent out a premonition of such a coming community whose primary ties would be through the Internet:

> Of my experience spending three years in jail so far for writing open source code (mainly), I can tell you how much authoritarian regimes feel the dangers of technology on their continuity. And they should be afraid of that, as code is much more than tools. It's an education that opens youthful minds, and moves nations forward. Who can stop that? No-one ... I'm in jail, but still have thousands if not millions of my hands and minds outside writing code and hacking and they will always keep doing that, no matter what stupid actions these regimes take to stop the motion.
>
> *(O'Brien 2017)*

In recent years, to shut down the Internet has become a common and devastating strategy for different governments in times of mass protests and social movements. Algeria, Bangladesh, Cameroon, Chad, Côte d'Ivoire, DR Congo, Ethiopia, India, Indonesia, Iraq, Kazakhstan, Mali, Nicaragua, Nigeria, Pakistan, Philippines, Russia, Sierra Leone, South Korea, Sri Lanka, Sudan, Syria, Togo, Turkey, and Yemen: in all these places, access to the Internet was limited or completely closed off by the government during mass protests in the year 2018 alone (Taye 2019). In 2019, the same happened in Ecuador (Netblocks 2019c), India (Netblocks 2019d), Iran (Netblocks 2019a), Iraq (Netblocks 2019b), and Sudan (Netblocks 2019e). According to Access Now, an organization fighting for free Internet access, the Internet has been shut down completely or partially in 29 countries (Access Now 2019).[11] Whether or not Bassel's dream for open access to knowledge lives or dies with him is now in our hands.

While the future of Syria and even the Internet itself may appear dark, there are reasons to be hopeful for access to knowledge. The Syrian social movements were at first limited to the nation, and while based in existential demand for dignity, politically they were limited and unorganized. Thus, it should be no surprise that regressive Islamist factions eventually usurped the Syrian revolution in the south of Syria. Yet in the north of Syria, the autonomous administration of Rojava is putting into practice a new post-Westphalian political ideology that is capable of explicitly taking on the political task of social self-organization of autonomous Internet access.

The Autonomous Administration of North-Eastern Syria (AANES) is built on democratic confederalism, where

> policymaking is exclusively the right of the popular community assemblies based on the practices of participatory democracy. Administration and coordination are the responsibility of confederal councils, which become the means of interlinking villages, towns, neighbors, and cities into confederal networks. Power thus flows from the bottom up instead from the top down.
>
> *(Bookchin 2015, 71)*

This form of popular self-organization is remarkably compatible with autonomous Internet access and mobile telephony. The technical infrastructure community can be controlled by the local community and networked over disparate and diverse communities in a bottom-up form, with the technical form of the network mirroring the social form of the democratic councils. Given the current chaos in Syria in terms of telecommunication and law enforcement, the main necessary ingredient to deploying an autonomous Internet is precisely the kind of social self-organization and political will that is provided by local councils based on democratic confederalism. Imagine if for every local democratic council in a village, there was within an economics or technology committee with the knowledge to control their own local mesh network or open-source mobile telephony base station, with this knowledge available to all via regularly offered trainings.

Although autonomous access to the Internet may have not reached realization in 2012, the dying dream of Bassel Khartabil may be reborn in Syria. Such access to the Internet was just not a priority in the YPJ/YPG's initial war against Daesh. With tensions rising with al-Assad and the shutdown of the Internet in Afrin by Turkey, AANES is keenly aware of the technical necessity to implement such an Internet access program as both a tactical short-term necessity for survival and as part of a longer strategy to rebuild a new democratic Syrian economy. Over the last few years, AANES has paid for new fiber-optic cables to be laid down throughout northeastern Syria, and the provisioning of a new mobile telephony company, called RCell, to be an autonomous competitor with TurkCell and Syriatel. RCell SIM cards are available throughout Rojava that provision data services, and during the October invasion in 2019 by various Islamic and Turkish-backed "Free Syrian Army" forces, often RCell continued operating against all odds.

Bassel's dream for autonomous, self-organized Internet lives, even if his specter remains in our nightmares. If the correct steps are taken to build a social foundation that goes beyond merely the technical components of routers and base stations to include basics such as the translation of the technical knowledge into the local language and long-term self-organization for the maintenance of the infrastructure, what happens—or *could* have happened—in Syria becomes of prime importance in the world. Although the experiments with democratic technical knowledge have just begun in AANES, it bodes well that this is even possible given the precarious politics of northeastern Syria.

Similar to the case put forward by Fanon in the remarkable case of the sudden mass adoption of the portable battery-powered radio due to its being tied to the anti-colonial struggle, access to knowledge of technical infrastructure could lead to a new radically democratic form of development. Countries and regions on the periphery of capitalist development, where the people are viewed as being left behind by technology developed in the core, are capable of "finding short-cuts and of achieving the most modern forms of news-communication without passing through the intermediary stages" (Fanon 1994, 83). A new form of politics based on the democratic control of knowledge and technology can fulfill Fanon's prophecy that "a disparity between the people and what is intended to speak for them will no longer be possible" (Fanon 1994, 97). Innovation in the kinds of technical tools and practices needed for democracy could be invented by necessity in places like Syria, given the collapse of their traditional infrastructure. This kind of knowledge would then be invaluable in the future, as no country is immune to crisis.

The first people to adopt democratic self-control of their own communication and knowledge infrastructure will serve as a model not only for other countries of the periphery, but also for core countries in North America and Western Europe that have monopolized technical development so far. Putting such ideas into practice would also lead to a deeper understanding of democracy in an increasingly technical age. One of the understandable blank spots in the philosophy of democratic confederalism is a lack of a practical plan for technical infrastructure, including but not limited to Internet access. Access to knowledge is a necessary but not sufficient condition for freedom. As access to the Internet is a vital part of our collective social affairs today, putting Internet access and eventually all technical infrastructure under democratic control is necessary for political autonomy. As put by Öcalan (2017, 284), "When communities are able to represent themselves and act on their own behalves concerning all their affairs, *then* they can be said to be democratic." This will require opening up the obscure knowledge of Internet protocols and the proprietary information of mobile telephony to be accessed by all. One step can be done by following the path of Bassel Khartabil. By working for the creation of free software for autonomous access to the Internet, programmers can play a small but vital role in the reconstruction of a new political project that goes beyond Syria: the awakening of a democratic civilization.

Notes

1 I would like to thank Dan Gorman for introducing me to Donnatella and Bassel in particular, and to Idil Onen and Seraf Kavak for organizing the workshop "Parallel Displacements: The Syrian Civil War & Kurdish Migration in Turkey, 2015–2018" on May 24, 2018 at the University of London Institute in Paris where I presented an earlier version of this writing.
2 For example, on August 1, 2011 it was reported in Asharq Al-Awsat that the military that defected against Bashar al-Assad said "we announce the formation of the free Syrian army to work hand in hand with the people to achieve freedom and dignity to bring this regime down, protect the revolution and the country's resources, and stand in the face of the irresponsible military machine that protects the regime."
3 AGPL stands for Affero General Public License and is a free software license.
4 Riseup is an organization that provides communication tools for people working on social change (Riseup n.d.).
5 APK is an abbreviation for Android Package Kit, a tool which allows installation of software without using Google Play.
6 As quoted in "The Johns Hopkins Foreign Affairs Symposium Presents: The Price of Privacy: Re-Evaluating the NSA." Video. Accessed September 30, 2019. https://www.youtube.com/watch?v=kV2HDM86XgI.
7 Riseup's security info page provides info under https://help.riseup.net/en/security.
8 For more information on Crabrgrass, see https://we.riseup.net/.
9 Global System for Mobile (GSM) Communications is a telephony standard developed primarily by large European telephone companies.
10 OpenBSC is the open-source implementation of a base station controller (BSC), which is upstream of the base station transceiver of OpenBTS (Rhizomatica 2015). For details of Rhizomatica's technical work, see https://wiki.rhizomatica.org/index.php/System_Architecture.
11 The Access Now website also lists Algeria, Bangladesh, Benin, Cameroon, Chad, China, Democratic Republic Congo, Eritrea, Ethiopia, Gabon, India, Indonesia, Iran, Iraq, Jordan, Kazakhstan, Liberia, Malawi, Mauritania, Myanmar, Pakistan, Russia, Somalia, Sri Lanka, Sudan, Syria, Tajikistan, United Kingdom, and Zimbabwe.

References

Access Now. 2019. "#KeepItOn: Resources." Accessed September 30, 2019. https://www.accessnow.org/keepiton/#resources.

Anonymous. 2016. *Revolutionary Echoes from Syria: Conversations with Two Anarchists from Aleppo*. Houriyya Press.

Benkler, Yochai. 1998. "Overcoming Agoraphobia: Building the Commons of the Digitally Networked Environment." *Harvard Journal of Law and Technology* 11 (2): 290–400.

Bookchin, Murray. 2015. "The Meaning of Confederalism." in *The Next Revolution: Popular Assemblies and the Promise of Direct Democracy*. London: Verso Books.

Coleman, Biella. 2005. "The Indymedia Era." *Multitudes* 2 (21): 41–48.

Fanon, Frantz. 1994. *A Dying Colonialism*. New York: Grove/Atlantic, Inc.

Ghattas, Kim 2011. "Syria's Spontaneously Organised Protests." BBC News. Accessed December 12, 2019. https://www.bbc.com/news/world-middle-east-13168276.

Greenberg, Andy. 2014. "Your iPhone Can Finally Make Free, Encrypted Calls." *Wired*, July 27. https://www.wired.com/2014/07/free-encrypted-calling-finally-comes-to-the-iphone/.

Kaspersky Labs, 2014. "Syrian Malware, the Ever-Evolving Threat." Accessed December 12, 2019. https://securelist.com/the-syrian-malware-house-of-cards/66051/.

LEAP Encryption Access Project. 2019. "About Us." Accessed October 4, 2019. https://leap.se/en/about-us.

Lagi, Marco, Karla Bertrand, and Yaneer Bar-Yam. 2011. "The Food Crises and Political Instability in North Africa and the Middle East." https://arxiv.org/abs/1108.2455.

Morozov, Evgeny. 2011. *The Net Delusion: How Not to Liberate the World*. London: Penguin UK.

Myers, Emily N. 2016. *Of Rhizomes and Radio: Networking Indigenous Community Media in Oaxaca, Mexico*. PhD diss., University of Oregon.

Netblocks. 2019a. "Reports: Internet Disrupted in Iran amid Fuel Protests in Multiple Cities." Accessed December 12, 2019. https://netblocks.org/reports/Internet-disrupted-in-iran-amid-fuel-protests-in-multiple-cities-pA25L18b.

Netblocks. 2019b. "Reports: Social Media Partially Unblocked in Iraq after 50 days." Accessed December 12, 2019. https://netblocks.org/reports/Internet-disrupted-in-iran-amid-fuel-protests-in-multiple-cities-pA25L18b.

Netblocks. 2019c. "Reports: Evidence of Social Media Disruptions in Ecuador as Crisis Deepens." Accessed December 12, 2019. https://netblocks.org/reports/evidence-of-social-media-disruptions-in-ecuador-as-crisis-deepens-oy9RN483.

Netblocks. 2019d. "Reports: Major Internet Shutdown Registered in Kashmir as Crisis Worsens." Accessed December 12, 2019. https://netblocks.org/reports/major-Internet-shutdown-registered-in-kashmir-as-crisis-worsens-xyMGzbAZ.

Netblocks. 2019e. "Reports: Sudan Internet shows Signs of Recovery after Month-Long Shutdown." Accessed December 12, 2019. https://netblocks.org/reports/sudan-Internet-recovery-after-month-long-shutdown-98aZpOAo.

O'Brien, Danny. 2017. "Bassel Khartabil, In Memoriam." Electronic Frontier Foundation. August 1, 2017. https://www.eff.org/deeplinks/2017/08/bassel-khartabil-memoriam.

Öcalan, Abdullah. 2017. *Manifesto for a Democratic Civilization*, Vol. 2: *Capitalism: The Age of Unmasked Gods and Naked Kings*. Cologne: New Compass Press.

OpenBTS. n.d. "About." Accessed September 30, 2019. http://openbts.org/about/.

OpenBTS. 2008. "The Unofficial Non-Carrier of Burning Man 2008." Accessed September 30, 2019. http://openbts.sourceforge.net/FieldTest/.

Preston, Jennifer. 2011. "Seeking to Disrupt Protesters, Syria Cracks Down on Social Media." *New York Times*. Accessed December 12, 2019. https://www.nytimes.com/2011/05/23/world/middleeast/23facebook.html.

Rhizomatica. 2015. "About: About Rhizomatica." Accessed December 12, 2019. https://www.rhizomatica.org/about/.

Riseup. n.d. "About Us." Accessed September 30, 2019. https://riseup.net/en/about-us.

Rizk, Nagla, and Lea Shaver. 2010. "Access to Knowledge: Economic, Global and Local Perspectives" in *Access to Knowledge in Egypt* edited by Nagla Rizk and Lea Shaver. London: Bloomsbury Academic.

SMEX. 2018. “Message from Afrin: We Can’t Wait for a Shutdown to Condemn Network Disruptions in Times of War.” SMEX, March 16. https://smex.org/message-from-afrin-we-cant-wait-for-a-shutdown-to-condemn-network-disruptions-in-times-of-war/.

Sparrow, Elijah, Harry Halpin, Kalı Kaneko, and Ruben Pollan. 2016. “*LEAP: A next-generation client VPN and encrypted email provider.*” In International Conference on Cryptology and Network Security, Milan, Italy, pp. 176–191. Springer.

Syrian Observatory for Human Rights. 2019. “Murder, Censorship and Syria: Crypto and the Future of Uprisings.” Last modified April 29, 2019. http://www.syriahr.com/en/?p=126076.

Taye, Berhan. 2019. “The State of Internet Shutdowns Around the World: The 2018 #KeepItOn Report.” *Access Now*. Accessed September 30, 2019. https://accessnow.org/kio-2018-report.

7

THE UNITED STATES AND GOVERNMENT-PROVIDED INTERNET ACCESS

Infrastructures of Free Expression and the Role of the State

Enrique Armijo

Introduction

Government-provided access to high-speed Internet in the United States is on the rise. This is due in large part, of course, to a smartphone-driven explosion in the demand for mobile wireless services. Smartphone ownership increased from 16 percent of Americans in 2009 to 56 percent in 2012 (White House OST and NEC 2013). Among the young, the numbers are even more pronounced. In 2017, more than nine in ten Americans between the ages of 18 and 29 owned smartphones (Smith 2017). This pervasiveness and the concomitant need for all of those devices and their users to be online, on-demand, at any time, has moved high-speed Internet access in the U.S. from a luxury to an expectation. And governments across the United States are stepping in not only to offer speeds that private cellular-based ISPs do not yet provide, and in places their networks do not yet reach, but also to offer alternatives to private networks and access providers (Cooper 2016).

More than 450 U.S. cities of all sizes have moved to try to meet this demand (Community Networks 2015). These offerings are taking a range of forms. One is a public utility model, i.e., purely government owned-and-operated "municipal broadband" networks. Other cities are adopting public–private partnership models; under one typical model, a private ISP provides free Internet access to the public in a particular public space such as a city park, town hall, or transportation hub in cooperation with a municipality or its administrative subsidiary (Flegenheimer 2013). Similarly, public utility companies have been building their own wholesale-only fiber-and-wireless-based broadband networks and making those networks available on an open access basis to ISPs, which can then use city-owned Internet infrastructure to offer in-home high-speed access to their subscribers for a fee; here, the government keeps the transport layer of the infrastructure for itself and offers the service layer to private ISP companies (Bode 2017).

Where city-wide networks have been cost-prohibitive or otherwise difficult to establish, municipalities have focused their efforts on aggregating smaller service areas within their city limits on their own or with corporate partners, usually via franchise agreements in the case of the latter (Kennesaw.com n.d.; MERAKI n.d.; Hinz 2012). Current infrastructure thus makes it possible for a visitor to New York City to enjoy free high-speed Wi-Fi Internet access on their iPad or Android Phone from Battery Park up to Central Park Zoo, across the East River, and back down to Prospect Park in Brooklyn—all without accessing their private carrier network (NYC Parks 2017).[1] On the other coast, San Francisco has begun serious consideration of a city-wide high-speed fiber-optic Internet network, including via a "public model" whereby the city would both manage construction of the network and serve as the ISP (City and County of San Francisco 2016). And this revolution is by no means limited to large cities like New York or San Francisco. Cities and counties of all sizes have undertaken or are considering municipal broadband projects or public–private partnerships to expand online access for their citizens (Office of Erie County 2015). Additionally, on the federal level, on March 21, 2017, the U.S. House Energy and Commerce's Subcommittee on Communications and Technology held a hearing on how to expand mobile broadband in rural America (U.S. House of Representatives Energy & Commerce Committee 2017).[2]

Underlying, and likely spurred by, this rise is an ongoing debate as to the proper role of governments in providing wired Internet access to their citizens. The entrenched incumbency of existing ISPs has had debilitating effects on start-up efforts in the market for broadband. If Google could not make Google Fiber work, it is difficult to conceive of any potential new entrant devising a business model that would permit it to even survive as a going concern, let alone compete against the incumbents on speed and price (Crawford 2017). Hence advocates call for a more aggressive government role, from the aforementioned building fiber networks and leasing access to ISPs on a wholesale basis to offering an Internet service itself.

Additionally, just like in the private market, the wireless service must at some point connect to wired infrastructure. The development of fiber networks and the capacity for wireless access are thus closely correlated. Greater wired capacity is a necessary predicate to greater wireless capacity. So once governments become involved in offering fiber-to-the-home, customers will demand mobile connectivity from those and other providers on the same terms (Institute for Local Self-Reliance 2007, 21). More ISPs and more networks lead to greater mobile connectivity.

The most important question with respect to this issue is how this "fundamental makeover" of public places from exclusively physical spaces to mixed spaces with both physical and online aspects, including the move of speech spaces from fixed spaces to mobile ones, is "alter[ing] the nature, character, and democratic functions of public places and public expression" (Zick 2007, 1–5).[3] The Access to Knowledge framework asks questions related to what Jack Balkin calls the "infrastructure of free expression," in particular whether "government policies promote the delivery of information and knowledge" (Kaminski and Prakash 2015, 9, quoting

Balkin 2007). Additionally, in the United States context, there is the First Amendment to the Constitution, which bars governments from interfering with speech on the basis of the speech's content or viewpoint—even when it is doing so for what it claims to be public-interest-related reasons. In all three models of government-provided Internet access set out above, a state actor is playing a significant role with respect to the infrastructure of the network and the traffic to be carried over it. When the traffic being carried is speech, the Access to Knowledge framework is directly implicated. And the record of these governments so far, at least with respect to the conditions they place on the speech traffic that is carried over their networks, is decidedly mixed.

If one's focus zooms out from the infrastructure and technology involved, Internet access networks are speech spaces—as Stacey Schesser (2006) says, a "new domain for public speech" (6). When the government is involved in their development or operation, these spaces are provided either in name or in fact by the state; to use the traditional parlance of First Amendment jurisprudence, these networks are publicly owned property over which citizen expression travels. There is no question that governments have a critical role to play in helping to bridge the digital divide, stepping in where privately provided service is uneconomical or lower quality due to near-monopoly power of private ISPs, particularly with respect to the "last mile" inefficiencies associated with privately provided Internet access and the high-cost, data-capped business model of mobile access in the United States. However, due to the pace of change, the U.S. runs the risk of accepting government-provided digital speech spaces unreservedly as part of our communications infrastructure without asking the fundamental questions of what law applies, what is permissible, and what the U.S. Constitution bars. Societies must not rush to embrace new technology and, in the process, leave behind all of the longstanding protections from government interference that are well established in every other context. It would be ironic, indeed tragic, if the 21st-century speaker loses the protections that were unquestionably enjoyed by the speaker who was communicating in government-provided speech spaces long before the iPhone was even invented.

Terms of service as speech rules

Comparing examples from two different points in time might illustrate the danger referred to immediately above. In the 1965 U.S. Supreme Court case of *Lamont v. Postmaster General,* a federal statute empowered the Postmaster General to confiscate foreign-originated mail that he deemed to be "Communist propaganda."[4] The *Lamont* petitioner, a pamphleteer who received notice of the Post Office's confiscation of his copy of the *Peking Review,* sought to enjoin the statute's enforcement, arguing that it violated his First Amendment right to receive information. Even though the statute provided that an addressee could request mail that the General had confiscated by returning an official reply card, the Supreme Court unanimously agreed with Lamont that the statute violated his First Amendment rights. The Court noted that "the United States may give up the post-office when it sees fit, but while it carries it on the use of the mails is almost as much a part of free speech as the right to use our tongues."

The principle affirmed in *Lamont*—that the government must carry the speech of its users without prejudice against the content of that speech—extends back to the founding of the postal service. Though the U.S. Supreme Court strayed from this foundational understanding for a time, finding that the government did have authority to make content-related decisions as to the mail it carried,[5] the provenance of the principle is not in dispute. As Ithiel de Sola Pool recounts in his seminal *Technologies of Freedom:*

> In 1836, President Andrew Jackson, concerned at the upsetting effect that the distribution of antislavery propaganda might have in the South, urged Congress to ban such matter from the mails. An ad hoc committee of the Senate chaired by [John] Calhoun, America's classic defender of slavery, rejected the President's request because, in his view, Congress had no such power: "If it be admitted that Congress has the right to discriminate … what papers shall or what shall not be transmitted by the mail, it would subject the freedom of the press, on all subjects, political, moral, and religious, completely to its will and pleasure."
>
> *(de Sola Pool 1984, 82)*

Compare the statute found unconstitutional in *Lamont*, as well as the historical basis underlying its invalidation, to the following proscriptions, all of which come directly from municipalities' terms of service for use of their publicly accessible broadband networks and all of which use blatantly content-based restrictions that would facially violate the United States Constitution's First Amendment in any other context:

- The "Acceptable Use Policy" for the municipal utility-owned and operated Chattanooga, Tennessee fiber-optic network bars users from using the network to "transmit, distribute, or store material … that is," in addition to illegal or obscene, "threatening, abusive or hateful," or that offends "the privacy, publicity or other personal rights of others." Nor may users of the network "post messages" on third-party blogs "that are excessive and/or intended to annoy or harass others"—"regardless of [the] policies" of the blogs on which the users post (Electric Power Board of Chattanooga 2017).[6]
- The Terms and Conditions for GOWEX, the private partner offering Internet access for New York City as part of city's Wireless Corridor Challenge, "bars the transmission of data … via Hotspots managed by GOWEX … whose content is threatening, derogatory, obscene, pornographic, or the transmission of any other type of material which constitutes or incites a conduct which may be considered a criminal offense, is prohibited." GOWEX also "reserves the right to prevent or block access to any user" who violates the content policy (GOWEX n.d.).

- The city of Miami's terms of use for its Miami Beach Wi-Fi network requires users to waive any claims against the city based on service disruptions:

  [Y]our access to the Service is completely at the discretion of the City, and your access to the Service may be blocked, suspended, or terminated at any time, at the sole discretion of the City, *without cause or for any reason including*, but not limited to, any violation of this Agreement, actions that may lead to liability for the City, disruption of access to other Users or networks, and violation of applicable laws or regulations... ., *and may be interrupted, refused, limited, or curtailed at any time.*
  (City of Miami Beach n.d.)

  Similarly, the city of Raleigh, North Carolina states that "under no circumstances shall the City be liable for any damages that arise or result in any way from use of, or inability to use, the service to or access to the Internet or any part thereof."
  (City of Raleigh n.d.)

- The City of Wilson, North Carolina's Terms of Service for its Greenlight network states that users may not "send[], post[], or host[] harassing [or] abusive" materials, or may not "engag[e] in any activities or actions intended to withhold or cloak any user's identity or contact information." Greenlight also may, in its "sole discretion," "temporarily or permanently remove content" that it believes violates its Terms of Use. Furthermore, Greenlight may, pending its investigation of a violation, "suspend the account or accounts involved and/or remove or block material that potentially violates this policy" (Greenlight Community Broadband 2017).

As should be clear, these networks, likely along with dozens if not hundreds of others, severely restrict users' speech on the network in exchange for access. First Amendment doctrine in the United States makes clear that outright bans on protected speech—even indecent speech, let alone "excessive," "derogatory," "abusive," or "hateful" speech—are never sufficiently narrowly tailored to survive constitutional scrutiny.[7] It is also black-letter free speech law that implements prior restraints—and there is no question that a network operator's "rejecting or removing" material because of its content before that material reaches its intended recipient is a prior restraint, as is the case here—are presumed unconstitutional.[8] And the right to speak anonymously is well enshrined in the Speech Clause's protections as well.[9] Terms of service such as those used in Chattanooga, Miami, Wilson, and potentially scores of other cities thus violate basic tenets of First Amendment law.

By defining what speech can and cannot be transmitted over the network and by setting out the grounds by which the state can refuse a user access, these terms define the contours of their users' First Amendment rights (Grimmelmann 2015, 49–75).[10] In *Lamont*, the Supreme Court declared that once the government decides to provide a mail service, it cannot discriminate in its delivery of that mail because of its objection to the content that users of the service seek to deliver. Yet that is exactly what is happening on dozens, or perhaps hundreds, of municipal broadband networks.

Government-provided internet access as free expression infrastructure

These restrictions on free expression are, to use another principle from the Access to Knowledge framework, a particularly pernicious mix of "old school" and "new school" speech regulation (Kaminski and Prakash 2015, 2, quoting Balkin 2007). They are "old school" because they use the power of the state to censor, based on what the state deems as harmful speech. It is Chattanooga's determination, not the speaker or listener's, as to which speech is, to quote from the Terms of Service for their network, "threatening, abusive or hateful," or that offends "the privacy, publicity or other personal rights of others," or "excessive and/or intended to annoy or harass others" (Electric Power 2017). They are "new school" because the consequences of the state's censorship take place *ex ante* to the speech being restricted rather than *ex post.*

As is common with state restrictions on information and communications technology (ICT) and unlike most interferences with speech in physical space, the tools for interference with online speech are embedded within the ICT, and the network operator has absolute control. Deleting an *en route* text or tweet for its failure to comply with a state-imposed term of service can go unnoticed by the speaker in a way that sending a police officer to shut down a protest in the park cannot. This also creates an intractable problem for judicial review, since the speaker may never know that the state has interfered with their speech for a content-based reason. As Seth Kreimer (2006) argues, in such a context "neither speakers nor listeners will know that the message has not been conveyed, and there is no way to determine how dialogue has been deformed" (16–27).

The state as first-order threat to freedom of expression

Given the characteristics of our current networked environment, the focus in Access to Knowledge-related scholarship on the acts and decisions of private intermediaries makes eminent sense. As I have noted in prior work, "through ICT, we have overcome temporal and spatial limitations on communication, but we need constant intermediation in order to do so" (Armijo 2015, 421; Armijo 2014). That trade-off, which was initially realized with the printing press and broadcast but which has become fully consummated with mobile telephony and ubiquitous Internet access, has come at a cost to speakers. And much of that cost is paid in the form of private intermediaries' control over expression. But First Amendment scholarship should never lose sight of the fact that governments represent the most serious challenges to citizens seeking to communicate online.

Through both direct censorship of user content through design, governance, network management-related decisions (Rosen 2012, 1525), and what Laura DeNardis calls "private industry mediation of delegated censorship" (DeNardis 2015, 16)—i.e., Internet service providers and application and website owners' enforcement of government content removal requests—the private telecommunications industry plays a critical and often negative role in establishing a freedom of expression-enabling infrastructure online. To the extent online expression is both a mediated and monitored experience, it is certainly so that private companies are doing much, if not most, of the mediating and the monitoring. But it is important to not lose sight of free expression first principles: it is governments, not private parties, which have historically represented the first-order threat to free speech and access to knowledge.

Another comparison across time, this one borrowed from prominent Internet critic Evgeny Morozov, might help to illustrate the point. As noted in Morozov's *The Net Delusion*, expression's move from physical space to online has been a boon for speakers, but it has also made it much easier to be a spy. In the 1970s, it literally took teams of KGB officers to drill holes for bugs, monitor workplaces, establish observation points below and above a single dissident's apartment, and listen to every conversation in order to collect speech and associations that the government believed to be incriminating. That is a lot of work to surveil one person. Now, however, a single officer of the modern-day secret police can run keyword searches of millions of intercepted emails by thousands of users without leaving his desk (Morozov 2011, 150–51). The overwhelming majority of those email accounts are provided by private companies and the emails themselves mostly travel over private networks, but private actors do not replace government interferences with privacy and association; rather, they facilitate it—so too with interferences with speech.

It is thus certainly the case that because of the mobile economy, the monitoring and mediating of speech has become cheaper, faster, and better, and the privatized nature of Internet infrastructure has enabled this to happen. But privatization can be a brake as well as a throttle. To be able to accomplish its desired results, the government must use its leverage over a private ISP to embed the functionality the state desires into its network, in much the same way the U.S.'s National Security Agency is alleged to have leveraged AT&T and other ISPs' cooperation as part of its FAIRVIEW program, whereby AT&T installed NSA surveillance equipment in at least 17 of its Internet hubs on U.S. soil (Angwin and Larson 2015; Ball 2013). Despite that notable example, however, companies can and increasingly do, especially post-Snowden, tell the government no (Rozenshtein 2018). If a government is providing an Internet service itself, however, there is no jawboning necessary. The state can design its *own* communications infrastructure in ways that compel users to waive their rights to be free from content-based interferences with their speech or from warrantless searches. As virtual public speech spaces emerge that are public as well as private, the risks of harm to access to knowledge multiply. And interferences with a virtual speech space can be much more efficient when the government cuts out altogether the middleman private ISP or network owner.[11] Accordingly, measures such as network neutrality, which seek to limit the interference private ISPs have over users' speech, are only a partial solution; meaningful limits must also be placed on governments' ability to do the same over their own networks.

In addition, the content-based terms of service discussed in the section above, though troubling, are just a small tool in the state's arsenal for *ex ante* interferences with mobile ICT-intermediated speech. Preemptive interferences with mobile users' online speech over private networks, from the blocking of websites and applications to shutting down networks altogether, are now common throughout the world. The civil society group AccessNow, as part of its #KeepItOn initiative, documented 56 Internet shutdowns by national governments in 2016—more than three times than the 15 that it documented the year prior (AccessNow 2017). Additionally, to claim these dangers are real only in countries with traditions of despotic regimes with historical enmity toward free expression in other contexts is dangerously false. The most comprehensive study of government interferences with users' connections to digital networks found that of the 566 instances of interference involving 101 countries between 1995 and 2010, 51 percent occurred in authoritarian regimes, but 39 percent occurred in democracies (Howard, Agarwal, and Hussain 2011, 222).

And even though government's attempts to enlist technology companies in the fight against extremist speech online have been longstanding (Yadron 2016), in 2015, the US President Donald J. Trump made his views on the issue explicitly known, stating while a candidate that in response to the spread of radical extremism online, "we have to talk [to the executives of private technology companies like Microsoft and Google] about, maybe in certain areas, closing that Internet up in some way" (Statat 2015). Even though ICT at the national level in the United States is highly privatized, it is very likely that the President has the power in the event of a national security emergency to shut down wire communications throughout the United States. The U.S. Communications Act states that the "war powers of President" include the ability to, "if he deems it necessary in the interest of the national security and defense, … cause the closing of any facility or station for wire communication."[12] So if President Trump had decided that he needed to turn off the Internet in the United States, he would not have needed Bill Gates's help—or, perhaps, even Congress's consent.

Again, private mobile technology companies are part of a highly regulated market, so government leverage over them will always exist. But when a government is administering its *own* networks, there is no need to exercise leverage at all. Even if a nationwide public Wi-Fi network in the United States may not be politically or economically feasible, individual municipalities and states' entry in the high-speed Internet market represents opportunities for great benefits but also great harms. We should temper our optimism over these developments with a healthy dose of caution, if not distrust.

Preserving an infrastructure of free expression

As argued above, promoting and preserving an infrastructure of freedom of expression remains a project of protection *from* governments as well as protections granted *by* them. As has long been the case when it comes to protecting speech more generally, civil society will continue to play an important role. For example, in collaboration with Tor, CitizenLab, and the international digital-rights advocacy group Access Now, The Open Observatory of Network Interference (OONI) has developed ooniprobe, a mobile application with the capability to test whether a network is censoring or blocking a mobile user's access to a particular URL (Waddell 2017). Internet-wide blackouts, rather than targets of specific URLs, are more difficult to demonstrate, but civil society is developing those tools as well.

In addition, the same private entity gatekeepers that have exercised significant control over online speech have also taken significant steps to protect it. In 2017, America's largest private ISPs successfully lobbied for legislative repeal of FCC (Federal Communications Commission) rules restricting the companies' use of their users' browsing information (Neidig 2017). But other private entities have taken more proactive approaches. Google's research and advocacy arm Jigsaw recently launched a suite of cybersecurity tools called "Protect Your Election," intended to help protect news sites and human rights groups from DDoS and other security-based attacks against elections-related speech by governments and their hackers (Newman 2017). And private intermediaries such as Twitter and Google commonly resist government requests for their users' information in the interests of free expression (Otarola 2017) and provide comprehensive information to the public concerning those requests (Twitter 2017; Rozenshtein 2018). As more of our discussions and accessing of information move to mobile platforms and technologies, these protections will play an increasingly important role.

Conclusion

I end with a thought experiment. Imagine a proposal for a nationwide high-speed wireless network in the United States, built by the federal government, with Internet access service provided to users' mobile phones over the network by local utilities, pursuant to terms of use adopted by those utilities and subject to whatever strings the feds would impose in exchange for network access. Imagine that this network was proposed in 2014, around the time the U.S. Court of Appeals for the D.C. Circuit struck down the FCC's first attempt at adopting net neutrality rules for private ISPs consistent with the policies of the Obama administration. Would you have been in favor? Would you have found the network consistent with, and promotive of, principles of free expression, innovation, and democratic discourse?

Now imagine the same project being proposed in 2018, with an anti-net neutrality, anti-media, and arguably anti-free speech President Trump in office. If you were in favor in 2014, would you be in support now? Do you still trust the government to provide nondiscriminatory access to the Internet, the way we have always presumed it offers access to other public goods like roads, water, sewers, and sidewalks? Or is mobile Internet infrastructure, where information is the public good on offer, somehow different? Would you consider the mobile device in your bag or pocket a speech engine or a tool the government could use to censor and surveil you?

It is certainly so that creating an infrastructure of free expression involves positive policymaking—affirmative acts by governments intended to fuel the production of knowledge and innovation and the interaction between diverse, and at times conflicting, ideas, cultures, and beliefs. Preserving and promoting Access to Knowledge, however, particularly in the ICT context, must also take into primary account the individual liberty-based principles that protect speakers and listeners from government interferences with speech. This constitutional norm may have been born with the First Amendment and intended for pamphleteers instead of bloggers. But as speech moves from physical to virtual space and from parks and streets to mobile phones, the United States, as well as rest of the world, needs to recognize and affirm those principles now more than ever.

Notes

1 These networks are often actually hodge-podged together, because of the challenges associated with city-wide municipal fiber networks in larger cities attributable to private incumbents' established infrastructure footprints (Burrington 2016).
2 A Bill discussed at the hearing proposed requiring the Department of Transportation to install needed broadband conduit underneath hard surfaces as part of any federally funded highway construction project.
3 Whether offering free high-speed Internet access is a good *economic decision* for cities is beyond the scope of this chapter. Some have argued that it is not, particularly since financing the construction of such a network is usually accomplished through debt funding via issuance of municipal bonds (Reason Magazine 2013), while others disagree (National Economic Council 2015).
4 Lamont v. Postmaster General, 381 U.S. 301 (1965).
5 Milwaukee Social Dem. Pub. Co. v. Burleson, 255 U.S. 407 (1921).
6 To be sure, such restrictions on Internet use and access would likely be more permissible in other countries, where governments have a freer rein with respect to barring hate speech or harassment. *See* Article 19, 1992, STRIKING A BALANCE: HATE SPEECH, FREEDOM OF EXPRESSION, AND NON-DISCRIMINATION (Sandra Coliver, ed.), at https://www.article19.org/data/files/pdfs/publications/striking-a-balance.pdf. But even in countries that tolerate greater restrictions on hate speech or harassing expression than the United States, the danger remains that those restrictions "become overbroad and are subject to abuse." Article 19, 2015, HATE SPEECH EXPLAINED: A TOOLKIT , https://www.article19.org/data/files/medialibrary/38231/'Hate-Speech'-Explained—A-Toolkit-%282015-Edition%29.pdf.
7 Sable Commc'ns. of Cal. v. FCC, 492 U.S. 115, 126–128 (1989) (upholding ban on obscene telephone messages but finding ban on indecent messages not narrowly tailored).
8 See Promotions, Ltd. v. Conrad, 420 U.S. 546, 553 (1975) (holding a city's denial of use of its theater for a production of *Hair* on the grounds the play was "not in the best interests of the community" was an invalid prior restraint).
9 McIntyre v. Ohio Elections Comm'n, 514 U.S. 334 (1995) (finding that a statute prohibiting anonymous political literature violated the First Amendment, on the ground that anonymity encourages open discourse and protects speakers from retaliation).
10 As Grimmelmann (2015, 42) writes, "owners occupy a privileged position because their control over [Internet] infrastructure gives them unappealable control over the community's software-based rules," and "can use their power over the infrastructure layer to make policy at the content layer, for good and for ill."
11 Under a mixed wholesale/retail model, leverage could of course work in a speech-promoting way; if a government builds its own network, it is free to insist on neutrality from any ISP seeking to provide retail service over it. But if many governments

themselves feel free and able to discriminate against user traffic on the basis of content on their own networks, it is difficult to imagine that most governments would insist on equal treatment of traffic from their partner private ISPs.

12 47 U.S.C. § 606. *See also*SENATE COMM. ON HOMELAND SEC. & GOV'T AFFAIRS, PROTECTING CYBERSPACE AS A NATIONAL ASSET ACT OF 2010, S. REP. NO. 111–368, at 10 (2010) ("The Committee understands that Section 706 gives the President the authority to take over wire communications in the United States and, if the President so chooses, shut a network down."). The Communications Act defines "wire communication" as "transmission of writing, signs, signals, pictures, and sounds of all kinds by aid of wire, cable, or other like connection between the points of origin and reception of transmission, including all instrumentalities, facilities, apparatus, and services (among other things, the receipt, forwarding, and delivery of communications) incidental to such transmission. 47 U.S.C. § 153 (51).

References

AccessNow. 2017. "#KeepItOn." Accessed August 11, 2017. https://www.accessnow.org/keepiton/ #problem.

Angwin, Julia, and Jeff Larson. 2015. "NSA Spying Relies on AT&T's 'Extreme Willingness to Help." *ProPublica*. August 15. https://www.propublica.org/article/nsa-spying-relies-on-atts-extreme-willingness-to-help.

Armijo, Enrique. 2014. "Kill Switches, Forum Doctrine, and the First Amendment's Digital Future." *Cardozo Arts and Entertainment Law Journal* 32: 411–469.

Armijo, Enrique. 2015. "Government-Provided Internet Access: Terms of Service as Speech Rules." *Fordham Urban Law Journal* 41: 1499–1525.

Article 19. 2015. "Hate Speech Explained: A Toolkit." Accessed August 11, 2017. https://www.article19.org/data/files/medialibrary/38231/'Hate-Speech'-Explained—A-Toolkit-%282015-Edition%29.pdf.

Article 19. 1992. *Striking a Balance: Hate Speech, Freedom of Expression, and Non-discrimination* (Sandra Coliver, ed.). Accessed August 11, 2017. https://www.article19.org/data/files/pdfs/publications/striking-a-balance.pdf.

Ball, James. 2013. "NSA's Prism Surveillance Program: How It Works and What It Can Do." *The Guardian*, June 8. https://www.theguardian.com/world/2013/jun/08/nsa-prism-server-collection-facebook-google.

Bode, Karl. 2017. "Huntsville, Alabama is Suddenly Awash in Broadband Competition, Showing Why Comcast is so Afraid of Municipal Broadband." *TechDirt*. February 16. https://www.techdirt.com/articles/20170214/10151036712/huntsville-alabama-is-suddenly-awash-broadband-competition-showing-why-comcast-is-so-afraid-municipal-roadband.shtml?mc_cid=d79017bcf3&mc_eid=2910c7b52b.

Burrington, Ingrid. 2016. *Networks of New York*. Brooklyn and London: Melville House.

City and County of San Francisco Board of Supervisors. 2016. "Financial Analysis of Options for Municipal Fiber Optic Network for Citywide Internet Access." http://sfbos.org/sites/default/files/FileCenter/Documents/55357-FAC1.pdf.

City of Miami Beach. n.d. "WiFi Miami Beach—Network Terms and Conditions" (on file with author).

City of Raleigh, North Carolina. n.d. "Downtown Raleigh Free WiFi Access Terms and Conditions" (on file with author).

Community Networks. 2015. "Community Network Map." Last modified October 2015. Accessed August 11, 2017. https://www.muninetworks.org/communitymap.

Cooper, Charles. 2016. "Why Municipal Broadband." *The Urbanist*, June 2. https://www.theurbanist.org/2016/06/02/why-municipal-broadband.

Crawford, Susan. 2017. "Google Fiber Was Doomed From the Start." *Backchannel*, March 14. https://backchannel.com/google-fiber-was-doomed-from-the-start-a5cdfacdd7f2?mc_cid= d76683f62f#.rxuus56sz.

de Sola Pool, Ithiel. 1984. *Technologies of Freedom*. Cambridge and London: Harvard University Press.

DeNardis, Laura. 2015. "The Privatization of Free Expression." In *Access to Knowledge: Global Censorship: Shifting Modes, Persisting Paradigms*, edited by Pranesh Prakash, Nagla Rizk & Carlos Affonso Souza. Yale Law School Access to Knowledge for Development Center, American University at Cairo, & Instituto de Technologia & Sociedade do Rio.

Electric Power Board of Chattanooga. 2017. "Acceptable Use Policy." Accessed August 11, 2017. https://epb.com/storage/app/media/uploaded-files/Acceptable%20Use%20Policy_0.pdf.

Flegenheimer, Matt. 2013. "Wi-Fi and Cellphone Service on Subway Trains? M.T.A. Says It May Happen." *New York Times*, September 17. http://www.nytimes.com/2013/09/18/nyregion/mta-plans-wi-fi-and-phone-service-on-subway-trains.html?partner=rss&emc=rss&smid=tw-nytimes&_r=0.

GOWEX. n.d. *Terms and Conditions for the New York City Wireless Corridor Challenge* (on file with author).

Greenlight Community Broadband. 2017. "Terms of Service." Accessed August 11, 2017. http://www.greenlightnc.com/termsofservice/.

Grimmelmann, James. 2015. "The Virtues of Moderation." *Yale Journal of Law & Technology* 17 (1): 42–109.

Hinz, Greg. 2012. "City Unveils Plan for Free Wi-Fi, Wider Super-fast Internet." *Crain's Chicago Business*, September 24. http://www.chicagobusiness.com/article/20120924/BLOGS02/120929936/city-unveils-plan-for-free-wi-fi-wider-super-fast-internet.

Howard, Philip N., Sheetal D. Agarwal, and Muzammil M. Hussain. 2011. "When Do States Disconnect Their Digital Networks? Regime Responses to the Political Uses of Social Media." *Communication Review* 14 (3): 216–232.

Institute for Local Self-Reliance. 2007. "Localizing the Internet: Five Ways Public Ownership Solves the U.S. Broadband Problem." http://community-wealth.org/sites/clone.community-wealth.org/files/downloads/report-daggett.pdf.

Kaminski, Margot, and Pranesh Prakash. 2015. "Introductory Framework." In *Access to Knowledge: Global Censorship: Shifting Modes, Persisting Paradigms*, edited by Pranesh Prakash, Nagla Rizk & Carlos Affonso Souza, 9. Yale Law School Access to Knowledge for Development Center, American University at Cairo, & Instituto de Technologia & Sociedade do Rio.

Kennesaw.com. n.d. "Wifi." http://www.kennesaw.com/information/wifi/. Accessed August 11, 2017.

MERAKI. n.d. "City of Newton." http://p13.meraki.com/network/CityofNewton. Accessed August 11, 2017.

Kreimer, Seth F. 2006. "Censorship by Proxy: The First Amendment, Internet Intermediaries, and the Problem of the Weakest Link." *University of Pennsylvania Law Review* 155: 11–101.

Morozov, Evgeny. 2011. *The Net Delusion: The Dark Side of Internet Freedom*. New York: PublicAffairs.

National Economic Council. 2015. *Community-Based Broadband Solutions: The Benefits of Competition and Choice for Community Development and High-speed Internet Access*. https://obamawhitehouse.archives.gov/sites/default/files/docs/community-based_broadband_report_by_executive_office_of_ the_president.pdf.

Neidig, Harper. 2017. "AT&T, Comcast Defend Repeal of Internet Privacy Rules." *The Hill*, March 31. http://thehill.com/policy/technology/326707-att-comcast-defend-repea l-of-internet-privacy-rules.

Newman, Lily Hay. 2017. "A Cybersecurity Arsenal That'll Help 'Protect Your Election'." *Wired*, March 7. https://www.wired.com/2017/03/cybersecurity-arsenal-thatll-help-pro tect-election/?mbid=social_twitter.

NYC Parks. 2017. "Wi-Fi in Parks." www.nycgovparks.org/facilities/wifi. Accessed August 11, 2017.

Office of Erie County Legislator Patrick Burke. 2015. "Municipal Broadband Project." http://www2.erie.gov/burke/sites/www2.erie.gov.burke/files/uploads/pdfs/MBN-Rep ort-Erie-County-20150316.pdf. Accessed August 11, 2017.

Otarola, Miguel. 2017. "Police Get Search Warrant for Everyone who Googled Edina Resident's Name." *StarTribune*, March 18. http://www.startribune.com/search-warra nt-issued-to-edina-police-raises-privacy-concerns-of-internet-users/416442113/.

Reason Magazine Policy Study. 2013. "Lessons in Broadband from Lafayette, Louisiana." (Policy Study 424, Nov.), http://reason.org/files/municipal_broadband_lafayette.pdf.

Rosen, Jeffrey. 2012. "The Deciders: The Future of Privacy and Free Speech in the Age of Google and Facebook." *Fordham Law Review* 80: 1525–1538.

Rozenshtein, Alan Z. 2018. "Surveillance Intermediaries." *Stanford Law Review* 70: 99–189.

Schesser, Stacey D. 2006. "A New Domain for Public Speech: Opening Public Spaces Online." *California Law Review* 94: 1791–1825.

Senate Comm. on Homeland Sec. & Gov't Affairs. 2010. *Protecting Cyberspace as a National Asset Act of 2010*, S. Rep. No. 111–368, at 10.

Smith, Aaron. 2017. "Record Shares of Americans Now Own Smartphones, Have Home Broadband." *Pew Research Center*, January 12. http://www.pewresearch.org/fact-tank/ 2017/01/12/evolution-of-technology/.

Statat, Nick. 2015. "Donald Trump Thinks He Can Call Bill Gates to 'Close Up' the Internet." *Verge*, December 7. http://www.theverge.com/2015/12/7/9869308/dona ld-trump-close-up-the-internet-bill-gates.

Twitter. 2017. "Transparency Report." Accessed August 11, 2017. https://transparency. twitter.com/en/countries/us.html.

U.S. House of Representatives Energy & Commerce Committee. 2017. "Broadband: Deploying America's 21ist Century Infrastructure." March 21. https://energycommerce.house.gov/ hearings-and-votes/hearings/broadband-deploying-americas-21st-century-infrastructure.

Waddell, Kaveh. 2017. "Mapping Countries that Censor the Internet." *The Atlantic*, February 9. https://www.theatlantic.com/technology/archive/2017/02/ooniprobe-censorship-mapp ing/516051/.

White House Office of Science and Technology Policy (White House OST) and The National Economic Council (NEC).2013. Four Years of Broadband Growth. https:// obamawhitehouse.archives.gov/sites/default/files/ broadband_report_final.pdf.

Yadron, Danny. 2016. "Revealed: White House Seeks to Enlist Silicon Valley to 'Disrupt Radicalization'." *The Guardian*, January 7. https://www.theguardian.com/technology/ 2016/jan/07/white-house-social-media-terrorism-meeting-facebook-apple-youtube-.

Zick, Timothy. 2007. "Clouds, Cameras, and Computers: The First Amendment and Networked Public Places." *Florida Law Review* 59: 1–69.

8

BRAZIL AND THE TREASURE TROVE'S TALE

A Study on the Evolution and Popularization of Phones and Law Enforcement Access to Communications

Dennys Antonialli and Jacqueline de Souza Abreu

Introduction

The arrival of mobile phones was certainly a breakthrough in real-time communications. The independence from fixed telephone devices enabled people to reach and be reachable at any time, revolutionizing the way people interacted with each other. The ability to carry telephone devices anywhere has also given rise to a number of different uses and applications, transforming mobile phones into (very) smart objects.

One of the most important features of mobile phone technology is Internet connectivity. In that sense, it is fair to say that the introduction of affordable smartphone devices and data plans had a significant impact on people's access to knowledge and communications. In Brazil, there are more than 100 million Internet users and about 89 percent access the Internet via mobile phones (Comitê Gestor da Internet no Brasil, 2016). According to data released by Facebook, out of the 120 million visits it receives monthly from Brazilian users, 91.6 percent comes from mobile connections.

While provoking a transformation in the way people communicate, making it possible to substitute traditional phone calls for instant messaging applications, emails, and even web-enabled voice over IP calls, mobile phones have also become a treasure trove of communications' information, particularly for law enforcement authorities. Apart from the detailed records about when, where, and for how long communications take place, these new forms of information exchange may also store their actual content.

Given that seeking access to the content of communications is a widespread investigation strategy of law enforcement in Brazil, this chapter describes the ways in which the "smartphone revolution" has enabled new forms of surveillance in Brazil. Even though the Brazilian Federal Constitution of 1988 guarantees the secrecy of communications, it carves out an exception for criminal investigation purposes. The rules governing communication interceptions were set forth by the Law of Interceptions of 1996.[1] Since then, the circumstances under which such access is granted have changed significantly and in large part because of the evolution of mobile phones.

Benefiting from outdated doctrines and broad interpretations, law enforcement authorities have been claiming that access to stored communications content and metadata should follow much less strict rules than those established in the Law of Interceptions. These claims and practices have been frequently deemed as adequate by the Judiciary branch, setting influential precedents. Moreover, the so-called "Car Wash Operation," an ongoing nationwide investigation regarding the biggest corruption scheme in history, has provided a momentum to the law enforcement narratives, consolidating a systematic expansion of their surveillance prerogatives, particularly the obtaining of evidence stored on digital devices (tablets, smartphones, etc.).

This chapter addresses the mismatch between the evolution of telephone usage and mobile phones and the protections provided to communications under Brazilian law. In order to do so, it presents empirical data on the evolution and usage of telephone technologies in Brazil and provides an overview of surveillance law, practices, and case law in the country, mapping out the main issues and loopholes that have arisen involving access to mobile phone data.

The mobile phone revolution in Brazil

The arrival of the first telephone in Brazil goes back to the end of the 19th century, but it was not until the 1950s that the industry started to flourish. At the end of that decade, about a thousand telephone companies offered services to urban areas in the country but were drowned in operational challenges given the lack of standardization and interoperability. For a population of 70 million, there were no more than 1 million installed telephone lines (Neves 2002). From the 1960s to 1996, the telecommunications sector was marked by strict state intervention towards social and economic development. Nonetheless, insufficient infrastructure still hindered mass expansion. In 1995, there were only 13 million active landline phones in Brazil and a population of 162 million (Figure 8.1).

It was not until the telecommunications sector was privatized in 1996 that universalization of telephony services really began. The introduction of mobile phone technology was of utmost importance for that change. The amount of active landline subscriptions tripled within 10 years (13 million in 1995 to 39 million in 2005), but since 2010 it has stabilized at around 43 million (Figure 8.2). On the other hand, the amount of mobile phone subscriptions increased dramatically, reaching a peak of 280 million in 2014. Brazil's population was 204 million that year.

Not only does the great majority of Brazilians (84 percent) now own mobile phones, but also the number of landlines is in decline, confirming that cell phones grew in importance as means of communication (Figure 8.3).

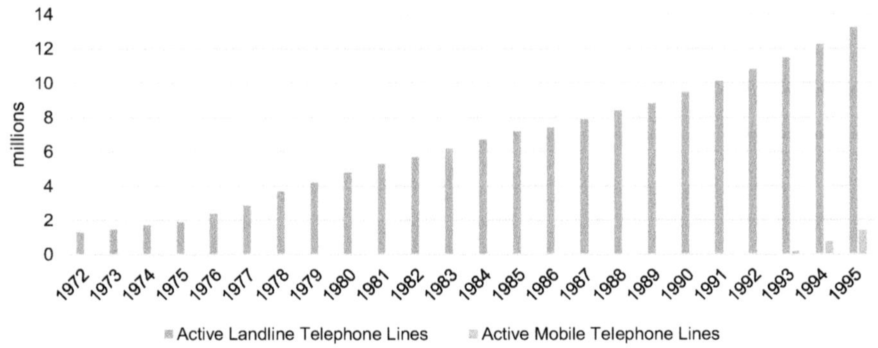

FIGURE 8.1 Telephone use in Brazil (1972–1995).
Source: Agência Nacional de Telecomunicações (2016, 192–194)

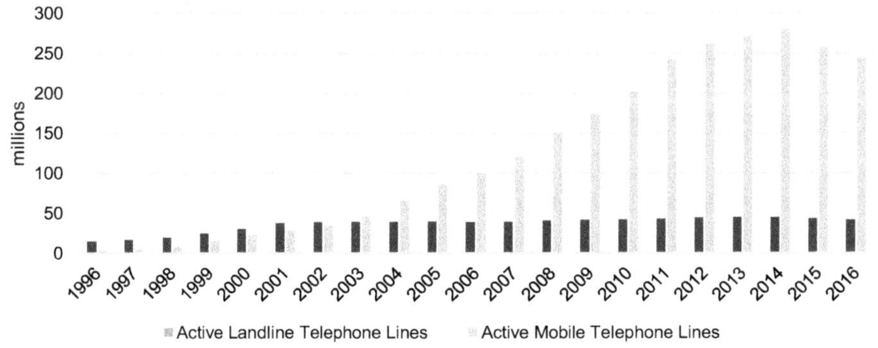

FIGURE 8.2 Telephone use in Brazil (1996–2016).
Source: Agência Nacional de Telecomunicações (2016, 192–194)

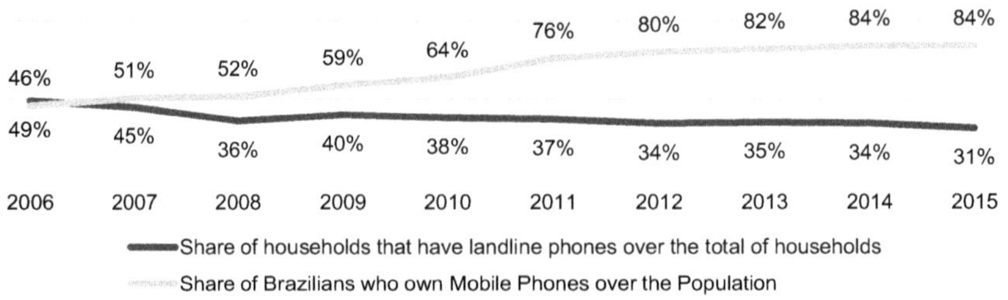

FIGURE 8.3 Landline and mobile phone ownership over time.
Source: Comitê Gestor da Internet no Brasil, 2006–2015

Following a global trend, in Brazil, smartphones are gaining a dominant presence. While there are no consolidated statistics available regarding the specific number of Brazilians that own smartphones, other empirical research data support the claim of the increased use of smartphones in Brazil. As the numbers below show (Figure 8.4), the percentage of Brazilians that use cell phones to go online—an activity typical of smartphone use—has rapidly grown. A 2016 survey conducted by the Brazilian Institute of Public Opinion and Statistics (IBOPE) and commissioned by Qualcomm indicated that the share of Brazilians who own a smartphone jumped from 19 percent in 2014 to 40 percent in 2016 (IBOPE Inteligência 2016). More recently, a Datafolha survey released in the beginning of 2017 and commissioned by WhatsApp Inc. has shown that 79 percent of adolescent and adult Brazilians use smartphones to access the Internet, attesting to the growth of this technology's penetration in Brazil (Datafolha 2016).

It is also worth mentioning that Brazil's social divide is also apparent in mobile phone technology use. According to a 2015 survey by the American think-tank Pew Research Center, the ratio of adult Brazilians who own a smartphone changes across different demographic groups (Poushter 2016). Younger, more educated, and higher-class Brazilians are more likely to own smartphones. For example, in the higher income group, 54 percent of the survey population owned a smartphone, while in the lower income group, this number dropped to 25 percent.

Nonetheless, the high penetration rate of mobile phone technology in Brazil represents, overall, a significant milestone not only in terms of expanding access to long distance communication but also to Internet-based services. The sharp increase shown in the graph in Figure 8.4 is notable in terms of access to knowledge.

However, the proliferation of smartphones has its dark side; it exposes more Brazilians to new forms of surveillance, both from the government and from the private sector. In terms of government surveillance, apart from the interceptions of

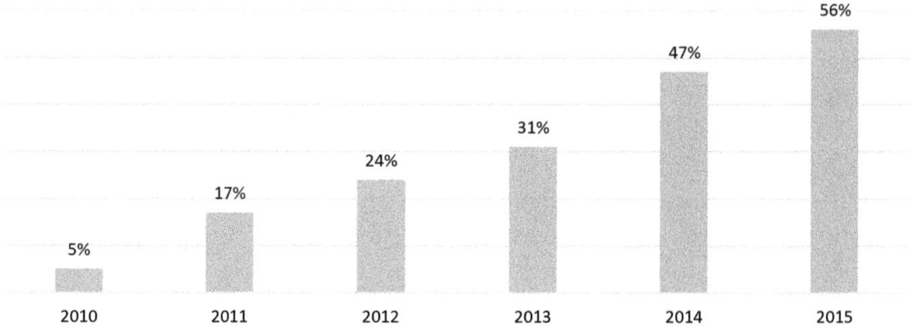

FIGURE 8.4 Brazilians who used a mobile phone to access the Internet within the last three months over the population.
Source: Comitê Gestor da Internet no Brasil, 2010–2015

the content of real-time communications ("wiretaps"),[2] access to metadata and to stored information has become a common practice. This occurs either by search and seizure of devices or by the turnover of these types of data by the telecommunication companies or application providers.

The potential threats of these greater surveillance capabilities would be far less worrying if Brazilian law provided citizens with robust human rights safeguards that could shield them from abusive or unlawful access to their communications data. However, as we demonstrate in the next section, Brazilian law has not kept up with the pace of mobile phone technology, leaving citizens, in particular mobile phone users, vulnerable to abusive surveillance. The next section offers a summary of the findings of a year-long research project about surveillance law and practices in Brazil, which provides an overview of the country's deficient legal framework. It also identifies the main issues that arise out of outdated interpretations, loopholes, and inappropriate checks and balances that are exploited by law enforcement.

Brazil's surveillance law: mapping out the main issues

Although the Brazilian 1988 Federal Constitution protects secrecy of communications and privacy, interpretation issues and outdated federal laws threaten the actual protection that the constitution affords against undue surveillance of communications by law enforcement authorities.

There is a long-standing dispute as to the scope of protection afforded under the unclear Subsection XII of Article 5 of the Brazilian Constitution, which states, "the secrecy of correspondence and of telegraphic communications, data and telephone communications is inviolable, except, in the latter case, under court order, in the events and as provided for in Law for purposes of criminal investigation or penal prosecution." This subsection provides for the protection of communications secrecy, but there is a long-standing disagreement as to whether the subject matter of protection is *information* transmitted through the media listed (correspondence, telegraphic messages, data, and telephone calls) or the *communication*, understood as the flow of such information (protection while in transit). The language of the subsection is also unclear about which categories out of the four listed are included in the constitutional exception that allows for "breach of secrecy."[3]

Leading scholars (Ferraz Junior 1993; Silva 2008, 438; Ferreira Filho 2009, 301) are of the view, endorsed in a decision of the Federal Supreme Court (STF)[4] that the protection referred to in Subsection XII of Article 5 does not refer to *information* transmitted through correspondence, telegraphic messages, data, and telephone calls but rather to its *communication*, i.e. to the flow thereof as it is taking place. A side effect of this weak understanding of Subsection XII is that the content of stored communications and the information generated about the circumstances in which these communications happened (metadata) are excluded from the scope of the provision's protection.

Moreover, the leading scholarly interpretation is that only the secrecy of *telephone* communication, while underway, could be breached for purposes of criminal investigation and prosecution; this possibility would not apply to the flow of data, telegrams, or letters. However, case law has accepted the "breach" of secrecy of communication flow of all types as long as it is "proportionate," whenever it is based on a fundamental right or the public interest.[5] Even the National Congress, in 1996, when establishing the circumstances for breach of secrecy of telephonic communications (*Law of Interceptions* 1996) as explicitly authorized by the Federal Constitution, included the possibility of making "telematic" interceptions, which encompasses "data" interception. In 2014, Congress once again explicitly admitted the real-time interception of electronic communications (which, equally involve "data") in the law known as the Brazilian Internet Civil Rights Framework, or *Marco Civil da Internet.*

Stemming from the constitution, other pieces of legislation address specific issues involving access to communications by law enforcement, particularly for criminal investigation purposes. Either because they were drafted for a different technological context or because they purposely adopted broad language, these pieces of legislation contain loopholes that have been heavily exploited by law enforcement authorities. In addition, gaps in such pieces of legislation leave many questions unanswered, exposing mobile users to even greater and more invasive surveillance. In the subsections below, we summarize the main circumstances that accentuate this problem.

Access to data stored on electronic devices upon search and seizure warrants

The restrictive constitutional interpretation given to the secrecy of communications, which only protects the (content of) communications as they are in transit, generates a regulatory discrepancy. Modern cell phones, tablets, and computers store an enormous quantity of information, photos, and communications that offer detailed profiles of their owners but that would not enjoy the same protection as *in transit* communication due to the mere fact of now being archived.

The Law of Interceptions (Federal Law n. 9.296) of 1996 regulated the constitutional exception to the secrecy of communications. It determined the circumstances in which state authorities may have access to telephonic and telematic communications in real time. The law also enumerated the means of the interception: whether with the aid of telephone companies or through the use of bugging devices. To do so, it established a rigorous legal regime, which involves the fulfillment of tougher requirements in recognition of this measure's invasiveness. These requirements are set forth in Article 2 of the law and demand (i) the existence of reasonable evidence of authorship or participation in a criminal act, (ii) the inexistence of other means of proof, and (iii) the involvement in highly seriousness offenses. The law also established a time limitation of 15 days (renewable) for the measure to be executed.

The protection afforded to (the content of) stored communications, or those which are no longer in transit, is different. The ordinary legislation approaches the issue in two different laws. When the access to these communications happens through an intermediate party which holds the data (such as Internet application providers), the enforceable provisions are those part of the Brazilian Internet Civil Rights Framework (Federal Law 12.965/2014), which determines that the access shall only happen upon a "court order"[6] in the hypotheses and in the way that "the law" establishes,[7] without, however, specifying the substantive requirements of evidential standard.

When the access to content of communications stored on apps (and to any other information stored on cell phones) happens directly on a seized device, the black letter law becomes grey. There is no specific legal framework designed and applied to the search of *electronic* devices, making room for judicial discretion, legal uncertainty, and abuse. One could say that, nowadays, communications which are stored on cell phones and computers, probably for years on end, enjoy a lesser degree of protection than in-transit communications, whose access is regulated in a more rigorous manner by the Law of Interceptions.

This paradox has been acknowledged and contested in some opinion articles (Antonialli, Brito Cruz, and Valente 2016; Maranhão 2016). In scholarship, arguments have also been put forward that Article 5, XII of the Brazilian Constitution should assure unrestricted protection to the *content* of communications, regardless of whether they are in transit or stored, with the implication that every breach of content secrecy should follow the strict requirements of the current Law of Interceptions (Sidi 2015, 111–118). However, the Superior Court of Justice (STJ), in a trial in September 2016, has already refuted this thesis. In the same decision, it affirmed the legality of evidence obtained from cell phones seized in the Car Wash Investigation upon a search and seizure warrant, even without a specific judicial authorization imposing limits to the "virtual search."[8] On the Recurso Extraordinário 418.416–8/SC, assessed in 2006, the Supreme Federal Court (STF) also admitted that a general search and seizure warrant validates the access to data stored on computers—an understanding extended to mobile phones as well.

In spite of being separated by ten years, the two court decisions endorse the assumption that stored data is not protected by the constitutional right to the secrecy of communications, which increases the regulatory discrepancy between the protection of communications in-transit and stored communications.

Access to data stored on electronic devices through searches incident to arrests

An equally problematic scenario is that of access to data stored on electronic devices—mainly mobile phones—in searches incident to arrests. When police authorities make *in flagrante* arrests, they proceed to search for objects and products of the crime carried by the detainee for the collection of elements that will constitute the writ of arrest and the elimination of any physical threats to officers and third parties. In this scenario, the possibility of police officers having access to data stored on the cell phone carried by the detainee has been questioned. Does the arrest *in flagrante* authorize the search not only of the person and/or their home, but also of everything that is electronically saved in devices in their possession? The answer to this question is a disputed matter. Once again, the debates on the protection of *stored* data (communication content and metadata) re-emerge.

There is no agreement in superior courts on the legality of access to stored data incident to arrests and of the evidence obtained from it. In a 2012 decision, the Supreme Federal Court (STF) held that the analysis of calling records (metadata) of a cell phone seized in an *in flagrante* arrest does not characterize a violation to the secrecy of communications (Article 5, item XII of the Brazilian Constitution), as its protection would encompass "communication of data and not the data itself" and "telephone communications and logs have a distinct legal protection."[9] In 2007, the Superior Court of Justice (STJ) had already decided in a similar manner that the inspection of call history after an *in flagrante* arrest does not configure an illegal breach of secrecy, because the information was not obtained through an intermediate party (telephone companies) nor was the content of the effectuated conversations revealed.[10] On the other hand, in 2016, now dealing with a smartphone and being aware of the enormous amount of data that modern cell phones produce and store, the STJ decided that the search of WhatsApp conversation history (communications content) in a cell phone seized after an arrest constitutes a breach of secrecy. The evidence collected is illegal when obtained in absence of an authorizing court order.[11]

In state courts, the appraisal of this question continues to vary case-by-case. In the Courts of Justice of Paraná,[12] Rio de Janeiro,[13] and Espírito Santo,[14] there are decisions from 2016 which consider that the access to data in cell phones seized *in flagrante* arrests does not require judicial authorization. The legal ground used was Article 6 of the Code of Criminal Procedure, which authorizes police authorities to seize objects related to the wrongdoing and to collect all evidence that can serve to clarify the fact and its circumstances. This stance is also supported in academic scholarship (see Barreto and Férrer 2016). In contrast, in the Court of Justice of the Distrito Federal[15] and in the Fourth Federal Criminal District of São Paulo, there are decisions in favor of the need of judicial authorization, holding that the access to data stored on seized cell phones constitutes a "virtual search" and therefore requires a court authorization. In the Seventh Federal Criminal District of São Paulo,[16] a judge also held that the evidence obtained through the inspection of WhatsApp messages without prior judicial authorization is illegal; on the other hand, the same court in the same decision held that police officers would be authorized to visualize the most recent calling history to discover "associates."[17]

Access to data protected by end-to-end encryption

WhatsApp is the most popular messaging application in the country. According to a survey commissioned by the company, nine out of ten cell phone owners in Brazil use the app (Datafolha 2016). Mainly after the implementation of end-to-end encryption by the app in April 2016, the use of this technology has also become reason for controversy in Brazil. This occurred because the implementation of end-to-end cryptography makes telematic interceptions—the real-time collection of conversations of specific targets—impossible, even with a court order. Since the company also does not store past messages on their servers, it is not possible to obtain any kind of conversation content from the company in an investigation. This technical obstacle was the reason why the application was temporarily blocked in Brazil (Abreu 2016). According to the judges involved in these cases, a technology that makes interceptions impossible does not accord with the exception provisioned in item XII of Article 5 of the Federal Constitution, which authorizes the access to telephone communications in real time for criminal investigations or instruction of criminal procedures. The STF, in *Ação Direta de Inconstitucionalidade 5527* and *Ação de Descumprimento de Preceito Fundamental* 403, will weigh in on the compatibility of WhatsApp shutdowns with the Federal Constitution and the *Marco Civil* and was also urged to manifest itself on the impasse (Barros 2016; Abreu 2017). At the time of writing it was impossible to predict when they would rule on the matter.

Once again, what was discussed in these cases was the scope of the constitutional protection to the secrecy of communications. Following the reasoning of the leading interpretation that Article 5, XII only admits the breach of secrecy of *in transit telephonic communications*, communications of data were supposed to be inviolable. It is also worth emphasizing that currently there is no enforceable obligation in the Brazilian legislation applicable to developers of messaging applications in the sense of building the architecture of their services in a surveillance-friendly way. Assistance obligations provisioned in the Law of Interceptions and in Brazil's telecommunications regulatory agency resolutions are only destined to telephone companies and connection providers but not to Internet application providers (Abreu and Antonialli 2016). The subject, nonetheless, stirs heated discussions, given the law enforcement powers at stake here. A decision against end-to-end encryption may have the effect of exposing almost all Brazilian mobile users to a number of cybersecurity and privacy risks, including that of increased illegal surveillance.

Access to data held by telephone companies

Aside from issues deriving from the interpretation of the constitution, federal laws governing state surveillance capacity for purposes of law enforcement also pose problems. Their lack of clarity, safeguards, and checks and balances potentially expose mobile phone users to abusive surveillance. One of them is the Criminal Organizations Law (Federal Law no. 12850/13), which exempted some officials from obtaining a court order to access subscriber information. Its Article 15 establishes that

> the chief of civil police and the Public Attorney's Office shall have access, irrespective of court order, only to such account information of the accused that indicates personal qualification, parents, and address retained by Electoral Courts, *telephone companies*, financial institutions, *Internet providers* and credit card administrators.
>
> *(Emphasis added)*

This provision repeats language existing in Article 17-B of the Money Laundering Crimes Law (Federal Law no. 9.613/99), which was added by Law no. 12.683/2012.

Even before the sanction of these legal provisions, police authorities already defended the interpretation that account information would not be safeguarded by the constitutional provisions that protect privacy and the secrecy of communications,[18] as they were not to be confused with the content of telephonic communications; telecommunications companies, however, challenged this interpretation. In 2016, upholding the law enforcement's view, the Federal Regional Court of the 3rd Region sustained that the provider Claro, which in 2013 filed a writ of mandamus against subpoenas from the Federal Police requesting account information associated with seized SIM-cards, has the obligation of revealing the account information even without a judicial order.[19]

Moreover, although legislation on *organized crime* and *money laundering* now allows them to access this information upon request, the authorities mentioned above are also working to expand their access to these data for other purposes, since the legislation did not expressly limit the purposes for which it could be used (Aras 2012). In practice, such authorities use these provisions to support data requests to telephone service providers in any case; the matter will only be submitted to a court for review if a company refuses to comply. The lack of any formal or material requirements for handing over the information leaves these procedures all the more discretionary.

Furthermore, since the enactment of the Criminal Organizations Law, authorities with appropriate jurisdiction, but especially chiefs of civil police, have tried to request telephone logs from telephone companies *without judicial authorization* based on their combined interpretation of Articles 15, 17, and 21 of that law.

Under Article 15, "chief of civil police and Public Attorney's Office shall have access, irrespective of court order, only to such account information of the accused that indicates personal qualification, parents and address" retained by telephone companies and Internet providers. Article 17, however, orders landline and mobile telephone companies to keep "identification logs of number of originating and destination telephone connection terminals" for five years "at the disposal of the authorities referred to in [A]rticle 15." In turn, the main clause of Article 21 criminalizes the refusal or failure to submit "account information, logs, documents and information demanded by the court, Public Attorney's Office or chief of civil police, in the course of investigation or proceedings," and establishes penalties ranging from six months to two years of incarceration, plus a fine. As a result, such authorities have demanded not only account information but also telephone logs (and even some location data) without court orders. Direct demands are made to companies under threat of punishment if they fail to comply.

Ação Direta de Inconstitucionalidade (ADI 5063/DF), a constitutional challenge, was filed in the Federal Supreme Court by the National Association of Cellular Carriers (ACEL) seeking to strike down these articles on grounds that they violate the right to privacy and the principle of legality since the rules' imprecision gives rise to legal uncertainty.[20] That action is still awaiting trial.

Access to data held by Internet service and application providers

Developed in the context of extensive public debate and enacted in 2014, the *Marco Civil da Internet* (Federal Law n. 12965/14) is of utmost importance, for it delineates the terms for legal surveillance on the Internet. Among its many principles and rules, the law crafts a clear regime for access to subscriber information, logs, and content of communications. Slowly, though, law enforcement has found ways to exploit loopholes under ambiguous provisions.

An illustration is that some state court decisions have determined the disclosure of information related to the "logical source port" by connection[21] and Internet application[22] providers (Brito Cruz 2016; Opice Blum 2016; Lopes 2016). That piece of information is not part of the statutory definitions of "connection logs" and "access to application logs," which encompass only IP address, date, and time, which must be retained. Claiming that this is necessary information to "identify" users, the "underlying goal" of data retention mandates, the disclosure of this information has been upheld by some courts. On a positive note, Article 10 § 3 of *Marco Civil da Internet* specifically establishes that access to Internet connection logs and to applications logs will depend on a court order, a protection that is reinforced by Articles 13 § 5 and 15 § 3. In turn, Article 22 limits its purposes to "production of the body of evidence in civil or criminal cases," and establishes the requirements that the "party in interest" must meet to be granted such a court order: solid indicia of wrongdoing, justification of the utility of the requested logs for the purposes of investigation or discovery, and the period to which such logs refer.

In terms of access to information, Article 10 § 3 of *Marco Civil da Internet* establishes that the protection of personal data and private communications "does not prevent access to account information that indicate personal identification, parents and address, as provided for by law, by administrative authorities that have appropriate jurisdiction to obtain such information." With regard to this provision, it is not settled who are these "administrative authorities" with power to directly request subscriber information. This ambiguity allows a wide range of government entities to claim this prerogative.

Finally, a "breach of secrecy" of electronic communications content in the possession of Internet application providers (such as Google and Facebook) is also covered by the *Marco Civil da Internet* under Articles 7, III and 10 § 2, which require a court order. In contrast to what happens for the disclosure of logs (Article 22), the law does not explicitly establish the formal and material requirements that should be fulfilled for a court order to be granted (Mendes and Pinheiro 2015), which again allows for abuses and discrepancies across similar cases.

Access to location data

There is no general framework for access to location data in Brazil. In practice, law enforcement authorities claim general investigatory powers to make location data requests; only if a company refuses to comply will the matter be submitted to a court for review. As most companies do challenge these demands when not accompanied by a judicial authorization, the protection afforded to this type of information is at the discretion of judges.

At least two examples illustrate how vulnerable the current situation is for mobile phone users. First is that of a decision from the Court of Justice of Rio Grande do Sul in July 2007 that allowed a breach of confidentiality of location data from a mobile user in a proceeding to enforce a child support obligation. The defendant under the proceeding was ordered to pay child support and failed to do so without cause; hence, a warrant was issued for his arrest. Identification of his location was attempted many times without success. In view of that and "to fully protect children and teenagers," the Appeals Court Judge allowed "telephone tapping," as it was called, to gather data on the location of the defendant based on his mobile phone number.[23] Given that there is no legal provision nor case law limiting breaches of confidentiality of location data in criminal cases such access was allowed.

The second example relates to a robbery of a security and money transportation company in Ribeirão Preto in July 2016. The police judicially asked Google, Apple, and Microsoft to supply data from all mobile phone users who had "connected" to their platforms from anywhere up to 500 meters from the victim's address within a period of four days leading up to the robbery. The police authorities wanted IMEI numbers (unique identifiers of cell phone devices), user data of email accounts, access logs, the list of places saved in Google Maps, the history of location and travels of these people, search history, and photos stored on the cloud from the last 30 days. The lower court judge agreed to only part of the request and authorized the breach of confidentiality of subscriber data, places saved in Google Maps, and of the location and travel history of the past 30 days from all unspecified users who had been in those surroundings. Google did not settle and filed a writ of mandamus in the São Paulo Court of Justice but only got a reduction of the order's scope. Still not settling, it took the case to the Superior Court of Justice. Only then, through a preliminary injunction, the order was revoked.[24]

The only parameters to handing over location data that do exist in Brazilian law were added to the Code of Criminal Procedure (CCP) in December 2016 and are very specific in their application. The new Article 13-B determines that

> if necessary to the prevention and the repression of the crimes related to human trafficking, the member of the Public Prosecutor's Office or the Chief of Police may request, upon a court order, for the telecommunication and/or telematic service providers to make available the adequate technical means—such as signals, information and others—that allow the location of the victim or of the suspects of the ongoing criminal act.

In the details, however, the wording of the provision has ambiguities that might allow abuses, such as: (i) the *caput* to article 13-B mentions "crimes related to human trafficking" without expressly indicating to which criminal types it is referring, and (ii) the same article also mentions "technical means" that enable the location of people ("signals, information and others") without specifying which would be the "information" or what should be understood by "others." Given the generic language of the law, it seems that any means are acceptable in order to achieve the end of locating someone—only the breach of secrecy of communication content would not be lawful, requiring a specific authorization.[25] According to Article 13-B § 2, the "signal" or the positioning of station of coverage, sectorization, and intensity of radio frequency should be provided to law enforcement authorities for a period no longer than 30 days (item II), renewable for an equal period. In a rather confusing wording, item III of the same paragraph sets forth that "for superior periods [than which item II addresses], a court order is necessary." The ambiguous language of the item could be maliciously exploited to support the interpretation that a court order would not be necessary for an inferior period, which contradicts the procedures established in the main section.

In January 2017, the ACEL proposed a direct action of unconstitutionality (ADI 5642) against these provisions, for violating Article 5, Items X and XII of the Constitution (Macedo and Coutinho 2017). It is unforeseeable when the Supreme Federal Court will rule on the matter.

Conclusion

The regulation of real-time interception of long-distance communications and of installation of bugging devices is a landmark in surveillance law in many countries. Brazil is no exception to that with its Law of Interceptions. The usage of telephony and phones themselves has, however, drastically changed since the enactment of such legislation in 1996.

Mobile phones, owned by the great majority of Brazilian citizens, are today a treasure trove of communications information and thus of valuable evidence to law enforcement. They are not used anymore just for calling. They store huge amounts of personal information we voluntarily produce (our texts, photos, notes, songs, contact's list, call's history). They also allow their holders to use Internet services through apps or browsers, which also produce and store data either on the device or in other locations. However, they are also constantly generating other kinds of information, such as location data, covertly for their own functioning.

Brazil, however, lacks a strong framework that establishes limits for law enforcement access to communications content and metadata stored on phones. This means that while the "smartphone revolution" represents a milestone in terms of access to knowledge and communications in Brazil, it also exposes Brazilian smartphone-using citizens to greater and more invasive surveillance due to outdated laws, loopholes, and surveillance-friendly case law. Rethinking this legal framework is key to safeguarding individual freedoms and avoiding the shrinking of civic space in a (smartphone) connected society.

Notes

1 The term "Law of Interceptions" is preferable here rather than "Wiretap Law" because it is more general. In some court decisions, judges have interpreted the term very broadly, encompassing different surveillance practices.
2 In Brazil, on average, more than 20,000 telephone lines are intercepted per month (Abreu and Antonialli 2017).
3 The term "breach of secrecy" is used in Brazil in a broad sense to refer to any act of disclosure (following subpoenas or court orders or any type of request or turning over of data) of any kind of information related to communications (user account information, metadata or content). In the particular case regarding the interpretation of Article 5, Subsection XII of the Constitution, it specifically refers to any interception procedure that breaches the secrecy of communications.
4 In the trial of Recurso Extraordinário 418.416–8/SC, of 10/May/2006, the case reported by the Justice Sepúlveda Pertence states that protection under Subsection XII of Article 5 does not refer to information transmitted in correspondence, telegraphic messages, data and telephone calls in itself but rather to communications in transit, to the flow of communications as they occur. Implicitly, the decision excludes application of the exception set forth in Subsection XII to Article 5 to data flow.
5 In habeas corpus 70814/SP (Case reported by the Justice Celso de Mello, tried on 1 Mar. 2004), for instance, the Federal Supreme Court accepted that a correctional administration may intercept an inmate's written correspondence for reasons of public safety, correctional discipline, or preservation of legal order with a basis in the sole paragraph of Article 41, of Law no. 7210/84, Criminal Corrections Law, which limits inmates' right "to have contact with the outside world through written correspondence" (Article 41, XV of the same law). If correspondence in transit were inviolable, to be coherent, the Court would have to have held this provision unconstitutional.
6 Brazilian Internet Civil Rights Framework, art 7, III.
7 Ibid., art 10 § 2.
8 SUPERIOR COURT OF JUSTICE. Appeal in Habeas Corpus no. 75.800-PR. Justice Felix Fischer, tried on 15.09.2016. Available at: http://www.internetlab.org.br/wp-content/uploads/2016/11/lavajato.pdf.
9 SUPERIOR FEDERAL COURT. Habeas Corpus no. 91.867/SP. Rap. judge Gilmar Mendes, tried. 24.04.2012.
10 SUPERIOR COURT OF JUSTICE. Habeas Corpus no. 66.368/PA. Rap. judge Gilson Dipp, 5th panel, tried on 05.06.2007.
11 SUPERIOR COURT OF JUSTICE. Ordinary appeal in Habeas Corpus n. 51.531/RO. Rap. judge Nefi Cordeiro. 6th Panel, tried on 19.04.2016.
12 PARANÁ COURT OF JUSTICE. Habeas Corpus no. 1547585–9/PR. Rap. Maria José de Toledo Marcondes Teixeira. 5th Criminal Court, tried on 14.07.2016.
13 RIO DE JANEIRO COURT OF JUSTICE. Criminal Appeal 01963693720158190001 RJ. Rap. Marcus Henrique Pinto Basílio, 1st Criminal Court, tried on 17.05.2016.
14 ESPÍRITO SANTO COURT OF JUSTICE. Apelação Criminal 00070812320148080030. Rap. Sérgio Luiz Teixeira Gama, 2nd Criminal Court, tried on 24.02.2016.
15 DISTRITO FEDERAL AND TERRITORY COURT OF JUSTICE. Criminal Appeal no. 20150110776509 0023326–92.2015.8.07.0001. Rap. João Timóteo de Oliveira, 2nd Criminal Panel, tried on 03.11.2016.
16 "Provas obtidas em celular de preso em flagrante são ilícitas", *Consultor Jurídico*, September 26, 2015, available at http://www.conjur.com.br/2015-set-26/provas-obtidas-celular-preso-flagrante-sao-ilicitas.
17 "Policiais causam anulação de provas por vasculharem WhatsApp sem autorização", *Consultor Jurídico*, March 10, 2017, available at http://www.conjur.com.br/2017-mar-10/policiais-vasculham-whatsapp-autorizacao-invalidam-provas. Accessed on May 5, 2017.
18 Brazilian Constitution, art. 5, items X and XII.

19 FEDERAL REGIONAL COURT OF THE 3rd DISTRICT. Appeal/Necessary Reassessment no. 0000108–56.2013.4.03.6110/SP. Rap. judge Johonson di Salvo, tried on 03.03.2016. Available at: http://web.trf3.jus.br/acordaos/Acordao/BuscarDocumentoGedpro/4976979. Accessed on 17.01.2017. The decision modified the lower court sentence in favor of Claro.

20 ACEL's motion and examples of notices received by operators based on that (interpretation of the) law may be found at "Operadoras reclamam de pedidos de delegados para quebra de sigilo telefônico", *Consultor Jurídico*, October 29, 2014, available at http://www.conjur.com.br/2014-out-29/telefonicas-reclamam-quebras-sigilo-pedidas-delegados.

21 SÃO PAULO COURT OF JUSTICE. Interlocutory Appeal no. 2150710–76.2015.8.26.0000. Appellant: Google Brasil Internet Ltda.; Appellee: Tim Celular S.A. Rapporteur judge. Alexandre Marcondes, tried on 31.08.2015, understanding that information on logical ports used on the access to Internet is proper of connection providers.

22 SÃO PAULO COURT OF JUSTICE. Interlocutory Appeal no. 2206954–25.2015.8.26.0000. Appellant: Google Brasil Internet Ltda.; Appellee: Itaú Unibanco S. A. Rapporteur judge Paulo Alcides, tried on 12.05.2016, determining that the application provider informs the logical port of origin.

23 COURT OF JUSTICE OF RIO GRANDE DO SUL. Agravo de Instrumento no. 70018683508, Appeals Court Judge Maria Berenice Dias, tried July 28, 2007. Available at: http://jus.com.br/jurisprudencia/16757/tjrs-authoriza-interceptacao-telefonica-para-localizar-devedor-de-alimentos Accessed on June 17, 2015.

24 SUPERIOR COURT OF JUSTICE. Pedido de Tutela Provisória nº 292-SP (2017-0034057-6), Justice Antonio Saldanha Palheiro, tried on February 24, 2017. Available at: http://www.internetlab.org.br/wp-content/uploads/2017/03/GooglevsMPSPnoSTJ_quebrageneralizadadesigilodelocalizacao.pdf.

25 Code of Criminal Procedure, art. 13-B, § 2º, I.

References

Abreu, Jacquelinede Souza. 2016. "From Jurisdictional Battles to Crypto Wars: Brazilian Courts v. WhatsApp." *Columbia Journal of Transnational Law Online Edition*. October 17. http://jtl.columbia.edu/from-jurisdictional-battles-to-crypto-wars-brazilian-courts-v-whatsapp/.

Abreu, Jacquelinede Souza. 2017. "Public Hearing on Encryption and WhatsApp Blockages: The Arguments before the STF." *Bloqueios.info*. June 26. http://bloqueios.info/en/public-hearing-on-encryption-and-whatsapp-blockages-the-arguments-before-the-stf/.

Abreu, Jacquelinede Souza, and Dennys Antonialli. 2016. "State Surveillance of Communications in Brazil FAQ." *Necessary and Proportionate*. July 7. https://necessaryandproportionate.org/state-surveillance-communications-brazil-faq.

Abreu, Jacquelinede Souza, and Dennys Antonialli. 2017. "State Surveillance of Communications in Brazil." July 13. www.internetlab.org.br/en/biblioteca. Agência Nacional de Telecomunicações. 2016. *Relatório Anual ANATEL 2016*. Agência Nacional de Telecomunicações.

Antonialli, Dennys, Francisco Brito Cruz, and Mariana Giorgetti Valente. 2016. "Smartphones: Treasure Chests of the Lava-Jato Investigation." *InternetLab*. November 24. http://www.internetlab.org.br/en/opinion/smartphones-treasure-chests-of-the-lava-jato-investigation/.

Aras, Vladimir. 2012. "A Investigação Criminal Na Nova Lei de Lavagem de Dinheiro." *Boletim IBCCRIM* 237, August. https://www.ibccrim.org.br/boletim_artigo/4671-A-investigao-criminal-na-nova-lei-de-lavagem-de-dinheiro.

Barreto, Alesandro Gonçalves, and Everton Ferreira de Almeida Férrer. 2016. "Perícia Em Celular: Necessidade de Autorização Judicial?" *Direito & TI*, June. http://direitoeti.com.br/artigos/pericia-em-celular-necessidade-de-autorizacao-judicial/.

Barros, Paula Pécora. 2016. "ADPF 403 in STF: Are WhatsApp Blockings Constitutional?" *Bloqueios.info*. November 21. http://bloqueios.info/en/adpf-403-in-stf-are-whatsapp-blockings-constitutional/.

Brito Cruz, Francisco. 2016. "Comentário, Porta Lógica E Provedores de Aplicação." June 1. http://omci.org.br/jurisprudencia/99/porta-logica-e-provedores-de-aplicacao/.

Comitê Gestor da Internet no Brasil. 2011. *TIC Domicílios E Empresas 2010 – Pesquisa Sobre O Uso Das Tecnologias de Informação E Comunicação No Brasil*. São Paulo: Comitê Gestor da Internet no Brasil. http://www.cetic.br/media/docs/publicacoes/2/tic-domicilios-e-empresas-2010.pdf.

Comitê Gestor da Internet no Brasil. 2012. *TIC Domicílios E Empresas 2011 – Pesquisa Sobre O Uso Das Tecnologias de Informação E Comunicação No Brasil*. São Paulo: Comitê Gestor da Internet no Brasil. http://www.cetic.br/media/docs/publicacoes/2/tic-domicilios-e-empresas-2011.pdf.

Comitê Gestor da Internet no Brasil. 2013. *TIC Domicílios E Empresas 2012 – Pesquisa Sobre O Uso Das Tecnologias de Informação E Comunicação No Brasil*. São Paulo: Comitê Gestor da Internet no Brasil. http://www.cetic.br/media/docs/publicacoes/2/tic-domicilios-e-empresas-2012.pdf.

Comitê Gestor da Internet no Brasil. 2014. *TIC Domicílios E Empresas 2013 – Pesquisa Sobre O Uso Das Tecnologias de Informação E Comunicação No Brasil*. São Paulo: Comitê Gestor da Internet no Brasil. http://www.cetic.br/media/docs/publicacoes/2/TIC_DOM_EMP_2013_livro_eletronico.pdf.

Comitê Gestor da Internet no Brasil. 2015. *TIC Domicílios E Empresas 2014 – Pesquisa Sobre O Uso Das Tecnologias de Informação E Comunicação No Brasil*. São Paulo: Comitê Gestor da Internet no Brasil. http://www.cetic.br/media/docs/publicacoes/2/TIC_Domicilios_2014_livro_eletronico.pdf.

Comitê Gestor da Internet no Brasil. 2016. *TIC Domicílios E Empresas 2015 – Pesquisa Sobre O Uso Das Tecnologias de Informação E Comunicação No Brasil*. São Paulo: Comitê Gestor da Internet no Brasil. http://www.cetic.br/media/docs/publicacoes/2/TIC_Domicilios_2014_livro_eletronico.pdf.

Datafolha. 2016. "Hábitos de Uso de Aplicativos, População Brasileira, 13 Anos Ou Mais." *Datafolha*. http://media.folha.uol.com.br/datafolha/2017/01/27/da39a3ee5e6b4b0d3255bfef95601890afd80709.pdf.

Ferraz Junior, Tercio Sampaio. 1993. "Sigilo de Dados: O Direito à Privacidade and Os Limites Da Função Fiscalizadora Do Estado." *Revista Da Faculdade de Direito Da Universidade de São Paulo* 88: 439–459.

Ferreira Filho, ManoelGonçalves. 2009. *Curso de Direito Constitucional*. 35th ed. São Paulo: Saraiva.

IBOPE Inteligência. 2016. "Usuários de Smartphones No Brasil Duplicam Em Dois Anos." *Notícias & Pesquisas IBOPE Inteligência*. August 29. http://www.ibopeinteligencia.com/noticias-e-pesquisas/usuarios-de-smartphones-no-brasil-duplicam-em-dois-anos/.

Lopes, Marcelo Frullani. 2016. "Entrave Tecnológico Provoca Impasse Sobre O Marco Civil E Anonimato." *Consultor Jurídico*. December 17. http://www.conjur.com.br/2016-dez-17/entrave-tecnologico-provoca-impasse-marco-civil-anonimato.

Macedo, Fausto, and Mateus Coutinho. 2017. "Operadoras de Celular Vão Ao Supremo Contra Lei Que Obriga Repasse de Dados a Delegados E Promotores." *O Estado de São Paulo*. January 25. http://politica.estadao.com.br/blogs/fausto-macedo/operadoras-de-celular-vao-ao-supremo-contra-lei-que-obriga-repasse-de-dados-a-delegados-e-promotores/.

Maranhão, Juliano. 2016. "O Acesso Ao WhatsApp Pela Operação Lava Jato." *Jota*. May 12. http://jota.info/artigos/o-acesso-ao-whatsapp-pela-operacao-lava-jato-05122016.

Mendes, Gilmar Ferreira, and Jurandi Borges Pinheiro. 2015. "Interceptações E Privacidade: Novas Tecnologias E a Constituição." In *Direito, Inovação E Tecnologia* Vol. 1, edited by Gilmar Ferreira Mendes and Ingo Wolfgang Sarlet. São Paulo: Saraiva.

Neves, Mauríciodos Santos. 2002. "O Setor de Telecomunicações." In *BNDES 50 Anos: Histórias Setoriais*, edited by Elizabeth Maria de São Paulo and Jorge Kalache Filho, 216–233. BNDES.

Opice Blum, Renato. 2016. "Portas Lógicas de Origem: Identificação E Caos Jurídico." *Jota*. October 26. http://jota.info/artigos/direito-digital-portas-logicas-de-origem-dificuldade-de-identificacao-e-o-caos-juridico-26102016.

Poushter, Jacob. 2016. "Smartphone Ownership and Internet Usage Continues to Climb in Emerging Economies." *Pew Research Center's Global Attitudes Project*. February 22. http://www.pewglobal.org/2016/02/22/smartphone-ownership-and-internet-usage-continues-to-climb-in-emerging-economies/.

Sidi, Ricardo. 2015. "A Interceptação de E-Mails E a Apreensão Física de E-Mails Armazenados." *Revista Fórum de Ciências Criminais* 4 (December): 101–121.

Silva, José Afonso. 2008. *Curso de Direito Constitucional Positivo*. 32nd ed. São Paulo: Malheiros Editores.

PART III

Social Change and Economic Opportunities

Social Change, Economic Opportunities, and Mobile Technologies

Stefanie Felsberger

Mobile technologies enable a different creation, sharing, and dissemination of culture and knowledge. These technologies have been used in social movements and have been entangled in profound changes in societies in different countries around the globe. Simultaneously, mobile technologies have been sites of innovation and their centrality to the sharing economy or gig economy cannot be overstated: mobile technologies have been at the center of disruptions to social and economic practices and structures. This has meant economic opportunities for some and grappling with social changes for others. A book on mobile technologies and the social transformations that occur in their wake cannot be complete without a part specifically addressing these transformations.

This final part analyses the ways in which the intersection between mobile technologies and access to knowledge can lead to social and economic opportunities but also questions the conditions under which these opportunities are realized and by whom. The chapters in this part also investigate the often-repeated claims that mobile technologies enable economic growth and positive social change. The authors provide analyses from the ground up of how such claims hold up against realities on the ground and show that context matters.

The three chapters analyze a range of social and economic changes and their entanglements with mobile technologies and access to knowledge. Colin Agur focuses on the use of mobile telephones and social media in the so-called "Umbrella Movement" of Hong Kong, a semi-autonomous territory of the Republic of China. Shubha Gokhale takes us to South Korea and analyses the train of events that led to the impeachment of President Park Geun-Hye for corruption. Gokhale traces the unfolding of the scandal and the government's efforts to censor news and curb the spread of information that accompany it. However, she shows that citizens responded by using mobile social media to spread news and awareness, plan and organize protests. Nagla Rizk looks at another extremely consequential social change that has occurred within the past decade: the advent of the "gig economy." Rizk studies the ride-sharing company Uber, which was founded in 2009. Within ten years, Uber expanded to over 600 cities spread over 65 countries and has been described as one of the most disruptive companies in the world. Rizk looks at Egypt where Uber was the country's first ride-sharing service offered in 2014.

Social media and mobile technologies have played crucial roles in protest movements in the last decades. Agur demonstrates the roots of Hong Kong's protest movement to September 1994 and similarly shows that the protests in Hong Kong did not erupt randomly. They can be traced back to the organizers of "Occupy Central with Love and Peace" (OCLP) who tested how social media could be used to plan actions and strategies some 18 months prior to the protests. Agur thus demonstrates that mobile technologies do not make a protest movement; people who make use of mobile technologies do. Gokhale takes a similar approach and provides an analysis of *how* activists and citizens in South Korea made use of social media and phones to spread information about corruption and protests. Neither of the chapters assumes an automatic connection between the introduction of mobile technologies and the emergence or unfolding of protest movements. In her chapter on Egypt, Rizk traces the unfolding of another monumental social change: the transformation of transportation. The chapter analyzes the legislative response to the emergence of ride-sharing applications in the country and discusses the effects of this legislative response on the different stakeholders in the transportation sector in Egypt from an A2K perspective. The chapter addresses both the social changes and economic opportunities that have arisen from how ride-sharing companies have made use of mobile technologies.

9

HONG KONG AND THE UMBRELLA MOVEMENT

Mobile Social Media, Activism, and Social Change

Colin Agur

Introduction

Hong Kong, a former British colony returned to China in 1997, is a "Special Administrative Region" of the People's Republic. The territory's semi-autonomous local government defers to the Central People's Government in Beijing on certain high-level diplomatic, security, and judicial matters. In the fall of 2014, after a decision by the Central Government blocked Hong Kongers from directly electing their own chief executive, protests erupted in the city streets. Before protestors took to the streets, starting as early as 18 months before, the organizers of the original Occupy Central with Love and Peace (OCLP) movement used social media as a tool for deliberative democracy to pressure the Hong Kong government on electoral reform. Strategies included public consultations, soliciting opinions online, and an informal "civil referendum" in which nearly a million people voted to proceed with a physical occupation movement in the streets. This non-binding, unofficial vote was seen by Beijing authorities as influential enough to merit a response of formal denunciations from Chinese state media and sustained cyber-attacks from hackers aligned with the mainland Chinese government.

This infrastructure of digital deliberative mechanisms was designed to lay the groundwork for a protest movement in the streets, which was not initially expected to draw major support or have a major impact on the civic life of Hong Kong. These platforms continued to operate after the largely spontaneous mass physical occupation of protest sites in central Hong Kong began in September of 2014, spurred by the Beijing Central Government's decision to limit promised direct elections for Hong Kong's chief executive and the subsequent use of tear gas by police to disperse a growing crowd of protesters. Compared to previous political demonstrations in Hong Kong, the Umbrella Movement was unprecedented in its scale and degree of contentiousness. It matched a significant digital discourse with physical protest encampments in two prominent locations: Admiralty (in the heart of Hong Kong Island's central business district) and Mong Kok (a densely populated working-class area on the Kowloon Peninsula).

In these events, social media played a major role in public deliberation about Hong Kong's political system. Activists drove debate on a range of issues in Hong Kong society, including inequality, job prospects, and political reform, taking to social media to communicate supporters, adversaries, and the local and global press. For several months in fall 2014, the Umbrella Movement commanded the attention of the eight million residents of Hong Kong, opposing forces in the Hong Kong Legislative Council, and in Mainland China, reporters (local and foreign) covering the events, and much of the surrounding region, which watched to see how the Beijing government would react to unrest in a territory whose autonomy it had guaranteed under treaty with the British government.

Literature review

The Umbrella Movement took place after a decade of scholarly efforts to understand the role and significance of social media in large-scale protests. One of the important shifts this chapter emphasizes is the migration of social media onto mobile devices. This change has brought a dramatic increase in the volume of user-generated content, as well as heightened scrutiny of actions by protesters and police. As scholars have noted in studies of several other protest movements, mobile social media have taken on significant roles for protesters, authorities, and reporters covering the action.

In their seminal work conceptualizing connected action, Bennet and Segerberg (2013) emphasize the importance of individuals sharing "personal frames" as part of a larger, kaleidoscopic movement. Importantly, they develop the concept of "power signatures" to explain "the degree to which recognition (prestige and influence) is concentrated or dispersed among actors in a network" (Bennet and Segerberg 2013, 152). They also outline a perennial challenge for protest movements: sustaining initial enthusiasm over time. Writing about Occupy Wall Street, they note that "fundamentally different ideals and ideologies of organisation and action" arose over online communication strategies (Bennet and Segerberg 2013, 200). For Evgeny Morozov (2009), social media pose a threat to social movements in the form of "slacktivism." This involves online activity that satisfies individuals' urges to speak their mind but does not translate into real-world outcomes. Questions about online and offline activism have a particular significance for authoritarian regimes, and the work of Philip Howard and Muzammil M. Hussain emphasizes that even in repressive contexts, social media and mobile communication can "alter the capacity of citizens and civil society actors to affect domestic politics" (2013, 66). In the protests Howard and Hussain studied, mobile communication proved to be especially important; activists could follow events and post content from any location. The mobile aspect of social media had the effects of allowing more participants to be in constant touch, speeding up replies, and creating new sources and content for news reporting (Belair-Gagnon et al. 2017, 2018). Zeynep Tufekci's (2017) book on the power and fragility of networked protest offers a more recent exploration of mobile communication in the context of protest movements. She explores the differentiated movements of the Arab Spring, Occupy Wall Street, and Gezi Park. Drawing on her studies of these movements, she finds that "[n]etworked protests have strengths and weaknesses that combine in novel ways and do not neatly conform to our understandings of the trajectory of protest movements before the advent of digital technologies" (2017, xxiii). This quote sums up what many scholars seek to understand about the role of social media and mobile communication in protest movements.

Methodology

This chapter explores the political significance of mobile social media in Hong Kong by interviewing a range of participants in the debates—online and on social media—centered on changes to elections for Hong Kong's Chief Executive. The interviews and analysis emphasize the complex interdependency of different social media platforms and apps and seek to understand both the relationships among types of social media and relationships between social media and the politics of Hong Kong. The chapter explores the ways participants used a range of social media platforms (Facebook, Twitter, Firechat, Snapchat, WhatsApp, WeChat, Telegram, and others) on mobile devices. It seeks to understand how participants used these platforms to interact with other participants in the debates and to convey digital narratives (in text, photo, and video formats) to audiences in Hong Kong and around the world. The mobile nature of these platforms is important. Even more so than in previous instances of political unrest (e.g. Howard and Hussain 2013), the Umbrella Movement depended on mobile devices to connect users in physically separate protest sites and coordinate the leadership team's media efforts. Similarly, reporters covering the Umbrella Movement made active and imaginative use of mobile technology to document events, share content in real-time with fellow reporters and editors, and verify user-generated content. Focusing on these mobile elements of social media usage, this chapter identifies patterns of usage as well as the degree and type of influence exercised by actors and analyzes (on each platform and collectively) the dynamics between different participant groups.

This study is distinct in several ways. It pays particular attention to mobile digital platforms, examining those used (WhatsApp and Facebook) during the Umbrella Movement, while also discussing other mobile platforms (WeChat, Firechat, and others) that played roles in the protests. It examines the places where most of the (online) discussions occurred, including semi-public venues like Facebook, as well as private chat groups. It also highlights the importance of protest leaders in the Umbrella Movement's communication on social media. Whereas many studies emphasize "leaderless" social movements (e.g. Castells 2012; Boler et al. 2014; Western 2014), the Umbrella Movement had visible leaders who played critical roles on social media, had distinct public personae on social media, and in some cases were "native" to social media. Methodologically, this study's use of in-depth interviews builds on studies that have used focus groups (Lee and Ting 2015), telephone interviews (Lee, So, and Leung 2015), and online surveys (Lee and Chan 2016).

This project is based on 40 in-depth interviews (in English, Cantonese, and Mandarin) with key participants in the protests, conducted in July–August 2015 and January 2016. Interviewees include leaders of Occupy Central, Scholarism (a prominent student activist group), and other groups: anti-Occupy organizations; reporters who covered the protests using social media; and local programmers, researchers, and journalists who have been archiving, mining, and visualizing data about the debates. This source base also includes regular monitoring of social media accounts and chat groups run by various organizations active in the protest movement and regular conversation with ordinary Hong Kongers who participated in but did not lead the movement, as well as routine consultation of their social media feeds.

Drawing on interview transcripts, this chapter identifies the ways that participants used social media to mobilize, organize, and persuade. Broadly speaking, Scholarism and local university students used Facebook, chat apps, and, more rarely, email. Occupy Central with Love and Peace (Benny Tai) were more responsive on email and initially emphasized traditional media such as newspaper columns, but they adapted to the media needed to reach younger protesters and built a savvy multi-platform media operation. Meanwhile, journalists from legacy media found their way to younger people like Joshua Wong, once they became key players in the main news narrative. Legacy media operations, especially those identified with centrist or pro-Occupy positions (*Ming Pao Daily News; Apple Daily*), built out robust social media operations. For example, *Apple Daily* specialized in viral memes. Also, the pro-government side eventually began adapting digital-first messaging tactics; thus, over the course of the protests, all actors gained some proficiency across platforms.

Unity and fragmentation on mobile chat apps: analysis of the Umbrella Movement

The Umbrella Movement encompassed several citizen protest movements and groups (including Occupy Central with Love and Peace (OCLP), Scholarism, and the Hong Kong Federation of Students) that became influential actors in protests occupying areas of central Hong Kong in 2014. Before the movement began, all major actors maintained some presence on Facebook (in the forms of personal pages, and professional individual and institutional pages for general communications) and WhatsApp (for targeted group and individual communications). This pre-existing use of social media was most pronounced among younger protesters (interviews with Nathan Law; Yvonne Leung) but also true of older academics and lawyers prominent in the lead-up to the protests. Before the protests, starting in early 2013, OCLP publicized and solicited public participation in a long process of public consultation to decide on the course of the movement. Strategies included public consultations, soliciting opinions online, and an informal "civil referendum" on political reform in which nearly a million Hong Kongers voted. This non-binding, unofficial vote was seen by Beijing authorities as influential enough to merit formal denunciations from Chinese state media and sustained cyber-attacks from hackers aligned with the mainland Chinese government.

As the protests started and evolved, participants experimented with numerous new tools. These included Firechat (briefly popular during rumors of mass signal outage due to its Bluetooth mesh connectivity but then rarely used in practice), Telegram (a chat app similar to WhatsApp but with more robust security features, which came to be widely adopted), Twitter (largely restricted to foreign correspondents and locals interacting with global press), and WeChat (a user-friendly chat app popular with many consumers worldwide but created by a mainland Chinese firm and thus seen as more exposed to Beijing's media control and security apparatus; WeChat was more widely used by Hong Kong citizens unsympathetic to the Umbrella Movement and more supportive of the local government and central government in Beijing).

Facebook was the default public medium for most activists on all sides (interviews by author with Po Chun Chung; Patrick Kao; Colman Li; Joshua Wong). The platform already has high penetration in Hong Kong, meaning that breaking news of social disruptions (from both news sources and affected individuals sharing their experiences) often first got to Hong Kong news consumers through their Facebook timelines. Many protest groups, especially those with younger, student-oriented constituencies and leadership, generally released statements and news on Facebook by default and only later or never by email and other legacy media.

Chat apps, mostly WhatsApp, are used by many Hong Kongers to communicate with small chat groups of users from family, school, and other real-life social institutions (interview by author with BBC journalist). "My boyfriend's family is [pro-government]," explained a BBC journalist who is a Hong Kong native. "My friends supported the protest, but I often saw pro-government points of view due to my boyfriend's family chat group" (interview by author with BBC journalist). When the protests began, pre-existing chat groups with no prior political function (e.g., a group of school alumni) were often taken over by political news and debates. Activists, meanwhile, created new special-purpose groups to mobilize supporters and inform the media. Concerns over data security led protest leaders to start using Telegram for operationally sensitive discussions, with the best practice guidelines dictating that the most sensitive deliberations conducted in person with phones stored in another location to deter surveillance (interviews by author with Joshua Wong; Colman Li; Yvonne Leung; Taurus Yip). While protest leaders made efforts to establish best practices for information security among protesters, observance was uneven.

Interviewees showed a strong preference for specific social media platforms, often to the exclusion of other, more conventional ones. Protest leaders, especially younger ones, prioritized Facebook and chat apps, rarely or never getting around to using email or Twitter. They felt more urgency in using media that reached to their immediate surroundings and did not craft a systematic legacy media communications strategy (emails, press releases, phone calls) to reach out to global media, most of whom were already physically located in Hong Kong and easily contacted en masse using dedicated WhatsApp groups for media. At the moment of mobilization, a social media discourse that was previously mainly limited to politically committed netizens and perennial protest figures shifted to a broader section of the population, making an unprecedented impact on Hong Kong's urban and media landscapes.

To press their case, protesters often created viral content, with eye-catching graphics and catchy slogans, designed to create momentum around a particular interpretation of events. These were designed to be easily shareable on Facebook and WhatsApp (to reach immediate participants, mostly younger) and shape a narrative that was often later echoed by legacy media outlets (which reach older audiences) (interview by author with Joshua WONG). Protesters also used social media to fight back against perceived mainstream media misinterpretations or misrepresentations of protest actions and motives (e.g., disowning the actions of a radical splinter group of protesters who used violent methods to break into a government building) (interview by author with Vincent LAU and Gilbert WAT). As a majority of older Hong Kongers were skeptical of the protesters' relative youth and civil disobedience methods, younger protest leaders made special efforts to shape legacy media coverage in the aftermath of incidents seen as reputationally damaging to the protests' image of nonviolent resistance. While dedicated social media teams affiliated with protest leadership centers often created this content, individual protestors without a leading role sometimes created popular viral content as well, in some cases becoming leading despite their pre-protest anonymity.

For most interviewees, time was a major factor in their participation. Since social media is produced on a different metabolism from most mainstream and legacy media, the ebbs and flows of social media follow those of participants' schedules. Many interviewees spoke about the importance of late-night (9pm onward) posts on WhatsApp, Telegram, WeChat, and Facebook and the comparative unimportance of early-morning posts (interview by author with Kin-man CHAN; Colman LI). Two interviewees pointed out that a power law developed among participants, with a significant percentage of the most forwarded and favorite content originating with a relatively small number of participants. When, for example, a group of these major players had dinner together and put away their smartphones, social media activity declined sharply. As one interviewee said, "there was exactly as much happening on the street as usual, so there was no real drop off in news. The only difference was that there was less happening online" (interview by author with Christian POON; Kris CHENG). This moment personifies Tufekci's (2017) observation about the fragility of networked social movements. The same technology that allows physically disperse users to communicate and share content in real time can also leave observers wondering if a movement has faltered, when all that happened was a dinner party involving a dozen key communicators. In the streets, the physical encampments remained unaffected, with their tents, banners, and occupants there as before. But for observers and participants not present—and dependent on social media for updates—it was easy to gain the impression that a lull in communication meant a weakening of the movement itself. Reflecting on Morozov's (2009) "slacktivism" argument, this event also shows the vulnerability of networked protests to supporters who are not physically present and whose contributions are exclusive to posts on social media.

Before and during the occupation, many average Hong Kongers were cautiously sympathetic to the political aims of the protests but dubious of their methods and of the advisability of using this form of public pressure against a local government ultimately answerable to the Central People's Government in Beijing. Protest leaders spent considerable effort attempting to shape a sympathetic media narrative to counter the government's negative portrayal of the protests, crafting statements posted to Facebook and creating viral memes that would resonate sympathetically with average Hong Kongers not active in the protests. A series of semi-private chat app groups in various languages gave the protest leaders immediate access to local and foreign reporters, while viral social media content was created to rally sympathizers and, to a lesser extent, persuade the unconvinced.

The question of time factored into the success and failure of the movement. Initially, the speed of social media favored the protesters: they were able to coordinate and mobilize the movement and (at least briefly) achieve considerable unity. But as time wore on, the speed of social media often worked against a unified protest movement; members of Occupy said they spent a significant amount of time *reacting* to social media and dispelling rumors and counter-arguments (interview by author with Alan LAI; Colman LI). This is in keeping with what Bennet and Segerberg (2013) found in their study of Occupy Wall Street. Networked collective action allows for a wide set of inputs by a wide set of users; this democratization can similarly lead to divergence in how a social movement should govern itself and pursue shared goals. While the Umbrella Movement was a more hierarchical movement than the famously "leaderless" Occupy Wall Street protest, this point is important. Over time, leaders of large-scale networked protests, especially those that make active use of mobile devices and networks, often find that the resulting cacophony of voices is difficult to unify. Conversely, opponents of these movements find that, over time, factions emerge amid the pluralism of the movement and the resulting divisions can be exploited.

Interviewees also emphasized the spatial characteristics of the debate. Very quickly, a local conversation went global, as overseas Hong Kong citizens, journalists, and others took an interest in what was happening. Some interviewees, especially those with considerable overseas experience and language skills, said they spent a significant amount of communication aimed at foreign audiences (interview by author with Kin-man CHAN; Christian POON; *Wall Street Journal* reporter). Several pointed out the importance of certain media spaces (e.g. Twitter) and practices (e.g. writing in English) in attracting scrutiny by international media, activists, and governments (interview by author with *Wall Street Journal* reporter; Kin-man CHAN). At the same time as the debate involved people around the world, it also took on hyper-local characteristics, which were unprecedented in Hong Kong's history of civil contention (interview by author with Vincent LAU 2015; Gilbert WAT 2015). This included high levels of linguistic and cultural specificity and local dialect and character usage that created a strand of discourse opaque not merely to English-speakers but to many Mandarin-speakers as well. In the context of Hong Kong's uncensored digital space, a robust local discourse emerged, asserting a local Hong Kong identity separate from mainland China. Even for Hong Kongers not persuaded by the movement's political objectives or protest tactics, this organic emergence of locally particularistic discourse, which relied on specialized local dialect characters, elaborate puns, and other cultural insider references, became a powerful assertion of a particular local Hong Kong identity, underscoring political and cultural separation from mainland China. Critically, this scale of local discourse was unprecedented in local legacy media, especially print media, which favors prestige Mandarin-influenced writing and makes only limited use of Cantonese dialect. Cultural defiance and contention online thus matched civil disobedience in the streets (Frisch et al., 2017).

The debate was also fractured by a split *among* social media platforms and mobile apps. Several interviewees who had been active in the Occupy movement described social media discussions as silos or echo chambers (interview by author with Vincent LAU; Gilbert WAT; Robert CHOW). Much of the conversation reinforced in-group bonds by "rallying the troops" but did little to persuade those beyond the group. As the movement wore on, the social media discourse became more chaotic, especially compared to the relative tidiness of the discourse on legacy media (interview with Benny TAI; Robert CHOW). Leaders of the Occupy movement, such as its founder and figurehead Benny Tai, said that on social media it was difficult to sustain unity beyond an initial rallying cry and mobilization (interview by author with Benny TAI; Kin-Man CHAN; Vincent LAU; Gilbert WAT; Robert CHOW). At the beginning of the protests, prominent opponents of the movement, such as Robert Chow, often advanced their favored narratives, unflattering to the protesters, through legacy media; as the protests continued and the media landscape evolved, however, more media-savvy opponents like Chow planned, created, and promoted new social media channels for anti-protest content that traveled outside legacy media, meeting protesters on their own digital turf.

The pluralistic and, over time, increasingly fragmented nature of the Umbrella Movement's social media presence also provided both a challenge and an opportunity for journalists covering the protests. As Belair-Gagnon et al. (2017) found, mobile tools such as chat apps allowed both small reporting teams and large-scale news organizations to cover the protests in more detail, at greater speed, and with a wider variety of multimedia content. This builds on the point by Bennet and Segerberg (2013) that, over time, social movements develop a divergent set of ideas and ideologies on how to achieve their goals (even if those end goals are shared). The resulting diversity in communication on social media—heightened by divergent experiences of participants in different places, surrounded by different sub-groups—can lead to reporting that emphasizes the kaleidoscopic nature of the movement. This coverage can, in turn, heighten a sense of disunity in the movement and magnify otherwise small differences among factions. The leaders of the Umbrella Movement sought to be seen as legitimate not only on friendly social media outlets but also—and in some ways more importantly—in legacy media. But as the months progressed, it became much more difficult for leaders to present a consistent, unified argument to media outlets.

Conclusion: toward a new model for mobile collective action in Hong Kong

Participants in the Umbrella Movement sought to reach potentially active demographics where they already live their lives—primarily in this online discourse, much less in legacy media. Beyond the overarching political objective, the movement's desired outcomes were: (a) effective mobilization and coordination of protest supporters in the physical space of the protest zones, (b) using digital platforms as a means of seeking consensus about key decisions for the protest movement, (c) attempting to keep a media spotlight on their cause and persuade persons beyond immediate supporters of the validity of their cause, and (d) establish, with "keyboard warriors," a strong digital presence to put the democracy movement's case forward to skeptics inside and outside Hong Kong and, if necessary, push back against negative discourse about the protest movement, including that incited by paid pro-government commenters.

Of these desired outcomes, the Umbrella Movement achieved the following: (a) some success in tactical coordination and blocking police advances for a period of several weeks; (b) little success forging a long-term political consensus within the movement; (c) limited success keeping protests in the global media spotlight and a concurrent loss of urgency in coverage of local media;, and (d) arguably, political failure, as the movement is now divided and its online discussions have come to be characterized by toxic recriminations, while the government did not concede on the protestors' key demand of electoral reform.

As the weeks ticked by, the Umbrella Movement struggled to persuade audiences outside the movement. Beyond the initial moment of unity, when the Umbrella Movement brought together different groups in a focused effort to defeat a government plan, it struggled to sustain what it had established. And as weeks passed and protests continued, the Umbrella Movement failed to subvert existing hierarchies and political networks in Hong Kong. For participants in the Umbrella Movement, the outcome was a reminder of the difficulty of achieving counterpower when existing political networks are strong and backed by powerful state institutions. For scholars of communication, the Umbrella Movement allows for a richer discussion about the reasons that protest movements use social media, the ways that factions within a movement can diverge in their approach to social media, and the ways online debate can play out in different social and cultural contexts. It also suggests the limits of movements who are unable to translate a robust digital discourse and even mass physical disobedience into political concessions or direct access to power.

Although the Umbrella Movement failed in its stated goals in terms of immediate political reform in the voting procedures for Hong Kong, social media content had a catalytic effect on mobilizing and organizing the protests. More than that, it also persuaded a large number of previously apathetic people that civil disobedience, formerly a tough sell to rule-abiding Hong Kongers, had a visible effect and was a legitimate form of collective action.

The movement created enduring networks of people who are no longer physically occupying the same site, but who have a transformed sense of civil discourse as a result of the simultaneous physical occupy movement and online conversation; moreover, the co-existence in the physical space created bonds of trust and community online that will be stronger for having been forged in a physical space. The Occupy Movement may not have persuaded an enduring majority of Hong Kongers that their movement and tactics were a valid or wise, but the existence of social media allowed protest leaders to document their motivations and conduct and avoid the tarnish of the least flattering narratives in legacy media. This preserves the movement's reputation if further repressive government actions in the future radicalize Hong Kong moderates who wish to preserve their freedoms while not actively antagonizing Beijing. By creating this discourse on social media, the original protest movement created an audience, a template, and clear rallying points for a potential future protest.

References

Belair-Gagnon, Valerie, Colin Agur, and Nicholas Frisch. 2017. "The Changing Physical and Social Environment of Newsgathering: A Case Study of Foreign Correspondents Using Chat Apps during Unrest." *Social Media + Society* 3 (1): 1–10.

Belair-Gagnon, Valerie, Colin Agur, and Nicholas Frisch. 2018. "Mobile Sourcing: Trust in Journalistic Sourcing on Mobile Chat Apps." *Mobile Media and Communication* 6 (1): 53–70.

Bennet, W. Lance, and Alexandra Segerberg. 2013. *The Logic of Connective Action*. New York: Cambridge University Press.

Boler, Megan, Averie Macdonald, Christina Nitsou, and Anne Harris. 2014. "Connective Labor and Social Media: Women's Roles in the 'Leaderless' Occupy Movement." *Convergence* 20 (4): 438–460.

Castells, Manuel. 2012. *Networks of Outrage and Hope: Social Movements in the Internet Age*. New York: Polity Press.

Frisch, Nicholas, Valerie Belair-Gagnon, and Colin Agur. 2017. "Media Capture with Chinese Characteristics: Changing Patterns in Hong Kong's News Media System." *Journalism*. Online First.

Howard, Philip N., and Muzammil M.Hussain. 2013. *Democracy's Fourth Wave: Digital Media and the Arab Spring*. Oxford University Press.

Lee, Francis L.F., and Joseph Man Chan. 2016. "Digital Media Activities and Mode of Participation in a Protest Campaign: A Study of the Umbrella Movement." *Information, Communication & Society* 19 (1): 4–22.

Lee, Alice Y. L., and Ka Wan Ting. 2015. "Media and Information Praxis of Young Activists in the Umbrella Movement." *Chinese Journal of Communication* 8 (4): 376–392.

Lee, Paul S. N., Clement Y. K.So, and Louis Leung. 2015. "Social Media and Umbrella Movement: Insurgent Public Sphere in Formation." *Chinese Journal of Communication* 8 (4): 356–375.

Morozov, Evgeny. 2009. "From Slacktivism to Activism." *Foreign Policy*, September 5.

Tufekci, Zeynep. 2017. *Twitter and Tear Gas: The Power and Fragility of Networked Protest*. New Haven, CT: Yale University Press.

Western, Simon. 2014. "Autonomist Leadership in Leaderless Movements: Anarchists Leading the Way." *Ephemera* 14 (4): 673–698.

Interviews

BBC journalist (not for attribution), in discussion with the author, June 12, 2015, Hong Kong.

Kin-manCHAN (Professor at Chinese University of Hong Kong and founder of Occupy Central With Love and Peace), in discussion with the author, May 15, 2015, Hong Kong.

DouglasBASTIEN, KrisCHENG, NatalieCHIU, AlanLAI, ChristianPOON (a group of young citizen journalists and activists present during main events of 2014 protests, group interview), in discussion with the author, May 21, 2015, Hong Kong.

RobertCHOW (founder of Silent Majority for Hong Kong, a pro-establishment and anti-protest movement seen as sympathetic to government), in discussion with the author, May 19, 2015, Hong Kong.

PatrickKAO (independent anti-Occupy organizer "Voice of Loving HK"), in discussion with the author, July 22, 2015, Hong Kong.

AlanLAI (citizen journalist), in discussion with the author, May 21, 2015, Hong Kong.

NathanLAW (student organizer active in Hong Kong Federation of Students and prominent personality during the protests), in discussion with the author, June 23, 2015, Hong Kong.

VincentLAU and GilbertYAP (co-founders of Code4HK and active "keyboard warriors" supporting protest, joint interview), in discussion with the author, May 18, 2015, Hong Kong.

YvonneLEUNG (former President, The Hong Kong University Students' Union, prominent protest leader), in discussion with the author, June 22, 2015, Hong Kong.

ColmanLI (former Vice-President (External) at Hong Kong University Students' Union, logistics organizer for protest movement with emphasis on technological tools), in discussion with the author, May 19, 2015, Hong Kong.

CharlesMOK (legislator in Hong Kong's Legislative Council (LegCo), representing Technology Functional Constituency), in discussion with the author, May 21, 2015, Hong Kong.

POChun Chung (founder and leading member of "Protect Hong Kong Movement" and frequent street protestor/heckler against Occupy movement actions, also prominent on Facebook), in discussion with the author, May 18, 2015, Hong Kong.

ChristianPOON (activist and prominent social media personality, formerly employed by Hong Kong University Journalism and Media Studies Centre as social media researcher), in discussion with the author, May 19, 2015, Hong Kong.

BennyTAI (Hong Kong University Professor of Law, co-founder of Occupy Central with Love and Peace), in discussion with the author, May 19, 2015, Hong Kong.

Wall Street Journal reporter (not for attribution), in discussion with the author, May 21, 2015, Hong Kong.

GilbertWAT (citizen journalist), in discussion with the author, May 18, 2015, Hong Kong.

JoshuaWONG (founder of Scholarism and prominent student leader of protest movement), in discussion with the author, June 22, 2015, Hong Kong.

TaurusYIP (former acting chairperson of the Current Affairs Committee of the Hong Kong University Students' Union), in discussion with the author, May 15, 2015, Hong Kong.

10

SOUTH KOREA AND A2K

The Role of Mobile Technologies in the 2016 Impeachment Scandal

Shubhangi Gokhale

Introduction

On April 6, 2018, South Korea's ex-President Park Geun-Hye was sentenced to 24 years in jail after being convicted of fraud, corruption, and nepotism. The corruption scandal emerged in 2016 and rippled through all of South Korea. It engulfed politicians, their advisers, and many heads of industry. It led to massive protests by citizens, who utilized social media and mobile technologies. As a result, the mobile technologies became a powerful means to keep the protests going. This chapter discusses the role of mobile technologies and social media in these South Korean protests.

In February 2013, Park Geun-Hye was elected President. She was the first female president in a country that ranks among the highest in the world for gender inequality (Editorial Board 2016). Yet, Park Geun-Hye was enormously popular in South Korea early in her term. Society's traditional views of womanhood and a single woman's place in society heavily influenced the public's perception of Park Geun-Hye, a president who actually grew up in the Blue House, her singlehood, and her relations with both men and women. As a young person, Park supporters viewed her as a tragic female victim of her parents' assassinations, in need of public support.[1] As an older, single female politician, she was seen as married to her father's legacy and to the state. Park's alleged past intimate relations with Choi Tae-Min, a Christian cult leader, which may have caused her to have publicly strained relations with her siblings later on, were not considered to be a relevant issue at the time of her candidacy (Gajdos and Bendini 2013). Over time, however, both her initial supporters and detractors viewed her presidency with certain gender biases that may have worsened their view of her mental fitness for office.

Once Park Geun-Hye became president, she was seen as the supreme leader, the person at the top of the hierarchy in South Korea. However, in contravention to this traditional respect for leaders, the country's ruler and daughter of a strong dictator soon faced revelations of being beholden to Choi Soon-Sil, Choi Tae-Min's daughter, a non-family member and childhood friend of dubious background and already mired in several scandals. She had apparently become heavily dependent on that friend's input on matters of national importance. These revelations led the public to lose trust in the mental fitness of the president and thus the legitimacy of her presidency itself. Such perceptions increased due to the government's lack of communication and transparency during scandals. In October 2016, every small misstep by the Park administration was chronicled. With almost instant access to information, the public had immense capacity to mobilize thousands of non-violent protesters at short notice. All of this added an impressive, escalating pressure on the administration's ability to control the public narrative of its scandals.

As a response, the Park administration sought to censor and manipulate perceptions of her administration by using old-school methods like intimidation, corruption, and abuse of questionably broad laws. However, sophisticated use of the available cutting-edge Internet infrastructure allowed the Korean public to quickly understand, explain, and share each new evidence of wrong-doing in real-time. The use of social media allowed spontaneous and wide-spread public protests to occur, which in turn gave additional support to critical "traditional media" investigators and the opposition to continue their push to successfully impeach the president. In other words, South Korean citizens, with the ability to access and use next generation knowledge goods, were able to make an informed political decision to ensure their own well-being.

The Access to Knowledge (A2K) framework helps us understand how mobile technologies can fuel public demand for increased government transparency. Analyzing the nature of the Korean public's participation in political protests through an A2K framework suggests that authoritarian policies that seek to restrict a digitally savvy public's access to knowledge may actually experience a strong public pushback to such actions. Despite the attempts of the Park administration to control the public opinion through censorship and limiting the dissemination of information, mobile technologies served as a tool and outlet for the public to express their opinion and engage in the political discourse.

This chapter will proceed through three main sections. The first section will further explain the A2K framework using Leah Shaver's seminal book on the matter. In a second stage this framework will be applied to analyze how South Korea fares in the area of A2K. The remaining sections of the chapter will take the reader through different instances of South Korea's recent history where mobile technologies were utilized to demand increased government transparency. The second section focuses on two disasters to which the government response proved dissatisfactory and that showcase how mobile technology enabled the citizenry to respond to the government's failure. The third section engages with two instances where photographic evidence of government corruption was shared with the help of mobile technologies and used to push back against government obscurity.

Access to knowledge in South Korea

The A2K movement advocates the need to establish and expand an individual's access to knowledge goods. Jack Balkin, the Knight Professor of Constitutional Law at Yale Law School, and Ramesh Subramanian, the Gabriel Ferucci Professor of Information Systems at the School of Business, Quinnipiac University, as leading scholars and advocates of the A2K movement, have placed the A2K framework within a social justice and international development context (Balkin 2006). While this framework has traditionally been applied by states to assess and advocate for access to critical knowledge goods like pharmaceuticals and medical equipment, it can also be deployed to explore the critical role of next-generation knowledge goods such as mobile technologies (Subramanian 2011).

Leah Shaver, Associate Professor at Indiana University School of Law, explains that access to knowledge is based on three principles: (1) knowledge is a resource that contributes to human welfare, (2) the disadvantaged need fair access to knowledge in order to be able to use it as a resource to further their well-being, and (3) governments should bear the responsibility to promote equitable access to knowledge and to ensure the well-being of their citizens. Only an educated and well-informed individual will have the capacity to participate in society and ensure that their political community promotes their wellbeing. Shaver lists nine measures that can generally determine whether a particular government promotes access to knowledge: educational achievement, informational literacy, linguistic fluency, Internet access, affordability of knowledge goods, purchasing power, freedom of expression, a balanced intellectual property regime, and new contributions to knowledge (Shaver 2008).

The South Korean government leads in seven of these nine measures, while lagging behind in two critical areas: support for freedom of speech and a more equitable intellectual property regime, due to the wide scope and strict enforcement of its defamation and copyright laws. The country has one of the highest linguistic and informational literacy rates in the world. It has more than 100 percent of mobile broadband penetration (OECD 2016), partly due to subsidized monthly subscription rates that are quite cheap by OECD[2] standards (generally less than 50 dollars per month). Thus, Korea falls in the enviably rare category of providing one of the cheapest and fastest Internet services in the world. Indeed, more than 60 percent of connections achieve more than double the global average Internet speed (OECD 2016). Cheap high-speed access to data has allowed its residents to become the heaviest data users in the world. Thus, besides linguistic fluency, Internet access, and informational literacy, Korea leads in its ability to provide affordable knowledge goods like smartphones.

Due to export-oriented, family-run, and generously subsidized big businesses (*chaebols*) like Samsung, Lotte, LG, and Hyundai, South Korea has been able to compete with both developed and developing states in the global export markets today. These *chaebols*, at least partially, owe their success to their highly sophisticated domestic market. Historically, these companies have viewed the Korean public to be a test-bed for new software and hardware products, and the successful ones are then produced for exportation. Recognizing this need for testing new software, Korean administrations have also consistently supported commercial innovation through consistent investments in cutting-edge infrastructure that continues to support the newest technological trends today (KISTEP 2017). Thus, the Korean public has enjoyed consistent access to futuristic software and hardware technology. As investors, inventors, employees, and consumers, the public plays a participatory role in shaping Korea's production of knowledge goods for export like smartphones, drones, and other AI (artificial intelligence)- and IoT (Internet of things)-enabled electronics.

Mobile technologies and access to knowledge

With current mobile technologies, the Korean public is both a creator and an amplifier of information. Social network platforms like YouTube, Twitter, and Facebook allow ordinary users to quickly broadcast their opinions about relevant information to both a domestic and foreign audience. As a consequence of the open sharing the Internet has enabled, the Korean public seems comfortable with a level of personal and professional transparency that comes with a digitally savvy society. The public's demand for greater government transparency began during the administration of President Roh Moo-hyun, who was president from 2003 to 2008. President Moo-hyun was a progressive who championed human rights and supported student protests against authoritarian rule. He is widely known as the "World's first Internet President" and had achieved a large following among young users who were very comfortable with the Internet and followed news websites such as "OhMyNews" (Watts 2003). Both availability as well as comfort with the Internet and web-based news continued to increase during the succeeding conservative governments of Lee Myung-bak and Park Geun-Hye. However, the demand for transparency has grown due to perceptions of increasing government corruption (OECD 2016). As a result, the Korean citizenry has relied on tools such as mobile technologies to voice their opinion and ensure transparency of the government. Below we provide examples of the use of mobile technologies by ordinary citizens of South Korea, and how these examples of public expression created enough momentum for the protests that lead to the impeachment of Park Geun-Hye.

Sewol Ferry Disaster and MERS epidemic: public reactions to Government incompetence

One event that sparked public criticism of the Park government was the Sewol Ferry Disaster. On April 16, 2014, the ferry MV Sewol was en route from Incheon to Jeju, carrying mostly school students, when it sank. The sinking of the ferry resulted in the drowning of more than three hundred passengers, mostly students from Danwon High School. The deaths were largely caused by structural flaws in the ferry that were exacerbated by a negligent crew as well as delayed actions from government agencies. Throughout the day, official accounts of the rescue changed from hopeful wishes to a dire note with media outlets finally admitting that perhaps the rescue mission was a failure (Park and Hancocks 2015). Some of the best documentation of the disaster as it was unfolding came from frantic calls and videos made by the students using their cell phones (Lee and Kim 2014; Robertson, Fantz, and Shoichet 2014). The continued information gaps between official rescue accounts and individual accounts, including recorded real-time calls and messages from the trapped students to their families, resulted in unnecessary anguish to the victims' families and increased public outrage (Kang 2014).

Within days, it became clear that these deaths had been entirely preventable. There are many scandalous facts associated with this preventable tragedy, involving the morally ambiguous behavior of the shipping company's staff, media representatives, and government officials. The public associated the failures with President Park's lack of leadership during the debacle (The Straits Times 2014). The public highlighted her delayed public appearance that day, her subsequent conflicting statements regarding her absence, the censorship of any media speculation regarding the cause of her absence, and the administration's blacklisting of individuals that criticized her handling of the disaster. These actions were seen as particularly egregious and darkly reminiscent of the dictatorial regime of her father Park Chung-Hee, who, as noted earlier, was a dictator and was often ruthless in his use of force to detain and torture protesters, activists, and dissidents (Denny 2015). In 2016, Park Geun-Hye continued to be blamed for her unexplained absence that day when her leadership was urgently needed. Although rejected by the Constitutional Court as a justification for impeachment, the prosecution even presented her conduct on that day as a particular example of her unfitness for office (Kim 2017).

After the ferry incident, the Park administration became notorious for its enthusiastic use of the defamation law to suppress criticism. Titled "The Act on Promotion of Information and Communications Network Utilization and Data Protection, Etc.," or the ICN Act of 2009, this still valid statute even includes within its scope truthful statements that can damage a person's reputation. In that sense, its scope is quite broad and thus ripe for abuse. The Park administration showed a record of personally directing punitive actions against critical media when scandals would break out with the apparent intention of promoting media self-censorship. Since the Ministry of Justice and its affiliated prosecutors fall under the direct authority of the President, media outlets and artistic expressions that linked Park Geun-Hye to the Sewol Ferry Disaster were met with strong government action ranging from unexplained censorship of the material to the aggressive use of defamation lawsuits against artists. Television shows, in particular comedy shows like Korea's *SNL* (licensed by its American counterpart) that generally include political satire, were also treated harshly by the administration.

In 2017, *The Hankyoreh*, a newspaper that supported her opposition and was a frequent target of the Park administration, later confirmed that the Blue House had a blacklist of more than 10,000 individuals, including sports people, intellectuals, artists, and organizations that were to be discriminated against based on their critical behavior towards the administration or support for an opposition party. Indeed, towards the end of 2016, the media and several non-governmental organizations had already protested the administration's push to silence critics, which led to a stifling of public expression about the administration and undermined one of the fundamental values of a thriving democracy (Hankyoreh 2017).

The MERS epidemic scandal is another example of the public's quick backlash against government secrecy. On May 20, 2015, South Korea first experienced an outbreak of the Middle Eastern Respiratory Syndrome (MERS) coronavirus. The virus had been transmitted through a businessman who had traveled from the Middle East to South Korea (Park, Han, and Kim 2015). This highly contagious disease could have been quickly contained had the government responded in a fast, transparent, and efficient manner. Instead, the government decided to withhold the names of the medical institutions that hosted the initial patients. Despite growing public outrage, the government delayed publicizing the hospitals with quarantined patients until June 7, 18 days later. The final list showed that the country's premier hospital, Samsung Medical Center, located in the Manhattan-like Gangnam district of Seoul, was hosting the most patients. Due to the center's negligence in quarantining of patients, many more contracted the virus. Although the government reasoned that the publication delay was to limit mass panic, *The Hankyoreh* and other critical media viewed it as an egregious example of the government protecting the hospital's reputation and its profits at the expense of public health. Its opinion polls confirmed that the public seemed to have similarly negative views of the administration's actions. In the absence of trust in the public health officials and the government, the public resorted to online news, interpersonal networks, and social media for acquiring MERS-related information (Jang and Baek 2019).

Government corruption, mobile technologies, and the transparency movements

The government of South Korea was formed in August 15, 1948, after gaining independence from Japanese rule. Throughout its almost 70 years of existence, successive South Korean presidents have been embroiled in various types of corruption scandals. Clint Work (2018) notes that the reasons for this could be a combination of an "imperial presidency" with informal networks, hierarchical exercise of power, and the establishment of a highly centralized and penetrating national security state, especially after the Korean war in 1950.

The roots of Park Geun-Hye's corruption scandal can be traced back to her father, Park Chung-Hee, who took power in a coup in 1963. Upon his assassination in 1979, Park Geun-Hye became close to her father's confidante, Choi Tae-Min, a colorful character who converted from Buddhism to Christianity and set up the "Church of Eternal Life." His daughter Choi Soon-Sil and Park Geun-Hye were childhood friends. After the death of Choi Tae-Min, Choi Soon-Sil became a close confidante and advisor of Park Geun-Hye, leading up to the latter's ascension to president. In 2016, Choi Soon-Sil was accused of using her influence with Park

Geun-Hye to interfere in state affairs, as well as leaning on big corporations (such as Samsung) for personal bribes (BBC News 2018).

Faced with accusations that could undermine her presidency, the Park government took restrictive legal and political actions to limit access to knowledge. However, current mobile technologies still allowed the public to quickly understand the corruption and the attempts at cover-up. These technologies also facilitated instant dissemination of such knowledge to a wide audience in a way that allowed the public to both make informed decisions about the authority figures, as well as have the capacity to organize mass protests against them.

In the sub-sections below, we provide two illustrative examples of how a digitally savvy public, through the use of mobile technologies, was able to push back against opacity and eventually generate a political movement that successfully impeached Park Geun-Hye.

The image of a former Senior Presidential Secretary

A good example of how mobile technologies and social media facilitated instant dissemination of information and shaped public opinion is the pictures relating to the interrogation of Woo Byung-Woo, who was Park Geun-Hye's senior secretary of civil affairs from early 2015 up to his resignation in late 2016. He was charged with aiding and abetting Park Geun-Hye and Choi Soon-Sil. On November 7, 2016, the newspaper *Chosun Ilbo* published two pictures of Woo Byung-Woo as he was being held for interrogation (Kim 2016). The photos were clandestinely captured by a freelance photo-journalist after a three-hour stakeout and then disseminated through traditional and social media and became an Internet sensation in South Korea. The photograph, which was taken from an adjacent building to the Seoul Prosecutorial Office, showed Woo Byung-Woo standing with "smugly folded arms while two prosecutors stood across from him looking deferential. The photo sparked an immediate Internet meme: "Questioning for the King" (Kang 2016). He seems to be relaxed and not required to face his interrogators who were his former employees. This photograph, along with the photographer's account of his investigation, was widely shared across TV news programs, newspapers, and social media.

As explained in *The Korea Times*, Woo Byung-Woo seemed to be smiling, while the two prosecutors seemed to be slightly bowing their heads, perhaps with their hands brought together. One may believe that this is a picture of a boss meeting his employees or younger friends, rather than an interrogation of the older man on a matter of national concern. Such an interpretation would not be speculative in nature. The photograph seemed to imply that his informal influence on the prosecution still remained. This influence, as well as implied pressure from the Blue House, seemed to protect him from a real investigation (Kim 2016).

In fact, the Korean public is well aware that both the judicial branch and the Ministry of Justice are more politicized, more prone to corruption, and weaker than their counterparts in other developed states. A November 2016 article in *The*

Diplomat magazine, for example, had to explain this internal history of corruption to its international readers in order to explain the public's particular outrage at this photograph (Fendos 2016). South Korea has a type of cronyism, termed 전관예우 (*jeong-gwang-ye-wu*), or "Chamberlain honor." For example, after retiring from their posts, former judges and prosecutors establish their own private practice and enjoy considerable preferential treatment when they litigate cases due to their previous relationships. In addition, they also benefit from their continued influence on younger professionals through the cultural values of *Sunbae-Hoobae* (Senior-Junior) loyalty and trust networks. Further, South Korea's mandatory military service for men, coupled with its long history of Confucian culture, has created a hierarchical society where employees tend to stay within certain hierarchical norms even when interacting with former superiors and inferiors. The informal and comparatively invisible nature of these relationships makes it harder to access information on the manner in which these former officers influence investigations and judicial outcomes.

The photograph of an abandoned shoe outside the Seoul Prosecutorial Office

On October 31, 2016, Choi Soon-Sil, friend and advisor to President Park, was hounded by reporters on her way to the Seoul Central Prosecutor's Office and lost her designer shoe while trying to get away from the crowds. The shoe was discovered by a photographer, and a picture of it was published in *The Korea Times* and other media the following day. *The Korea Times* and other traditional and social media outlets emphasized how the designer shoe highlighted Choi Soon-Sil's elite status in contrast to former President Park's habit, as advised by Choi, of wearing simple clothes and shoes from local and cheaper brands (Park 2016). The picture of the shoe added fuel to the public outrage and criticism about Choi's disproportionate influence over the president and her alleged profits from this relationship. Since this news was released before Halloween weekend, many used the opportunity to channel this outrage into numerous parodies and satires of Choi and Park's relationship. Even international newspapers, like *The South China Morning Post*, covered the various Halloween costumes that were inspired by the scandal. Choi Soon-Sil's inordinate influence on president Park Geun-Hye, and the possible reasons for that, are discussed below (Tai 2016).

At the time the scandal surfaced, president Park Geun-Hye was 64 years old, five years older than Choi Soon-Sil. As the daughter of a former president, as well as the financial benefactor of Choi Soon-Sil's family, Park Geun-Hye was widely considered to have an elder-sister-like relationship with Choi Soon-Sil. Korea's Confucian-influenced culture guides the dynamics of such a relationship along certain formalistic lines. For example, an elder of a higher economic status may treat their junior confidant to dinner, while the junior may express their deference and gratitude through assisting the elder in some capacity. The elder may be considered to be a mentor in the relationship. Although Korea is not completely defined by traditional Confucian values, they have heavily influenced perspectives of proper professional relationships. This is the reason that the Park–Choi relationship was shocking to the public for the leaked communications between the two women showed a role reversal of assumed Confucian values. In the leaked communications, the former president seemed intent on receiving wide-ranging and detailed advice from Choi, while Choi seemed to entertain a condescending attitude towards Park (Kim 2017).

Previous to the shoe scandal, Choi was already infamous because of her use of a fraudulent admissions strategy and grade inflation scheme to ensure the academic success of her daughter at a local elite university. The public had also been recently made aware of her management of two new non-profit organizations that were rumored (then later confirmed) to be money-laundering vehicles to move government bribes to private offshore accounts. These allegations were buttressed by a former young male associate's salacious interview, explaining how his dubious past with Choi Soon-Sil helped him land a managing role at one of these non-profits and also establish his current career as the personal fashion designer of President Park and other celebrities.

The photograph of Choi's shoe and those of Woo Byung-Woo at his interrogation were widely disseminated throughout the Internet, social media, and cell phones. They cemented the hypocritical image of a presidential advisor who apparently wore clothes allegedly derived from government bribes while directing the South Korean president to wear clothes of an amateur designer.

Conclusion

In the above narrative, we have discussed at length the role of mobile communications technologies in the impeachment of president Park Geun-Hye. South Korea is a contradiction. It is technologically advanced, yet its people and politics are governed by traditional loyalties, hierarchical and patriarchal societal structures, and corrupt oligarchies. In such an environment, it has been very difficult to accuse the nation's leaders of corruption, and further, to get them impeached. Yet, that is what happened in South Korea in the period 2016 to 2018. It was achieved by peaceful means by the people of South Korea who were able to use communications to collect and disseminate information of the government's scandals quickly and effectively and organize protests that eventually led to the impeachment of president Park Geun-Hye.

The volume and intensity of the humorous and peaceful outrage was unprecedented, considering the fact that the administration had spent two years trying to limit public criticism of its administration. This outrage was partly instigated by the sudden awareness of Park and Choi's non-traditional relationship. Meanwhile, the unofficial artist blacklist and the government's use of defamation lawsuits had led to two years of media self-censorship until October 2016. Anger over Choi Soon-Sil and the gossipy nature of Choi's unofficial machinations created a sea of parodies and satire.

In November 2016, with online and offline protests, one suddenly saw parody posters, games, even songs, and scenes in Korean dramas, increasingly satirizing the whole controversy. As the protests grew more diverse and gained momentum, political satire suddenly became prevalent on television. Although *SNL Korea*, which has a similar format to and is derived from the American *Saturday Night Live*, largely stayed away from political satire under pressure from the Blue House for many years, it joined in with enthusiasm. In that sense, her diminishing control over a publicly cheered enraged media, allowed free criticism of her actions. Thankfully, political satire still continues in the media today.

Unfortunately, despite South Korea's transition to democracy in 1987, violations of democratic principles of law still occur today (Heo and Hahm 2014). Thus, despite an excellent infrastructure, Internet access has not significantly lessened the strong enforcement of defamation and copyright laws. Nor did the right to freedom of expression improve, despite the November 2016 mass movements that forced the then legislature to protect the public's right to protest and criticize the government.

Notes

1 Park Geun-Hye's father, Park Chung-Hee was the third president of South Korea. He was also a military general and dictator who ruled South Korea with an iron fist from 1963 to 1979, when he was assassinated. Park Geun-Hye had faced tragedy even earlier. In 1974, her mother Yuk Young-soo was killed by a North Korean assassin. At that time, Park Geun-Hye became a stand-in first-lady to her father (BBC News 2018).

2 "OECD" stands for the Organization for Economic Development and Cooperation. Formed in 1961, its membership consists of 37 countries at present. The organization was formed to promote the economies of, and trade among, the members.

References

Balkin, Jack. 2006. "What is Access to Knowledge?" *Balkinization: An Unexpected Consequence of Jack Balkin*. Blog. https://balkin.blogspot.jp/2006/04/what-is-access-to-knowledge.html.

BBC News. 2018. "South Korea's Presidential Scandal." *BBC News*, April 6. http://www.bbc.com/news/world-asia-37971085.

Denny, Steven. 2015. "The Mixed Legacy of a South Korean Dictator." *The Diplomat*, September 17. https://thediplomat.com/2015/09/the-mixed-legacy-of-a-south-korean-dictator/.

Editorial Board. 2016. "The Saga of Park Geun-hye." *New York Times*, November 24. https://www.nytimes.com/2016/11/24/opinion/the-saga-of-park-geun-hye.html.

Fendos, Justin. 2016. "South Korea's Corruption Culture." *The Diplomat*, November 17. https://thediplomat.com/2016/11/south-koreas-corruption-culture/.

Gajdos, Lukas and Roberto Bendini. 2013. "Quick Policy Insight: The 2012 South Korea Election." Policy Department, Directorate-General for External Policies. briefing note. European Parliament. http://www.europarl.europa.eu/RegData/etudes/briefing_note/join/2013/491471/EXPO-AFET_SP(2013)491471_EN.pdf.

Hankyoreh. 2017. "Government blacklist stretched beyond culture, across South Korean society." *Hankyoreh*, February 1. http://english.hani.co.kr/arti/english_edition/e_national/780870.html.

Heo, Uk and Deuk Sung Hahm. 2014. "Political Culture and Democratic Consolidation in South Korea." *Asian Survey* 54 (5): 918–940.
Jang, Kyungeun and Young Min Baek. 2019. "When Information from Public Health Officials Is Untrustworthy: The Use of Online News, Interpersonal Networks, and Social Media during the MERS Outbreak in South Korea." *Health Communication* 34 (9): 991–998. Pub. online March 2018: https://doi.org/10.1080/10410236.2018.1449552.
Kang, Jin-Kyu. 2014. "Videos at Ferry Disaster Give Glimpses of Doom." *Korea JoongAng Daily*, April 30. http://koreajoongangdaily.joins.com/news/article/article.aspx?aid=2988632.
Kang, Jin-Kyu. 2016. "Prosecutors Suspected of Going Easy on Woo." *Korea JoongAng Daily*, November 8. http://koreajoongangdaily.joins.com/news/article/article.aspx?aid=3025881.
Kim, Nan. 2017. "Candlelight and the Yellow Ribbon: Catalyzing Re-democratization in South Korea." *The Asia-Pacific Journal: Japan Focus* 15 (4): 1–17.
Kim, Sejeong. 2016. "Public losing trust in prosecution's probe." *Koreatimes*, November 7. https://www.koreatimes.co.kr/www/nation/2017/11/113_217722.html.
KISTEP (Korea Institute of Science & Technology Evaluation and Planning). 2017. *Main Science and Technology Indicators of Korea*. Part 1. Seoul: Center for International Affairs. http://www.kistep.re.kr/en/c3/sub2.jsp#none.
Lee, Kyung-mi, and Kim Young-dong. 2014. "Student Made First Call for Rescue from Sinking Sewol Ferry." *Hankyoreh*, April 24. http://english.hani.co.kr/arti/english_edition/e_national/634369.html.
OECD. 2016. "Open and Transparent Government in Korea." In *Government at a Glance: How Korea Compares*, 67–81. Paris: OECD Publishing. doi:10.1787/9789264259003-7-en.
Park, Madison, Sol Han, and Jung-eun Kim. 2015. "South Korea MERS Outbreak: 9 Dead; 3,000 Quarantined." *CNN*, June 11. https://www.cnn.com/2015/06/10/world/south-korea-mers-outbreak/index.html.
Park, Madison, and Paula Hancocks. 2015. "Sewol Ferry Disaster: One Year on Families Want Answers." *CNN*, April 16. https://www.cnn.com/2015/04/15/asia/sewol-ferry-korea-anniversary/index.html.
Park, Sae-jin. 2016. "Prada Shoes of President Park's Friend Become Internet Topic." *AJU Business Daily*, October 31. http://ajudaily.com/view/20161031171855040.
Robertson, Nic, Ashley Fantz, and Katherine E. Shoichet. 2014. "Videos Capture South Korean Ferry's Final Moments, Fuel Fresh Outrage." *CNN*, May 14. https://www.cnn.com/2014/04/27/world/asia/south-korea-ferry-video/index.html.
Shaver, Lea. 2008. "Defining and Measuring A2K: A Blueprint for an Index of Access to Knowledge." *I/S: A Journal of Law and Policy for the Information Society* 4 (2): 235–269.
Subramanian, Ramesh. 2011. "ICTs and Access to Knowledge in Rural India: A Comparative Study of Two Models of Deployment." In *Access to Knowledge in India: New Research on Intellectual Property, Innovation & Development*. edited by Lea Shaver and Ramesh Subramanian, 109–147. London: Bloomsbury Academic.
Tai, Crystal. 2016. "Unleash the memes: how South Koreans are mocking president's scandal with humour." *South China Morning Post*, November 3. http://www.scmp.com/news/asia/east-asia/article/2042602/unleash-memes-how-south-koreans-are-mocking-presidents-scandal.
The Straits Times. 2014. "South Korea Ferry Disaster: Distrust, Anger over President's Actions." *The Straits Times*, May 2. https://www.straitstimes.com/asia/east-asia/south-korea-ferry-disaster-distrust-anger-over-presidents-actions-0.
Watts, Jonathan. 2003. "World's First Internet President Logs On." *The Guardian*, February 24. http://www.theguardian.com/technology/2003/feb/24/newmedia.koreanews.
Work, Clint. 2018. "Park, Lee and the Plight of Korean Presidents." *The Diplomat*, April 14. https://thediplomat.com/2018/04/park-lee-and-the-plight-of-korean-presidents/.

11

EGYPT AND THE CASE OF UBER

An A2K Perspective on Ride-Sharing Legislation

Nagla Rizk

Introduction

Egypt's first ride-sharing service emerged in November 2014, when Uber initially started operating in specific areas of the capital city, Cairo. Since then, Uber has expanded to cover a total of seven Egyptian cities, as well as a limited service in Egypt's upscale North Coast and resort town El Gouna during seasonal months. The launch of Uber in Cairo was followed by at least three other ride-sharing companies spanning various different cities in Egypt (Uber Egypt 2018). As in many other parts of the world, the introduction of ride-sharing services triggered reactions from taxi drivers, which necessitated legislative action to respond to the ensuing market disruption. Both the introduction of ride-sharing services and the government response in Egypt provide a story that warrants investigation. The purpose of this chapter is to examine the case of ride-sharing services in Egypt and the government's legal response, known as the *Ride Hailing Apps Act*, from an Access to Knowledge (A2K) perspective. The chapter analyzes the effects of the legislation on various stakeholders in the ride-sharing and public transport market in Egypt, including newly emerging ride-sharing platforms, with Uber as the central focus as the largest player in the Egyptian ride-sharing market and a principle party in the legislation forming process.

The analysis throughout the chapter is framed within the A2K paradigm which refers to "a collection of public policies and private initiatives that help promote the growth, spread and distribution of knowledge and knowledge goods and tools around the world" (Balkin 2010, xix–xxi). The "knowledge" aspect of the A2K paradigm applies to a range of elements much broader than solely access to education or learning. It includes access to information such as news, data, and information about the government and its processes, but also includes human knowledge, such as education and skills. A2K expands to constitute access to information about the legislative process conducted by governments (Balkin 2010, xix–xxi). A2K covers the range of public policies and private initiatives that aim to promote a more equitable distribution of knowledge and knowledge goods. Distribution in this sense is not limited to the dissemination of knowledge goods as commodities widely and fairly, but also with providing citizens with the skills and practical abilities to participate in creation and innovation.

The chapter focuses on the impact of legislation. Law and legal regulation are deeply intertwined with access to knowledge because the "law often sets the basic conditions of access" (Balkin 2010, xix–xxi). Legislation plays a large role in determining the extent to which innovation and knowledge production are shared widely for the benefit of society as a whole. In order for the law to fill its potential as a guarantor of justice, legislative processes must be inclusive of a variety of players as producers in the creation of policy. Law and law-making play a fundamental role in ensuring that the process of knowledge-making, is open, inclusive, and distributed for the benefit of all, or monopolized for the benefit of certain segments or stakeholders (Balkin 2008, 2). It is therefore crucial to promote participatory law-making processes that acts as a bridge between governments, stakeholders, and the public. The chapter explores whether, and the extent to which, legislation regarding ride-sharing in Egypt has been inclusive enough to promote participatory development.

The chapter is composed of six sections. After the introduction, section two gives an overview of ride-sharing apps, particularly Uber, in the global sharing economy. This is followed by a perspective on the distinctive role ride-sharing companies have in the specific Egyptian socio-economic context and transportation realities. Section three focuses on the process of market disruption and the opportunities offered by ride-sharing platforms. Section four then focuses on the Egyptian legal framework for public transport and clarifies the timeline of events that led to conflict arising between traditional white taxis and ride-sharing companies in Egypt. The section also presents the subsequent legal developments and the ultimate outcome of Egypt's Ride Hailing Apps Act. Section five offers an A2K perspective on the legislation itself and the way in which it was drafted. It considers how law making in this context could affect other smaller players like local, emerging ride-sharing platforms, as well as entrepreneurship in general. The final section provides concluding remarks and recommendations for the future of ride sharing legislation in Egypt.

Ride-sharing platforms in the global sharing economy and Egypt

The concept of ride-sharing is an alternative to individual car ownership not by sharing access to cars, but rather access to a ride in a car in order to reach a specific destination chosen by the passenger. Drivers make an income from their ownership of an otherwise idle good, the car (Morency 2006). This model is enabled by technology, as ride-sharing transactions are fully completed on smartphone application platforms, in addition to being facilitated by the use of smartphones' GPS location services that allow consumers to find nearby drivers (Kapoor 2014).

San Francisco-based Uber is a pioneer and currently the most popular ride-sharing company in more than 100 countries. To use Uber, consumers download Uber's smartphone app, which connects user requesting rides based on GPS pickup location with available drivers nearby (Uber 2018). Uber sets the price of the ride, and transactions happen through mobile payment on the online platform; 70–80 percent of each fare goes to the driver, and the rest goes to Uber (Posen 2016). This is the traditional model used by ride-sharing companies, and it has revolutionized the manner in which on-demand transport is conducted.

While Uber and other ride-sharing platforms seem to offer consumers a service similar to that of a taxi, Uber's Terms and Conditions explain that they do not provide a transportation service, but a "technology platform" that connects drivers with private cars to passengers seeking them online (Uber 2017). Uber's business model, therefore, resembles that of a "middle man" that uses software in the form of a smartphone application to connect driver partners with people looking for rides. Uber promises quality and safety standards through driver background checks, vehicle inspections, and real-time customer ratings that can be made directly on its smartphone application. As of 2017, Uber was valued at more than $68 billion and is continuing to grow at a rate of 8.4 percent. Today, Uber provides more than 1 million rides a day worldwide (Bensinger 2017).

Arguments have also been made against Uber's disruption of the traditional transportation industry model using its technological infrastructure. For those competing with these new ride-sharing services, such as taxi drivers, it has been stated that the playing field is not level. A report by the Grattan Institute put forth that taxi regulations and license fees in most countries "force taxi fares to be higher than Uber's" (Jericho 2016). In fact, arguments have been made that Uber's business model itself, which is that of a technology platform acting as intermediary between "those willing to sell spare capacity of cars to those willing to pay for this capacity," allows it to capitalize on the transportation sector without being subject to the regulations that traditional businesses within the same sector face (Schneider 2017). This has led to conflict in a variety of contexts over discrepancies in licensing and operation fees between taxi drivers and Uber (Minifie and Blowers 2016).

Uber and other ride-sharing platforms are part of the larger phenomenon of the sharing economy, greatly facilitated by mobile technologies. While consumers previously preferred ownership to sheer access, technological developments throughout the last decade have allowed for greater and easier access to products and services. The use of mobile technology is a key component. Technology has created platforms that have allowed for owners of various goods to make money by sharing these goods with others who do not own these goods themselves (Credit Suisse 2015). Most specifically, advances in mobile technology have allowed for the creation of online marketplaces involving the easy completion of immediate transactions between multiple parties online. Smartphone mobile apps connect supply with demand in a manner that is timely and cost-effective. Moreover, these transactions are easily concluded through one-click mobile payments (Kapoor 2014).

On the one hand, this new "sharing economy" focuses on facilitating "community ownership, sharing, cooperation and the regeneration of economic and natural abundance" (Posen 2016, 412). Along with the rise of the information and knowledge society, the main driving force of the sharing economy is the realization that idle goods can generate significant income while catering to demand in a mutually beneficial manner. On the other hand, businesses in the sharing economy experience unique benefits as well. The required resources and technology for forming business within the sharing economy are lower than they are for traditional business, making the sharing economy attractive for entrepreneurs (Dervojeda et al. 2013).

A challenging socio-economic context: ride-sharing in Egypt

The discussion of ride-sharing business models takes on a new flavor when seen in the context of a country like Egypt. On the one hand, the country has witnessed numerous and substantial socio-economic challenges over the past decade. On the other, Egypt's largest city, Cairo, experiences pervasive transport and traffic difficulties. Against this backdrop, ride-sharing services present opportunities that are unique.

Episodes of economic growth in Egypt have often been non-inclusive and the effects of this growth have trickled down only to particular segments of its growing population. The global financial crisis of 2009 caused a decline of 4.7 percent in Egypt's economic growth and exacerbated already high levels of income inequality (The World Bank n.d.). The uprisings of January 2011, which resulted in political unrest, economic turmoil, and multiple periods of transition, contributed to a further decrease in the rate of annual growth to 1.8 percent while amplifying existing socio-economic issues (CAPMAS 2016). By 2016, Egypt's Central Agency for Public Mobilization and Statistics (CAPMAS) found that 27.8 percent of the population lived beyond the poverty line, with the unemployment rate at 12.5 percent of the population and inflation reaching 20.2 percent (CAPMAS 2016).

Moreover, the Central Bank of Egypt's free floating of the Egyptian pound in late 2016, which resulted in a depreciation of 48 percent of the currency's value, caused a severe decline in purchasing power, with prices of basic goods rising by 200–300 percent (Ayesh 2016). Shortly after the floatation of the Egyptian pound, the International Monetary Fund (IMF) and the Egyptian government reached an agreement on a $12 billion IMF loan to support the government's economic reform program. The program consisted largely of austerity measures that included the cutting of subsidies on fuel and electricity, as well as the introduction of a Value Added Tax (VAT) of 13 percent (International Monetary Fund n.d.).

Finally, unemployment remains a central problem for the country's population, and even more so due to the crippling economic effects of ongoing fiscal reforms. In a population with a large youth bulge, with 33.8 percent of the population falling between the ages of 18 and 35, unemployment in 2015 reached 19.2 percent for youth of this age bracket (CAPMAS 2016). Perhaps even more significantly, the unemployment rate for holders of university degrees or higher was reported at 25.7 percent in 2016 (CAPMAS 2016). Unemployment in Egypt is a predominantly structural issue, meaning that it affects new, young, and educated entrants to the job market more frequently than being indicative of job loss due to economic downturns (Said 2015, 12).

The chronic lack of job opportunities has also led to the creation of a substantial informal sector within the Egyptian labor market. By 2012, 40 percent of total employment in Egypt came from informal work (Kassem 2014, 27). Informal employment in Egypt ranges from self-employment in any unregistered enterprise to selling goods as a street vendor. Various disadvantages arise from informal work, including irregularity of being paid, or lack of job security and contractual protection or employment benefits (ILO 2012, Main Findings). These disadvantages are often imposed on less privileged segments of the population, as figures show that there is a 35.5 percent probability of irregular wage workers to be part of the poorest 20 percent of the population in Egypt (Assaad and Krafft 2015).

Also central to the emergence of ride-sharing in Egypt has been mobile technology, and smartphone mobile applications in particular. There is no doubt that increasing rates of mobile usage and internet penetration in Egypt have paved the way for ride-sharing companies to experience high growth in the Egyptian market. A 2018 report by the Egyptian Ministry of Communication and Information Technology (MCIT) revealed that by April 2017, the number of Internet users in Egypt had reached 33.19 million, representing an increase of 7 million users within one year (Ministry of Communications and Information Technology 2018). Moreover, data collected in December 2017 showed that the number of mobile subscriptions was more than 100 million, therefore exceeding the actual population of Egypt and putting the percentage of mobile penetration in Egypt at 111 percent by the end of 2017 (Ministry of Communications and Information Technology 2018). As for internet penetration, the 2018 MCIT report revealed that by December 2017, there were 33 million mobile internet users, and an overall 41 percent Internet penetration rate in Egypt. With the number of mobile internet users increasing at a rate of approximately 14 percent annually, Egypt's growing rates of mobile and internet penetration undoubtedly serve as enablers for the boom of ride-sharing platforms in the Egyptian market (Ministry of Communications and Information Technology 2018).

Market disruption: ride-sharing in Egypt

The above-discussed socio-economic situation is compounded by transport and traffic realities in Egypt's largest city and capital: Cairo. In 2016, the United Nations ranked the Greater Cairo Metropolitan Area (GCMA) as the ninth largest global megacity. Today, Cairo continues to be one of the world's most heavily congested capital cities. Cairo alone comprises more than 20 million inhabitants, with an overall Egyptian population of nearly 100 million (Worldometers 2018). Traffic congestion in Cairo, and Egypt in general, is a result of various factors. Cheap fuel due to government subsidies has traditionally encouraged high rates of private car ownership, although subsidy cuts, including those on fuel, have recently changed this phenomenon.

A 2014 World Bank study found that private cars dominate the transportation context, constituting 55 percent of vehicles in Cairo, with a 7.8 percent increase in car licensing per year. Simultaneously, still only about 10 percent of Egyptians have access to a private car, meaning that the remaining 90 percent of the population resort to public transportation, "micro" buses or traditional white taxis (Werr 2017). While rates of car ownership in and of themselves might appear low, however, the ratio of cars to kilometers of existing roads is one of the highest in the world (The World Bank 2012). A 2013 World Bank Report stated that Greater Cairo had approximately 120,000 licensed taxis. While white taxis and microbuses sometimes compensate for the lack of public transportation capacity, these vehicles only contribute to further congestion and sub-par quality and reliability (Nakat, Herrera, and Cherkaoui 2014, 4). Government efforts to address this problem have targeted the expansion of public transportation options, but the pace of development has lagged behind the steadfast growth of the city.

Furthermore, complaints are rampant among those who do own privately owned cars about road safety, poor implementation of traffic laws, and excessive hours spent maneuvering traffic. In this context, ride-sharing services have emerged as viable transportation options for those who can afford it (Farid 2017). These services provide the opportunity to cater to the demand for novel and safe means of transportation in Egypt's dense and traffic-aggravated cities, especially in Cairo.

Uber first entered the Egyptian market with a soft launch in Cairo in November 2014 that catered to selected neighborhoods in the city, later expanding to the rest of the metropolis and rolling out the service to a number of other major Egyptian cities. Regional competitor Careem also launched in 2014. The Dubai-based ride-sharing company currently operates in 13 countries and over 90 cities across the Middle East and Asia. As of August 2017, Careem had invested $10 million in Egypt and boasted a 30 percent monthly growth rate since launching in the country. The company stated that it employed more than 60,000 drivers across the Middle East, with the target being 200,000 drivers throughout the Middle East by 2018 (Egypt Today Staff 2017).

In March 2016, Egypt's first local ride-sharing application, Ousta, was launched. The company looked to be a local alternative to the dominance of Uber and Careem and quickly expanded across eleven cities in Egypt. Five months after its launch, Ousta locked in $1.25 million in bridge investment in one of the largest investment deals for a tech startup in Egypt (Rashad 2016). But Ousta's growth plateaued and the company stopped their services in Egypt.

Another local startup is Swvl, a bus ride-sharing application, launched in May 2017 looking to transform the concept of urban mass transit in Egypt. Through their mobile app, the company connects users with private buses on fixed-route trips based on users' GPS location, at prices 60–80 percent lower than competing ride-sharing services. The company aims to utilize the standard ride-sharing model with the twist of applying it to vehicles that can transport multiple passengers, thereby also addressing issues of congestion (Elserty 2017). Months after its launch, Swvl received $500,000 in seed funding from ride-sharing company Careem. By

April 2018, shortly prior to the passing of Egypt's Ride Hailing Apps Act, Swvl had received $8 million in Series A Funding, the largest funding an Egyptian tech startup has ever received (Mabrouk 2018).

Launched in late 2017, Halan is Cairo-based ride-sharing app for tuk-tuks (three-wheeled small vehicles), motorcycles, and tricycles in Cairo. Halan looks to fill the gap for on-demand transportation in low-income and slum areas in Cairo, where tuk-tuks are already highly prevalent and practical with streets too narrow for regular cars. The app only comes in Arabic and places an emphasis on its affordable prices (El-Sayed 2018). By March 2018, Halan had successfully expanded to several major Egyptian cities. That same month, Halan closed $2 million in pre-series A funding (Enterprise Ventures 2018a).

While the ride-sharing scene in Egypt includes multiple players, Uber currently occupies the largest segment, with more than 150,000 drivers working on the platform in 2017 alone and more than 4 million riders in Egypt using the ride-sharing application since its launch (Al-Aees 2018). Only a year after its launch, Cairo became the fastest growing city for Uber. Today, Egypt continues to be one of the San Francisco-based company's fastest growing markets in the world (Zawya 2015). The app proved especially popular with women, who face widespread sexual harassment, often including harassment from traditional "white taxi" drivers, as well as on various modes of public transportation. Complaints about taxi drivers also commonly include lack of cleanliness and general safety, use of rickety vehicles, rejection of rides based on requested destination, and tampering with meters or claiming meter defectiveness in order to charge higher rates (Business Insider 2018). Uber's business model, however, gives customers a greater sense of power and trust; customers are able to monitor their route, review each trip and easily file reports on violations of Uber's quality and safety standards (Jericho 2016).[1]

Previous research by Rizk (2017) on Uber driver partners in Cairo shows why many Uber drivers prefer the platform to the often labor-intensive, low-skill jobs of the informal employment sector in Egypt. The benefits of working with a reputable company, as well the driver-partner's use of technology and incentive for self-improvement driven by the model's rating system, mean that working with the ride-sharing service is often much more attractive. Other comparative advantages include sustainability in earnings whenever driver-partners choose to use the platform and the chance to improve soft skills that are transferable to other job markets. In the Egyptian context, therefore, the story of Uber and other ride-sharing companies can be examined from the lens of opportunity against a backdrop of rampant economic challenges. As of late 2017, Uber stated that more than 150,000 drivers worked on the platform just that year (Al-Aees 2018).

Ride-sharing and Egypt's legal responses

In the particular context of Egypt, ride sharing platforms like Uber offer novel solutions to unique challenges. They provide an alternative to formal and informal employment during times of widespread economic difficulties. They are a new form of opportunity for a large and growing number of young and educated youth to either earn or supplement their income, especially with the flexibility of driver-partners to select the times they drive with the platform. With their emergence comes the challenge of integrating a novel model into pre-existing legislative infrastructure. The section below offers more details on the Egyptian legal framework before the emergence of ride sharing platform and on the timeline of events surrounding the different legal responses from the Egyptian government.

Egypt's legal framework

Ride-sharing companies seem to perform a similar function as taxis, but they are not licensed as such and were not faced with many of the regulations imposed on taxi drivers. Uber, in fact, defines its service not as transportation, but as connecting drivers and users. This highlights a key challenge for the sharing economy: sharing platforms often do not fit within existing legal frameworks. On the contrary, most legal systems are designed to manage economic relationships in a "binary" manner, such as landlord and tenant, or employer and employee (Crespo 2016, 79–110). In the sharing economy, however, "many of these relationships overlap," creating difficulties in determining applicable laws or regulations, if any. This legal "grey area" is one that multiple players, including Uber and other rider sharing players, traditional taxis, and the government, found themselves in, in the context of Egypt (Crespo 2016, 79–110). Because Uber's model operates via the ride-sharing of privately owned vehicles, it does and cannot fall entirely within existing legal dichotomy of either private or commercial vehicle use.

Prior to the Ride Hailing Act of 2018, regulations governing licensing and fees for various vehicles were outlined under Law No. 155 of 1999, amending Law No. 66 of 1973, commonly known as "the Traffic Law." Article 3 of the law categorizes vehicles as either private or commercial vehicles. Private vehicles are defined as those intended solely to transport passengers for personal use. Commercial vehicles are defined either as "taxis," intended to transport passengers in return for a fee, or "vehicles intended to transport passengers," mainly encompassing public buses, tourist buses, and school buses (Egyptian Central Traffic Department 1999, Article 3).

Article 51 of the law dictates that an attached annex outlines the taxes and fees required by vehicle owners. Under the annex, drivers of commercial vehicles, under which white taxis are categorized, are required to pay two types of insurance. The first is regular vehicle insurance, which is required both for private and commercial vehicles. However, the law imposes a second commercial insurance on drivers of commercial vehicles. In order to obtain the required taxi license needed to operate as such, the law stipulated that taxi drivers must show proof of payment for both regular vehicle insurance and commercial insurance. Taxi licenses were then valid for one year. Moreover, specifically with regards to commercial vehicle licensing, the law requires drivers of such vehicles, including taxis, to indicate whether more than one driver will operate the vehicle. If this is the case, an additional social insurance fee is required by the commercial vehicle owner for each additional driver (Egyptian Central Traffic Department 1999, Article 51). Therefore, in addition to the "gap" in the law regarding ride-sharing regulation, pre-existing legislation imposes burdensome requirements on commercial white-taxi drivers.

The white-taxi response: protests 2014–2016

In February 2016, white-taxi drivers began protesting the status of ride-sharing platforms in Egypt. The paragraphs below elaborate on and provide key features of the legislative process that began as the government moved to respond to this market disruption. This section also presents examples from other countries for purposes of comparison. Because of the "legal grey area" faced by ride-sharing platforms in Egypt, along with taxi drivers' growing frustration with what they perceived as unfair competition, Uber's rapid growth in Cairo and other Egyptian cities has not been without problems. In February 2016, slightly more than a year after the company first launched in Cairo, Egypt's traditional, or "white-taxi" drivers organized a mass protest to demand the government immediately ban both Uber, along with Careem. The protests against both applications were based on the allegations that vehicles operating through these ride-sharing apps "operated as taxis yet were not licensed as such" under the Traffic Law (Alaa El-Din 2016). Uber initially responded to these allegations by stating that the company was operating legally in Egypt by relying on drivers sourced from domestic registered limousine and rental service providers that have valid commercial licenses and tax IDs, in addition to fulfilling their taxation requirements accordingly (Ragheb 2016). Moreover, the Authority on Investment and Free Zones affirmed that Uber was licensed as an Internet and mobile phone applications company under the Egyptian Investment Law No. 159. This statement was subsequently affirmed by both Uber and Careem.

Maintaining that ride-sharing services were both illegal in Egypt, as well as a threat to their livelihoods, hundreds of white-taxi drivers continued to protest with the backing of the land transportation workers' union. In response, during a coinciding visit to Egypt, Uber's Senior Vice President of Policy and Strategy David Plouffe stated that taxi drivers in many of Uber's markets have been misled into believing their livelihoods are being jeopardized by Uber, but that the ride-sharing application, in fact, can help "create an additional and flexible avenue of income for taxi drivers who otherwise would be bound to taxi companies" (Elkadeem 2017). In the case of Egypt, however, neither of these claims has yet to be confirmed by independent research or available data.

In August 2016, however, the Egyptian House Communication and Information Technology (CIT) Committee responded to increasing pressure from white-taxi drivers by holding hearings with both Uber and Careem to examine an acceptable framework for ride hailing applications in the Egyptian context. The hearings found that Uber drivers are indeed obliged to file tax returns locally, but that due to a dual-taxation agreement, Uber as a company did not pay taxes in Egypt, but rather is taxed in the Netherlands, where one of its international headquarters is based (Elshowaikhy 2017). At the hearing, representatives of both Uber and Careem called for special permits to be provided to their drivers to counter allegations of illegal licensing. Based on the outcome of these hearings, the House of Representatives' ICT Committee set forth a plan to draft legislation to regulate car-hailing apps. Meanwhile, the Committee pushed ride-sharing companies to incorporate white-taxi drivers into their business model by allowing users the option to order a white taxi (Salah 2016).

Taxi drivers were frustrated by the failure to integrate taxis into ride-sharing business models due to a lack of user interest in selecting white taxis through the apps, as well as by the continuing growth of Uber and other ride-sharing applications in Egypt. Subsequently, 42 white-taxi drivers filed a class action in Egypt's Administrative Court in early 2017, calling for a complete shutdown of operations of both Uber and Careem. Taxi drivers argued that ride-sharing apps illegally used private cars to function as taxis. They stated that due to Article 54 of the Traffic Law, which stipulates that owners of vehicles used in transporting individuals pay various taxes and fees, Uber and other ride-sharing applications had an unfair advantage because they did not have to pay the same kinds of taxes or fees imposed on taxi drivers.

The government's response: towards a draft bill for ride hailing applications

In an effort to authorize the operation of ride-sharing platforms, the Egyptian cabinet approved a draft Ride Hailing Apps Act in April 2017. The draft bill stipulated that ride sharing service providers would need to acquire specific permits for vehicles used under these apps and would also be made to pay taxes locally. However, the bill continued to be pending sign-off from the Cabinet and House of Representatives for over a year (Elshowaikhy 2017). Meanwhile, Uber and other ride-sharing applications continued operating under their status as a licensed technology company under the Investment Law.

In parallel, while the Ride Hailing Apps bill remained unsigned, Egypt's Administrative Court ruled on the case raised by white-taxi drivers and initially ordered the suspension of licenses for ride-sharing apps in March 2018. However, Uber and other ride-sharing apps swiftly appealed the ruling with the Supreme Administrative Court, challenging charges by taxi drivers of the companies operating illegally by stating that the apps were operating legally within the existing legal framework and had received licenses to operate from both the Egyptian government and the Ministry of Investment (Reuters Staff 2018). The ride-sharing companies added that they operated under these licenses while awaiting the passage of the Ride-Hailing Apps Act to fully regulate their operations. It seemed that the Executive and Legislative were at odds: while the House of Representatives was clearly trying to conciliate white-taxi drivers, the government was more interested in securing economic and future investment interests.

In an attempt to complement its development strategy, initiate regulations on the sharing economy and protect investment, as well as remedy the clearly divergent decision made by the Administrative Court, the government rushed to legalize ride-hailing apps by pushing for the Ride-Hailing Apps Act to pass before the Supreme Administrative Court decided on the ride-sharing companies' appeal (Aman 2018). Due to heavy backlash against data-sharing clauses in the Act mandating that ride-hailing companies store user data on their servers abroad for a period of 180 days and make information accessible to government agencies, final voting by the House on the Ride-Hailing Apps Act was postponed several times despite an imminent hearing scheduled to decide on the appeal by ride-sharing companies of the lower court decision. Meanwhile, the companies continued to operate under a Court of Urgent Matters ruling that allowed for temporary operations (Abdelaziz 2018).

Key features of the Egyptian Ride Hailing Apps Act

Days before the Egyptian Supreme Administrative Court was scheduled to decide on the appeal case raised by ride-sharing applications against the lower court's decision that decided on the suspension of their operations, the House of Representatives approved its Ride Hailing Apps Act on May 7, 2018 (Abdel Qader et al. 2018). The Act, consisting of 20 articles, outlines the procedures and conditions necessary for ride-sharing companies to operate legally in Egypt. Parliament initially passed the law without amending its most controversial clauses on access to user data, namely Articles 9 and 10 of the Act (Rabea 2018).

The Act created a specific licensing framework for ride sharing companies and gave companies a three-month period after receiving their operating licenses to design a strategy to incorporate white taxis in their fleets and train white-taxi drivers to meet companies' quality standards. The law in its final form imposed higher licensing fees than the initial bill specified. It required ride-sharing companies to pay up to EGP 30 million (USD 1.71 million) to receive their five-year operating license. Ride sharing companies have to pay a 25 percent down payment on these licenses, with the remaining portion of the fees delivered in installments over the five-year licensing period. In addition, drivers working under ride-sharing applications are required to pay up to EGP 2000 for annual licenses, in addition to paying taxes at a rate 25 percent higher than that paid by white-taxi drivers via their obligations under the Traffic Law. Finally, ride-sharing companies must also pay a one-time fee "lower than the cost of the operating license" in order to legalize their status under the Ride-Hailing Apps Act. The Law set a penalty between EGP 200,000 and 5 million on ride sharing companies operating without receiving the required licenses. The bill gave the Minister of Transport authority to decide on the number of operating licenses that would be issued to vehicles working within ride-sharing companies, up to a maximum of 10 million licenses (Rabea 2018).

Uber representatives in Cairo seemed accommodating of the law. The Egyptian Ministry of Investment and International Cooperation praised the Act as "encouraging" for the ride-sharing industry, adding that the legislation will also protect competition within the transport sector. As for numerous Uber drivers, however, among them government employees, the law was felt to be unfair and restrictive, mostly due to the law's requirement that ride-sharing drivers display the ride-sharing company's logo on their private cars. Under Egyptian Law, government employees are prohibited to be employed elsewhere (Almasry Alyoum 2018). According to Khaled El-Gammal, the lawyer representing the class action initially brought forth by taxi drivers in Egypt's Administrative Court, the number of taxi drivers involved in the lawsuit dwindled incrementally due to a growing realization by taxi drivers that the government would not ban ride hailing apps. Instead, he stated that taxi drivers preferred allocating their time realistically towards "working, not fighting" (interview by author with El-Gammal).

Little more than a month after being passed by Parliament, the Ride Hailing Apps Act was ratified by Egyptian President Abdel Fattah El Sisi. After generating controversy over Articles 9 and 10 that allowed government access to private user data, the Act was modified to allow governmental authorities to access data on a case-by-case basis, resulting in a watered-down version of the initial clauses allowing for access to real-time user data (Youm7 2018). In short, the legislative process seemed very accommodating towards large players, but it is useful to evaluate the extent to which Egyptian legislation was mindful of the budding trend of successful local ride-sharing startups that offer opportunities for sustainable, inclusive development, and the degree to which the emergence of these Egyptian companies was embraced as part of the legislative drafting process and outcome. The next section utilizes an access to knowledge perspective to analyze the degree of comprehensiveness of the Ride Hailing Apps Act, and the extent to which it is truly inclusive of all players in the ride-sharing market.

An A2K perspective: towards more openness and inclusion

The Egyptian government responded relatively quickly to the issue at hand. Nevertheless, in applying an A2K framework to the case of the Ride Hailing Apps Act, it is important to examine the degree of inclusiveness of different stakeholders in the legislative process. Based on the above analysis it shows that the final outcome of ride-sharing legislation in Egypt, and the process through which it was created, was centered on large players. These were international ride-sharing players like Uber and its regional counterpart Careem, on the one hand, and on the other hand white-taxi drivers and union representatives. Mostly overlooked, however, were local ride-sharing and carpooling companies, part of Egypt's growing entrepreneurial, and especially tech-based, ecosystem.

The Ride Hailing Apps Act was coined as the "Uber and Careem Law" not only by the media, but by lawmakers as well. Participants in the process of creating the law included the House of Representatives ICT Committee, taxi drivers, and large ride-sharing companies Uber and Careem. However, the legislative process did not incorporate a sufficient range of ride sharing companies in Egypt to ensure the creation of a truly inclusive law that fairly represented a variety of ride-sharing services in Egypt. Notably, smaller local ride-sharing companies were excluded in the process. Given the entrepreneurial potential of technology-based transport solutions for Cairo and for other sharing economy platforms, a more inclusive process could have also brought representatives of the entrepreneurial ecosystem on board.

Uber's statement following the passing of the Ride Hailing Apps Act deemed the law "a major step forward for the ride-sharing industry as Egypt becomes one of the first countries in the Middle East to pass progressive regulations" (Minifie and Blowers 2016). Uber's reaction to the law in Egypt is similar to the rhetoric it has used in reaction to legislative action in a variety of countries, such as Brazil or France. The case of Uber in Egypt reflects the clear benefits that can arise from the sharing economy, including "boosting employment and incomes for those on the fringe of the labor market, and putting thousands of underused [...] assets to work," as described by the Grattan Institute (Minifie and Blowers 2016). In a unique context where Uber has served as a safe, reliable, and novel alternative in a city with heavy congestion, large gaps in modes of public transportation, poor infrastructure, and rampant sexual harassment, the Ride Hailing Apps Act has served to comprehensively legalize and regulate the operation of Uber in Egypt. The Act has served to substantiate Uber's presence in the Egyptian market, allowing the company to continue to provide alternative means of employment and transportation.

While it is a positive and favorable step for larger players such as Uber, there is room for more openness and inclusiveness in terms of accommodating home-grown entrepreneurship in ride-sharing and in the sharing economy in general. The legislation certainly provides increased opportunities and encouragement for foreign investment, but it is crucial that new legislation find a balance between providing incentives for established international players in the ride-sharing market, such as Uber, and prioritizing the needs of nascent, local entrepreneurs attempting to enter the market.

The current Ride Hailing Apps Act's clauses certainly include barriers to entry for smaller local ride-sharing applications (Enterprise Ventures 2018c). While Uber and Careem, around which the law was formed, are major multinational companies that are able to bear the heavy licensing, taxation, and penalty costs that the Act imposes on ride-sharing services, local startups with comparatively minimal funding will undoubtedly find it much more difficult to comply with the burdensome financial requirements of the law.

Aware of this discrepancy, Mostafa Kandil, founder of local ride-sharing platform Swvl, stated that while the Ride Hailing Apps Act was a positive step towards creating a legitimate space for ride-sharing platforms in general, the regulations imposed by it did not necessarily encourage the prosperity of smaller local players, or provide incentives for their growth (interview by author with Kandil). He made the point that the Egyptian market is currently extremely price sensitive, and increased licensing and taxation fees on both companies and drivers only mean that prices will have to be raised for consumers.

Kandil confirmed that while Swvl was the only local startup invited to participate in the process of drafting the Ride Hailing Apps Act, their actual input was not requested. His experience witnessing the drafting process of the Act made it clear that the legislative process as a whole was not geared towards the inclusion of small, local startups (interview by author with Kandil).

Important to note is that the Ride Hailing Apps Act does not only apply to traditional passenger cars, but "land vehicles and mass transit" in general. This means that the Act affects novel services that utilize private bus sharing services, including Swvl. Local ride-sharing companies based on the use of tuk-tuks or motorcycles, such as Halan, are likely to remain unaffected, however. The Egyptian House of Representatives Transport Committee confirmed that while the Act applies to "land vehicles and mass transit," this definition does not include tuk-tuks. Instead, they confirmed that tuk-tuks are regulated through their respective municipalities (Enterprise Ventures 2018b).

The Ride Hailing Apps Act put forth regulation that incontestably facilitated the smooth operation of ride-sharing companies, such as Uber, which has provided positive alternatives for transportation, as well as socio-economic solutions in Egypt's unique context. In order for regulation to avoid harming small business looking to compete in the ride-sharing market, however, the law must aim at reforms that are inclusive of smaller businesses. This can be done by ensuring that the financial policies of the law vary based on different tiers of company size. While the Egyptian Ride Hailing Apps Act does include a tier-based financial regulation model, the lowest tier included in the law begins with fleet sizes much larger than those of small startups (Rabea 2018).

It would thus be beneficial for the law to include several lower tiers in this section of the law in order to offset the competitive advantage possessed by large ride-sharing companies and become accurately inclusive of smaller players. By doing this, the law would better capitalize on the prospective benefits local ride-sharing startups could provide. In addition to creating jobs locally, successful Egyptian ride-sharing platforms promise to bring increased foreign direct investment to the country. Swvl's Kandil put forth that the company has already raised more than $10 million, and are likely to raise another $40–50 million, with plans of expanding globally, in the near future. Startups that experience local success that enables them to branch out globally also bring the additional benefit of generating revenue in foreign currency, which would then be funneled back into the Egyptian market.

Conclusion

The case of Uber's confrontation with legislation in Egypt and around the globe undeniably sheds light on the dichotomy of innovation versus legislation in the new sharing economy era. The focus of innovation in the sharing economy is no longer limited to its traditional sense of "creating new things;" instead, it seeks to revolutionize the way in which business is traditionally done by fostering participation and communal ownership. More specifically, the sharing economy focuses on consumer wants and needs. Uber and other ride-sharing services have provided alternatives to the traditional transportation industry in a manner that has demonstrably filled various consumer demand for these services.

The challenges, therefore, that Uber has faced both from traditional taxi drivers and governmental bodies around the world, seem to miss the point of this new sharing economy. The recent creation of regulation in Egypt serves the important function of creating legitimacy for the novel alternatives provided by the ride-sharing market. Moreover, the establishment of clearly defined legislation allows for rules than promote fair competition, increased guarantees to secure and protect consumer experience, and a system to ensure safety-oriented guidelines.

Legislation, however, should not be selective in encouraging fair competition in the transport market. While laws that legalize, and regulate, ride-sharing services such as Uber are successful in providing space for these applications to compete with traditional players in the area of transportation, it is important for regulation to be inclusive of different tiers in the ride-sharing market. In order to avoid passing legislation that erroneously only caters to, and allows for monopolization of, the ride-sharing market by large, high-valued companies, laws must be created or reformed to become inclusive of smaller ride-sharing startups that create valuable competition in the new ride-sharing market.

Note

1 No evidence has shown that Uber or other ride-sharing platforms have completely solved issues of sexual harassment.

References

Abdel Qader, Mohammed, Mohammed Ghareeb, and Khaled Elshamy. 2018. "Parliament Passes "Uber and Careem" and Requires to Provide Data for «National Security» When Needed." *Almasry Alyoum*, May 7. http://www.almasryalyoum.com/new/details/1288490.

Abdelaziz, Nagwa. 2018. "Ruling Against Uber and Careem Being Considered." *Almal News*, 12 May. http://www.almalnews.com/Story/374884/19/نظر-طعن-أوبر-وكريم-على-حكم-منع-نشاطهما—12-مايو.

Adghirni, Samy, and Simone Preissler Iglesias. 2018. "Uber Scores Victory With New Brazil Legislation." *Bloomberg*, March 1. https://www.bloomberg.com/news/articles/2018-03-01/uber-scores-victory-with-new-brazil-legislation-in-major-market.

Al-Aees, Shaimaa. 2018. "150,000 Drivers Joined Uber Egypt in 2017." *Daily News Egypt*, February 15. https://www.pressreader.com/egypt/the-daily-news-egypt/20180215/281621010803775.

Alaa El-Din, Menna. 2016. "Cairo Taxi Drivers Call for Protests to Ban Uber, Careem Services." *Ahram Online*, February 3. http://english.ahram.org.eg/NewsContent/1/64/186586/Egypt/Politics-/Cairo-taxi-drivers-call-for-protests-and-suspensio.aspx.

Almasry Alyoum. 2018. "Uber and Careem Drivers Say New Law 'Unfair'." *Egypt Independent*, April 1. https://www.egyptindependent.com/uber-careem-drivers-say-new-law-unfair/.

Aman, Aya. 2018. "The Government Refers the Law on the Regulation of Land Transport Using Information Technology to the Parliament." *Shorouk News*, March 21. http://www.shorouknews.com/news/view.aspx?cdate=21032018&id=440e5436-de30-430e-91fe-0676344cb9c3.

Assaad, Ragui, and Caroline Krafft. 2015. *The Egyptian Labor Market in an Era of Revolution*. Oxford: Oxford University Press.

Ayesh, Mohammed. 2016. "Egypt Economic Crisis: Four Ways Currency Flotation Will Cause More Problems Than It Solves." *Middle East Eye*, November 23. http://www.middleeasteye.net/columns/four-ways-egypt-s-pound-flotation-will-cause-more-problems-it-solves-2013820354. Balkin, Jack. 2008. "Foreword." In *Access to Knowledge in Brazil: New Research on Intellectual Property, Innovation and Development*. Edited by Lea Shaver. New Haven, CT: Information Society Project.

Balkin, Jack. 2010. "Foreword." In *Access to Knowledge in Egypt: New Research on Intellectual Property, Innovation and Development*. Edited by Nagla Rizk and Lea Shaver, xix–xxi. London: Bloomsbury Academic.

Bensinger, Greg. 2017. "What is Uber Really Worth?" *The Wall Street Journal*, November 15. https://www.wsj.com/articles/with-two-price-tags-from-softbank-what-is-uber-really-worth-1510741802.

Business Insider. 2018. "Egypt's president approves law for ride-hailing apps." *Business Insider*, June 24. http://www.businessinsider.com/ap-egypts-president-approves-law-for-ride-hailing-apps-2018-6.

Central Agency for Public Mobilization and Statistics (CAPMAS). 2016. "Egypt in Figures." Central Agency for Public Mobilization and Statistics (CAPMAS). Last Accessed July 24, 2018. http://www.capmas.gov.eg/Pages/StaticPages.aspx?page_id=5035.

Credit Suisse. 2015. *Global Investor: The Sharing Economy, New Opportunities, New Questions*. Zürich: Investment Strategy &Research. https://www.oxfordmartin.ox.ac.uk/downloads/GI_215_e_GesamtPDF_01_high.pdf.

Crespo, Yanelys. 2016. "Uber v. Regulation: "Ride-Sharing" Creates a Legal Gray Area." *University of Miami Business Law Review* 25 (1): 79–110. https://repository.law.miami.edu/cgi/viewcontent.cgi?article=1285&context=umblr.

Dervojeda, Kristina, Diederik Verzijl, Fabian Nagtegaal, Mark Lengton, Elco Rouwmaat, Erica Monfardini and Laurent Frideres. 2013. "The Sharing Economy: Accessibility Based Business Models for Peer to Peer Markets". The European Commission. http://ec.europa.eu/growth/content/accessibility-based-business-models-peer-peer-markets_en.

Egypt Today Staff. 2017. "Careem Invests $10M in Egypt Since Opening, 30% Growth Monthly." *Egypt Today*, August 1. https://www.egypttoday.com/Article/3/14990/Careem-invests-10M-in-Egypt-since-opening-30-growth-monthly.

Egyptian Central Traffic Department. 1999. "Article 4." In *The Law No. 155 of 1999, Amending Law No. 66 of 1973*. Cairo: Egyptian Central Traffic Department. http://www.moiegypt.gov.eg/Arabic/Departments+Sites/Traffic/trafficlaw/66/puplicWay/types/.

Elkadeem, Maha. 2017. "David Plouffe, Uber SVP Talk about the Importance of the Sharing Economy". The American University in Cairo, n.d. http://schools.aucegypt.edu/Business/aucvlab/Pages/David-Plouffe-talks-about-the-Sharing-Economy.aspx.

El-Sayed, Jehad. 2018. "Halan' app hails tuk-tuks, motorbikes, tricycles in slums." *Egypt Today*, April 5. https://www.egypttoday.com/Article/1/47056/%E2%80%98Halan%E2%80%99-app-hails-tuk-tuks-motorbikes-tricycles-in-slums.

Elserty, Amro. 2017. "Careem Invests in Egyptian Transportation Startup Swvl." *Forbes Middle East*. July 17. https://www.forbesmiddleeast.com/en/careem-invests-in-egyptian-transportation-startup-swvl/.

Elshowaikhy, Abdel Razek. 2017. "'Egyptian Parliament is Preparing to Draft a Law to Reconcile the Conditions of "Uber' and "Careem'." *Al Borsa News*, February 2. https://www.alborsanews.com/2017/02/02/970557.

Enterprise Ventures LLC. 2016. "House Holds Hearing on Legal Status of Uber and Careem." *Enterprise*. Last Modified August 9, 2016. https://enterprise.press/stories/2016/08/09/house-holds-hearing-on-legal-status-of-uber-and-careem/.

Enterprise Ventures LLC. 2018a. "Halan, a Ridesharing App for Tuktuks and Motorcycles, Closes in on USD 2 MN Fundraising Round." *Enterprise*. Last Modified March 25, 2018. https://enterprise.press/stories/2018/03/25/halan-a-ridesharing-app-for-tuktuks-and-motor cycles-closes-in-on-usd-2-mn-fundraising-round/.

Enterprise Ventures LLC. 2018b. "Final vote on Ride-Hailing Apps Act postponed in House on account of controversial clauses." *Enterprise*. Last Modified May 7, 2018. https://enterp rise.press/stories/2018/05/07/final-vote-on-ride-hailing-apps-act-postponed-in-house-on-a ccount-of-controversial-clauses/.

Enterprise Ventures LLC. 2018c. "Parliament Looks to Smother Ride-Hailing in The Baby Crib by Approving an Even Worse Version of The Ride-Hailing Apps Act." *Enterprise*. Last Modified May 8, 2018. https://enterprise.press/stories/2018/05/08/parliam ent-looks-to-smother-ride-hailing-in-the-baby-crib-by-approving-an-even-worse-version-of-the-ride-hailing-apps-act/.

Farid, Doaa. 2017. "Is Egypt Finally Ready for Ride-Sharing?." *Wamda*. Last Modified April 09, 201. https://www.wamda.com/memakersge/2017/04/egypt-finally-ready-for-ride-sharing.

ILO Department of Statistics. 2012. "Statistical Update on Employment in the Informal Economy." International Labor Organization. http://laborsta.ilo.org/applv8/data/INFORMAL_ECONOMY/2012-06-Statistical%20update%20-%20v2.pdf [Accessed 19 Jul. 2018].

International Monetary Fund. n.d. "Arab Republic of Egypt." http://www.imf.org/en/Countries/EGY.

Jericho, Greg. 2016. "The Dark Side of Uber." *The Guardian*. https://www.theguardian.com/business/grogonomics/2016/apr/18/uber-airbnb-sharing-economy-tougher-rules-australia.

Kapoor, Raj. 2014. "Lessons from the Sharing Economy." *Tech Crunch*, August 31. https://techcrunch.com/2014/08/30/critical-lessons-from-the-sharing-economy/.

Kassem, Taha. 2014. "Formalizing the Informal Economy: A Required State Regulatory and Institutional Approach – Egypt as a Case Study." *International Journal of Humanities & Social Sciences* 4 (1): 27–48. https://enterprise.press/wp-content/uploads/2016/08/50535_77_17_Formalizing-the-Informal-Economy-2.pdf.

Mabrouk, Ahmed. 2018. "Egypt-Based SWVL Raises $8 Million In Series A Funding." *Forbes Middle East*, April 23. https://www.forbesmiddleeast.com/en/egypt-based-swvl-ra ises-8-million-in-series-a-funding/.

Minifie, Jim, and David Blowers. 2016. *Peer-To-peer Pressure: Policy for the Sharing Economy*. Carlton, Victoria: Grattan Institute.

Ministry of Communications and Information Technology. 2018. "ICT Indicators in Brief: January 2018 | Monthly Issue." Egyptian Ministry of Communications and Information Technology. January. http://www.mcit.gov.eg/Upcont/Documents/Publications_1532018000_En_ICT_Indicators_in_Brief_January_2018.pdf.

Morency, Catherine. 2006. "The Ambivalence of Ridesharing." *Transportation* 34 (2): 239–253. doi:10.1007/s11116-006-9101-9..

Nakat, Ziad, Santiago Herrera, and Yassine Cherkaoui. 2014. *Cairo Traffic Congestion Study: Executive Note*. Washington, DC: The World Bank Group. http://www.worldbank.org/content/dam/Worldbank/TWB-Executive-Note-Eng.pdf.

Posen, Hannah A. 2016. "*Ridesharing in the Sharing Economy: Should Regulators Impose Über Regulations on Uber?*." *Iowa Law Review* 101 (1): 405–433. https://ilr.law.uiowa.edu/print/volume-101-issue-1/ridesharing-in-the-sharing-economy-should-regulators-impose-ueber-regulations-on-uber/.

Rabea, Rania. 2018. "We Publish the Text of The "Uber and Careem" Law After The Approval of the Parliament." *Shorouk News*, May 6. http://www.shorouknews.com/news/view.aspx?cdate=06052018&id=680064f7-b364-44d7-a06c-c84a335de5a7.

Ragheb, Shereen. 2016. "Uber: We Operate Legally." *Almal News*, March 8. http://www.almalnews.com/Story/273761/18/أوبر-نعمل-بشكل-قانونى—والمرور-تتحايل.

Rashad, Radwa. 2016. "Ousta is Driving Ride-Hailing Expansion in Egypt." *Tech Crunch*. June 5. https://techcrunch.com/2016/06/05/ousta-egypts-first-local-ride-hailing-app-grows-to-expand-in-5-cities-in-fewer-than-3-months/.

Reuters Staff. 2018. "UPDATE 3-Egypt Court Orders Suspension of Uber, Careem Services in Victory for Taxis –Sources." *Reuters*, March 20. https://af.reuters.com/article/commoditiesNews/idAFL8N1R24A4.

Rizk, Nagla. 2017. "A Glimpse into the Sharing Economy: An Analysis of Uber Driver-Partners in Egypt." *SSRN Papers*, February 22. http://dx.doi.org/10.2139/ssrn.2946083.

Said, Mona. 2015. "Policies and Interventions on Youth Employment in Egypt." European Training Foundation. http://www.etf.europa.eu/webatt.nsf/0/8B7FE470410B4DB8C1257E28004C06CA/$file/Employment%20policies_Egypt.pdf.

Salah, Kareem. 2016. "Chairman of the Communications Committee at the Parliament: Bill to Protect the Confidentiality of Data Soon." *Al Borsa News*, September 28. https://www.alborsanews.com/2016/09/28/904673.

Schneider, Henrique. 2017. "What is Uber's Business Model?" In *Creative Destruction and the Sharing Economy: Uber as Disruptive Innovation*. Cheltenham: Edward Elgar Publishing Limited.

The World Bank. N.d. "GDP growth (annual %) – Egypt, Arab Rep. Data Catalog." The World Bank. Last Accessed July 24, 2018. https://data.worldbank.org/indicator/NY.GDP.MKTP.KD.ZG?contextual=default&end=2015&locations=EG&name_desc=true&start=2000%20&view=chart.

The World Bank. 2012. "Cairo Traffic is Much More Than a Nuisance." The World Bank. Last Modified August 21, 2012. http://www.worldbank.org/en/news/feature/2012/08/21/cairo-traffic-much-more-than-nuisance.

Uber. 2017. "U.S. Terms of Use." Uber Technologies Inc. Modified December 13, 2017. https://www.uber.com/legal/terms/us/. Uber. 2018. "How Uber Works." Uber Technologies Inc. Last Accessed July 25, 2018. https://www.uber.com/en-EG/about/how-does-uber-work/.

Uber Egypt. 2018. "Drive with Uber in Egypt". Uber. Last Accessed September 12, 2018. https://www.uber.com/en-EG/drive/.

Werr, Patrick. 2017. "Egypt's Public Transport a Matter of Real Urgency." *The National*. April 19. https://www.thenational.ae/business/egypt-s-public-transport-a-matter-of-real-urgency-1.4791.

Worldometers. 2018. "Egypt Population (Live)." *Worldometers*. http://www.worldometers.info/world-population/egypt-population/.

Youm7. 2018. "El Sisi Issues Law Regulation Transport Services Using Information Technology". *Youm7*, 24 June.https://www.youm7.com/story/2018/6/24/3845982/السيسى-يصدر-قانون-تنظيم-خدمات-النقل-البرى-للركاب-باستخدام-تكنولوجيا.

Zawya. 2015. "Uber in Egypt Creates Over 2000 Job Opportunities a Month." *Zawya*, December 27. https://www.zawya.com/mena/en/story/Uber_in_Egypt_creates_over_2000_job_opportunities_a_month-ZAWYA20151227095115/.

Interviews

Khaled El-Gammal (lawyer representing the class action brought forth by taxi drivers in Egypt's Administrative Court), in discussion with the author, February 19, 2018.
Mostafa Kandil (founder of local ride-sharing platform Swvl), in discussion with the author, July 5, 2018.

12

CONTRADICTIONS AND TENSIONS IN MOBILE TECHNOLOGIES AND A2K

Stefanie Felsberger

Mobile technologies have had a stellar history of success. The mobile phone has made access to the Internet and communications technology in general more affordable and accessible to a much larger group of people than ever before. This is the story that has been repeated in reports and newspaper articles around the world. Since the mobile phone has become the most commonly used avenue for people to access information and knowledge, this book has aimed to ask how this transformation has played out in different places around the world. The chapters in this book paint very different pictures of how mobile technologies have shaped and have been shaped by their specific contexts. They complicate the notion that mobile phones have simply increased access to information or knowledge.

The different chapters provided detailed snapshots of the different discussions and conversations around mobile technologies as they played out in each of their contexts. The chapters did not all come to the same conclusions, instead they gave us seemingly contradictory insights into the politics, histories, and different lived realities of mobile technologies. One example is how mobile technologies have simultaneously enabled access and control. In their respective chapters on Hong Kong and South Korea, authors Colin Agur and Shubhangi Gokhale outlined how mobile phones were used by people to mobilize against oppression and for more rights. On the contrary, the chapter on Brazil by Dennys Antonialli and Jacqueline de Souza as well as the chapter on Syria by Harry Halpin elucidated how mobile technologies were used by the powerful to suppress dissent. Others brought to the fore the economic opportunities or legal challenges posed by the swiftly developing technological landscapes. Nagla Rizk's chapter, for example, examined the former and demonstrates Uber's economic success in Egypt.

It was important to us as editors of this volume not to take a stance on whether mobile technologies either further or hamper access to knowledge. As the different chapters clearly show, mobile technologies can lead to both. The chapters in this book come to seemingly contradictory conclusions about the potential of mobile technologies for empowerment or control due to the multifaceted nature of mobile technologies' impact around the world. They showcase how differently the discourses around the potentials and pitfalls of mobile technologies manifest in the different sites of investigation our authors have chosen or written from. Combined, these ten chapters provide a multilayered and complex picture of the different ways in which mobile technologies have impacted access to knowledge around the world.

The chapters together raise many questions about the conflicting and sometimes murky "agencies and urgencies" in relation to mobile technologies and access to knowledge (Franklin and Roberts 2006, 2): can mobile technologies enable better access to knowledge and at what cost? How have states promoted or demoted the spread of mobile technologies and what role have international intellectual property regimes played in this? What is the impact of international or local tech companies in the spread of mobile technologies and as intermediary to people's access to knowledge? Are the people who use these technologies able to shape and contribute to their production and implementation?

Each chapter has provided different answers to these questions and thus contributed differently to the overall Access to Knowledge (A2K) framework. Lourdusamy and Czarzasta's study on enhancing the study of a foreign language in India through mobile technologies provided an example of how mobile technologies could encourage the access to knowledge, specifically language, through immersion. Matthew, Kumar, and Subramanian's chapter looked at efforts to increase people's access to ICT in rural India and cautioned that access to (mobile) technology does not equal access to knowledge. In a chapter on the diffusion of mobile technology in Botswana, Lesitaokana looked at the ways in which access to mobile technologies has enabled access to public services. Bottino, Souza, and Nunes analyzed the intersections and trade-offs between access to knowledge and arguments about safety they identified in a debate on blocking non-approved cell phones in Brazil. They showed how access to knowledge could be at odds with economic and regulatory interests. Halpin's chapter argued, based on insights gained from Syria, that access to knowledge needed to also entail access to the means of communication, if that access were to be free and uncontrolled. Armijo argued that rights over access to knowledge must not be promoted at the expense of other rights such as freedom of expression, instead human rights need to be enshrined into the infrastructures that enable access to knowledge. Antonialli and de Souza Abreu's chapter on Brazil showed us how access to knowledge enabled by the quick spread of mobile technologies, needed to be legally protected, otherwise law enforcement would abuse loopholes to violate people's privacy rights. Agur's chapter traced the ways in which mobile technologies were utilized in Hong Kong's social and political movements. Gokhale took a similar approach and investigated the role of mobile technologies in spreading information about corruption in South Korea. Both chapters are important contributions that analyze to the scale and speed with which information can be spread through mobile technologies. Finally, Rizk took the A2K framework to analyze how different ride-sharing companies managed to participate in shaping legislation in Egypt.

What unites all chapters is the question how mobile technologies have changed the ways in which people in different places around the planet access knowledge and how mobile technologies have disrupted well-established dynamics of access. The way I have learned to understand access to knowledge has been shaped by the five years I worked at the Access to Knowledge for Development Centre (A2K4D) at the American University in Cairo and center director Nagla Rizk. Access to Knowledge in its basic tenets refers to physical access to sources of knowledge, such as a book—or in our case, a mobile phone—and the ability to understand said knowledge. At A2K4D, this definition was always understood to also include the ability to participate in the creation and sharing of knowledge based on one's personal context and understanding (Rizk and Shaver 2010). This definition shifts our understanding of access to knowledge mediated through mobile technologies.

This is also the definition that has been applied throughout the different chapters. The authors explored what happens when (mobile) infrastructures mediate access to knowledge. Already in the past, access to knowledge has depended on and been structured by different infrastructures: knowledge that is accessed through a book—a seemingly "neutral" way to access knowledge—was produced by printing presses and distributed through different infrastructures. Every kind of infrastructure enables different modes of access, control, social change, and economic opportunity. This book has been interested in the particular modes of access and control mobile technologies enable and the social and economic changes that develop as a consequence. How are mobile technologies set up and how does this configuration affect the proliferation and accessibility of cellular devices and knowledge.

We have divided the chapters into three parts, which each highlight a different aspect of how mobile technologies have impacted A2K: access, control, and social and economic opportunities. In the following pages, I will contrast and compare the insights from and conflicts between the three different parts in light of this understanding of access to knowledge.

Contrasting themes: access to knowledge vs. control

Technology, in general, and specifically information, communication, and technology (ICT) are presumed and theorized to have great potential to bring about positive change to people's lives: to increase access to knowledge but also to improve material wealth (Fuchs 2013). This is evident in the many initiatives in the development sector (ICT4D) and within societies of the Global North, to improve access to technologies. After installing the first transatlantic cable, there was hope this new technology would connect "all the nations of the earth" and eliminate "old prejudices and hostilities" (boyd 2014, 156). Today, this idea that the telegram could have had such an effect might seem shortsighted, if not outright ridiculous, but when the Internet was developed, similar hopes and dreams were voiced (Chun 2006, 2). These dreams about the Internet have also become stale today, but yet again the onset of mobile technology and smartphones spurred comparable excitement for the technology's empowering potential. This excitement is especially noticeable in the development industry which has put great emphasis on the positive potential of ICT.

Mobile technologies *can* have fantastic benefits and *can* make people's lives easier, but it is crucial to repeat that this is not always the case but specific to certain contexts and people. It is a conclusion that can only be reached after investigating who has benefited (as well as where, when, and how) from mobile technologies. This is definitely not a new insight, but a point that needs to be made again and again—especially, in the face of constantly repeating rounds of excitement over new technologies and its potentials to solve the world's problems. William Lesitaokana, in this volume, has not taken such an approach, instead he detailed how the government of Botswana significantly pushed access to mobile devices and services across the country. In his interviews with young citizens, he outlined how mobile technologies facilitated access to public services and civic participation. His chapter also provides an important counter argument to widely repeated assumptions about information-poor citizens across "Africa" and evidence that the oft-repeated arguments about the global digital divide sometimes help to entrench generalizations about the Global South, instead of providing deeper insights into global inequalities and their intersections with technology. Colin Agur and Subhangi Gohkale showed how mobile technologies have been used in Hong Kong and South Korea to organize and mobilize against oppressive governments and for greater access to information. Mobile phones were, thus, used for an empowering purpose by a group of people. In these cases, mobile technologies enabled people to participate in a meaningful way in producing and sharing information and knowledge about their political realities. By accessing and sharing the truths about their own realities people in Hong Kong and South Korea were able to mobilize and make use of mobile technologies, but in both countries, technologies have also been used towards opposite ends. The chapters detail specific snapshots in which mobile technologies enabled greater access to knowledge, but on the flipside, Harry Halpin's and Enrique Armijo's chapters are warnings against the use of mobile technologies to control access to information.

Halpin wrote about the early days of the Syrian uprising when attempts to use mobile and communications technologies to mobilize failed, because the local and international infrastructure around mobile technology enabled government control, repression, and the arrest of many activists. Based on discussions with the Syrian programmer and activist Bassel Safadi, Halpin showed how communications and mobile technologies in Syria were structured around government control. Importantly, Halpin also discussed how the global app market and the international regulations it is subject to intersected with the control exerted by the Syrian government. When sanctions were placed on Syria, the few available apps that provided safe and encrypted means of communications were not accessible through the app store anymore, leaving Syrians even more vulnerable to government surveillance. Thus, the restrictions imposed by Western governments further restricted access to safe means of communication and information. Halpin's chapter implores us to learn from Bassel's insights to build safer technologies for activists and people around the world. Enrique Armijo's chapter is a case against the assumption that increased access to mobile technologies will have an empowering effect. He wrote about publicly provided WiFi in the United States but warned that not all providers respect the rights outlined in the US constitution. He argued that providing access to the Internet must not be seen as more important than doing so in line with the rights granted by the Constitution, specifically. In short, access to the Internet must not come at the expense of freedom of speech. Armijo pointed out how a change in government could additionally lead to a fundamental change in how governments honor basic human rights such as freedom of speech, making it all the more important to enshrine human rights and social justice into the very infrastructure of communication.

The supposed contradiction between access and control which I have outlined above has been theorized by Wendy Chun (2006) in her book on *Control and Freedom.* She looks at communications technologies more broadly, and "traces the ways in which a technology, which thrives on control, has been accepted, however briefly, as a mass medium of freedom" (2006, vii). By thriving on control, Chun refers to the fact that communication technologies rely on the tracking and storing of all data in order to function, thus enabling an apparatus of control. This is the argument Dennys Antonialli and Jacqueline de Souza Abreu made in their chapter. They described how the success of smartphones has enabled new forms of surveillance due to the fact that legislative protections for online communications have lagged far behind social realities.

Chun argues that the contradiction between technology's supposed potential for emancipation or control stems from the belief in technological solutions for social or political problems (2006, 3). Is the Internet an empowering technology? Are mobile technologies a tool for freedom or control? Or more recently: Is artificial intelligence a force for good? Questions like these can only be asked when we believe that technology will provide the answer. The chapters in this volume showed that different questions need to be asked, such as: when and where and how are mobile technologies used for social good? How do we build mobile technology infrastructures that enshrine protections for human rights, people's active participation, and informed consent? How can infrastructures devoid of this inherent control potential be built so that most people have access to the social and economic opportunities these technologies provide? This question brings us to the next intersection of themes: access versus social change and economic opportunities.

Contrasting themes: social and economic opportunities vs. access to knowledge

In this section, I will outline how the chapters in this book put access in conversation with social and economic opportunities and how the insights from the different chapters bring out tensions between access to knowledge and social and economic opportunities. There are two obvious sides to this conversation: on one hand, how does access to knowledge change one's social and economic opportunities, and on the other hand, how does economic and social status influence the knowledge you can access? The line of thinking that access to technologies equals access to and thus enables better economic and social opportunities has become part of the core assumptions in the development literature (Fuchs 2013). The phone is imbued with the potential to facilitate the "circulation of 'useful information'," such as information about health care public services, and business (Archambault 2017). In light of this presupposition about the transformative potential of mobile phones, the need to close the global digital divide has become more urgent. But the insight that this relationship is not as straightforward has gained traction (Unwin 2017). Julie Archambault reminds us that "access [to mobile phones] in no way guarantees that user will use their phones in development-inducing ways" (2017, 4). The chapters in this volume take this argument seriously and investigate how different attempts to increase access to knowledge though mobile devices have played out on the ground: John Bosco Lourdusamy and Rishika Czarzasta analyzed how mobile technologies and information and communications technologies in general supported students learning a new language when it was impossible for them to physically immerse themselves in the country where the language was spoken. They came to the conclusion that these technologies helped to widen students' horizons and allowed them to better acquire language skills. Their study focused on Indian students in Chennai studying French; mobile technologies, in this case, through access to knowledge opened the students up to social and economic opportunities.

Some chapters highlighted that the relationship between access to knowledge and social as well as economic opportunities was not always as linear as sometimes presumed. I want to point out the chapter by Celina Bottino, Carlos Affonso Souza, and Beatriz Nunez, which studied debates in Brazil over a proposal to block non-approved cell phones due to—as officially stated—safety concerns. They analyze the interplay between connectivity and economic and social opportunities: banning non-approved cell phones would have disproportionally affected lowest-income segments in the population living in rural areas who were most likely to exclusively access the Internet through these mobile devices. While no technical studies were presented by the Brazilian government agency proposing the ban, the authors highlight other factors that could have motivated the ban. The non-approved devices were often cheaper, imported from China, and allowed the owner the simultaneous use of several SIM cards, enabling them to take advantage of all promotional offers of different carriers. While the state argued the phones were not safe, the ban would have amounted to an attempt by the state to control the Brazilian phone market by utilizing intellectual property regimes. Bottino, Souza, and Nunez provided us with an example where access to knowledge did not enable economic opportunities, but instead they described a trade-off between access to knowledge and economic opportunities. Economic opportunities (of different local and international companies) were played against the needs to access the Internet by the most marginalized groups in society. Enrique Armijo's chapter also addressed the intersection between access and economic opportunities in the field of mobile technologies. In the US, publicly provided WiFi networks only emerged because Internet Service Providers incentivized by the market did not provide equal access to the Internet. Access here was seen as more important than market-driven solutions but was pushed at the expense of protection for human rights. In Brazil, the state chose to intervene in the market to support local companies but at the expense of its citizens' access to the Internet. The chapters pose important questions such as: who can benefit the most from new technology? Who is left out and at whose expense?

Mobile technologies have provided enormous economic and social opportunities to those who were able to capitalize on these possibilities. The chapters in this volume highlighted another crucial question: how do social and economic differences impact how people or other actors experience technology? In her chapter, Nagla Rizk analyzed how local and international start-ups and companies accessed knowledge and how they were able to leverage this. She argued that Uber was much better situated to provide the Egyptian legislative with advice on how a new proposed Ride-Hailing Act would influence them, than other local start-ups. While Uber's privileged status enabled the company to better influence legislation, the question remains how social and economic inequalities influence impact *people's* experience of mobile technologies?

Mathew, Kumar, and Subramanian provided a crucial take on this question in their chapter on "The Last Mile," which described different efforts to connect people from the lowest income level in India. The chapter highlighted the failures and mistakes made in providing access to the Internet but also provides valuable lessons to be learned from these mistakes. What is evident from the chapter is that social and economic context shapes how people use or want to use technologies and that top-down approaches need to take marginalized people's realities seriously. Mathew, Kumar, and Subramanian made a strong case that acceptance of a new technology did not only depend on existing ICT infrastructure, but on whether people think a technology will "obviously improve their economic opportunities or quality of life." When they refer to quality of life, this means not just material improvements, but they spoke of joy. Just as Maya Indira Ganesh (2011) argues in her article "'Mobile Love Videos Make Me Feel Healthy': Rethinking ICTs for Development," Mathew, Kumar, and, Subramanian reminded us not to take a paternalistic and reductive approach when dealing with impoverished communities: technology is not just useful, but it is entertaining and brings joy, and this will factor into whether it will be accepted or not.

Mathew, Kumar, and Subramanian also provided an interesting example of how citizens seized upon the economic opportunities that ICTs can provide: one kiosk owner turned his Internet access into success. He charged people for checking exam results published on the State Examination Board's website where they were available 24 hours earlier. This example illustrates something that is indicative of this particular moment in time when knowledge and value have become almost inseparable and access to knowledge and economic and social opportunities more closely intertwined than ever. The very infrastructure that fuels the digital economy, namely mobile technology infrastructure, intimately connects A2K and economic opportunities. By accessing (knowledge on) our phones, we inadvertently produce data. This data is both a source of new knowledge we can access and a source of value for companies. How does this change how we access knowledge when each time we do we also generate more data that can be turned into value for someone else? How this intersection interacts with pressures for control will be explored in the next section.

Contrasting themes: control vs. social and economic opportunity

By analyzing the chapters through the nexus between social and economic opportunities and control, a new set of issues and tensions are illuminated. How and where do motivations for control or for providing opportunities contradict or intersect? What is the role of companies seeking economic opportunities operating in an environment focused on controlling mobile technologies? Uber's activities in Egypt fall under this category. While the chapter in this book focuses on how different ride-sharing companies participated in the legislative process, the Egyptian government attempted to gain access to Uber's data on people's movements by adding a clause to the law that would have regulated Uber's activities in the country. Fortunately, this data-sharing clause faced much backlash and was dropped. This dilemma is by no means unique to Egypt: the US government has routinely requested information from ICT companies (Angwin et al. 2015). Google has until 2019 decided to stay outside the Chinese market to avoid similar dilemmas (Gallagher 2019).

Tensions between government control and people's social or economic opportunities were apparent in several of the chapters in this volume. Mathew, Kumar, and Subramanian's chapter described efforts to further people's access to technologies and knowledge in order to provide opportunities for economic and social development. Among the many examples they drew from was a story from Bangladesh where women's access to the Internet via telecenters was denied out of fear they would be used to access pornography. Here, it appears, social opportunities were less important than controlling what kind of contents could be accessed. In Halpin's chapter on Syria, the Syrian government's overriding need to control communications infrastructure by any means necessary was the main focus. In the case of Syria, the government violently and brutally suppressed people's hopes to (use mobile technologies to) mobilize.

What next: tensions between access, opportunities, and control

The chapters in this volume illuminate much by themselves and even more in conversation with each other. There are apparent tensions between motivations to promote access, social or economic opportunities, or control which play out differently in the many contexts investigated in this book. I have addressed some of these tensions in this conclusion. In addition, there are many lessons to be learned from each chapter and from the book as a whole.

The most important lesson for myself is the renewed reminder that technology is not a solution to social, economic, or political problems. Technology, as Leila

Green argues (2001, 3), is not something neutral or "outside society". It is not society's role "adapt to (and benefit from) technological change" (Green 2001, 2). Technological progress and development are not inevitable, but mobile technologies do in fact *have politics* (Winner 1980)[1] and social, economic, and political environments, geography, race, class, and gender rather than technology itself determine its use, adoption, and consequences (MacKenzie and Wajcman 1999, Archambault 2017). How then do we apply these insights to build technologies without the inherent tensions between access, control, and social and economic opportunities? There are lessons in each chapter which can help to create parameters for "better" mobile technologies; technologies that enable access for as many as possible but do not enable pervasive tracking, that people can use to demand social change but cannot be used against them by global tech companies or governments, and that are accessible but do not force us to relinquish control over the data we produce.

The chapters have illuminated particular cases of how mobile technologies have fundamentally altered access to knowledge in Brazil, India, Hong Kong, Syria, South Korea, Botswana, the United States of America, and Egypt. But there are many areas, contexts, and issues that this book did not address that remain on the research agenda. Much more is left to be illuminated about how the commodification of people's data shifts the dynamics around access to knowledge. Can access to knowledge be free when data itself is value? Another set of issues involves the ecological costs of mobile technologies and ICT in general. What are the tensions between preserving the planet and increasing access to knowledge? How can these tensions be eliminated? Finally, how does gender intersect with access to knowledge?

The access to knowledge framework is also how I would like to end this conclusion. To recap, I understand access to knowledge as everyone's right to participate in the creation and sharing of knowledge that is specific to one's social, economic, and political reality. If we apply this framework to different contexts, it is crucial to keep in mind that knowledge and participation can take many forms and shapes depending on the race, gender, class, ability, sexuality, or history of different people. With this framework comes the possibility to pave a way towards finding solutions to the tensions challenges and tensions outlined in this book, towards building technologies for social justice, equity, and freedom.

Note

1 In reference to Langdon Winner's (1980) article "Do Artifacts Have Politics?"

References

Angwin, Julia, Charlie Savage, Jeff Larson, Henrik Moltke, Laura Poitras and James Risen. 2015. "AT&T Helped U.S. Spy on Internet on a Vast Scale." *The New York Times*, August 15. https://www.nytimes.com/2015/08/16/us/politics/att-helped-nsa-spy-on-an-array-of-internet-traffic.html?_r=0.

Archambault, Julie Soleil. 2017. *Mobile Secrets: Youth, Intimacy, and the Politics of Pretense in Mozambique*. Chicago: University of Chicago Press.

boyd, danah. 2014. *It's Complicated: The Social Lives of Networked Teens*. New Haven, CT and London: Yale University Press.

Chun, Wendy HuiKyong. 2006. *Control and Freedom: Power and Paranoia in the Age of Fiber Optics*. Cambridge, MA and London: The MIT Press.

Franklin, Sarah and Celia Roberts. 2006. *Born and Made: An Ethnography of Preimplantation Genetic Diagnosis*. Princeton, NJ and Woodstock: Princeton University Press.

Fuchs, Richard. 2013. "From Heresy to Orthodoxy: ICT4D at IDRC." In *Connecting ICTs to Development: The IDRC Experience*, edited by Laurent Elder, Heloise Emdon, Richard Fuchs, and Ben Petrazzini, 1–17. London: Anthem Press.

Gallagher, Ryan. 2019. "Google Employees Uncover Ongoing War on Censored China Search." *The Intercept*, March 4. https://theintercept.com/2019/03/04/google-ongoing-project-dragonfly/.

Ganesh, Indira Maya. 2011. "'Mobile Love Videos Make Me Feel Healthy': Rethinking ICTs for Development." *IDS Working Papers* 2010, no. 352: 1–43. https://doi.org/10.1111/j.2040-0209.2010.00352_2.x.

Green, Lelia. 2001. *Technoculture: From Alphabet to Cybersex*. Crows Nest, NSW: Allen & Unwin.

MacKenzie, Donald and Judy Wajcman, eds. 1999. *The Social Shaping of Technology: How the Refrigerator Got its Hum*. Milton Keynes: Open University Press.

Rizk, Nagla, and Lea Shaver. 2010. "Access to Knowledge: Economic, Global and Local Perspectives." In *Access to Knowledge in Egypt*, edited by Nagla Rizk and Lea Shaver, 1–15. London: Bloomsbury Academic.

Unwin, Tim. 2017. *Reclaiming Information and Communication Technologies for Development*. Oxford: Oxford University Press.

Winner, Landon. 1980. "Do Artifacts Have Politics?" *Daedalus*, 109, no. 1: 121–136.

INDEX

For Product Safety Concerns and Information please contact our EU representative GPSR@taylorandfrancis.com
Taylor & Francis Verlag GmbH, Kaufingerstraße 24, 80331 München, Germany

www.ingramcontent.com/pod-product-compliance
Ingram Content Group UK Ltd.
Pitfield, Milton Keynes, MK11 3LW, UK
UKHW022031061126
477531UK00003B/164
9780367545222